T0137347

The Information Retrieval Series Volume 38

More information about this series at http://www.springer.com/series/6128

Chirag Shah

Social Information Seeking

Leveraging the Wisdom of the Crowd

Chirag Shah
School of Communication & Information
Rutgers University
New Brunswick, NJ
USA

ISSN 1387-5264
The Information Retrieval Series
ISBN 978-3-319-85993-4 ISBN 978-3-319-56756-3 (eBook)
DOI 10.1007/978-3-319-56756-3

Softcover reprint of the hardcover 1st edition 2017

Printed on acid-free paper

This Springer imprint is published by Springer Nature
The registered company is Springer International Publishing AG
The registered company address is: Gewerbestrasse 11, 6330 Cham, Switzerland

For my wife Lori for her unconditional love and unwavering support that make projects like this book possible.

Foreword

Now, it is probably impossible for college students to imagine what people had to do in order to get a question answered before the Web. Imagine, for a moment, that it is 1990, when none of the current university students are yet born, and well before the age of search engines, and of course Wikipedia. You have no easy access to a library, and the reference books nearby are not enough. You might have a simple question like "what movies are good to watch tonight?" The only option you might have is to call up a friend who might know the answer. In fact, this option is so important, it is baked into the game *Who Wants to be a Millionaire?* as one of the three lifeline options to take when you're stumped for an answer. This natural instinct to call someone is what is baked into how we search for information and make sense of it.

Interestingly, even with the Web search engines at our fingertips, we still find the opinions of others, even strangers, to be quite valuable for decision-making. For example, in our many purchasing decisions, we seek the reviews and recommendations of others. We like to understand the average experiences of others for a given movie—how they felt about the acting, the storyline, and the production value of the film. In buying a lawn mower recently, I wanted to understand not just whether the product is well-built, but also whether it tends to break down over time, what kind of maintenance costs are associated with it, and whether the manufacturer stands behind their warranty when something goes wrong.

With the above in mind, let me first lay out the general research challenges in social information seeking from the perspective of a system builder.

First, gathering all of these opinions from people is challenging in multiple ways. For example, how do we incentivize users to contribute opinions and review and then to curate it? How do we build systems for processing, indexing, and extracting useful bits of information from the gathered data?

Second, we need to process a huge amount of social signals so that helpful bits are surfaced. For example, when we turn to social sources for information, we expect it to be free of unhelpful bias. However, every personalized source of information is somewhat subjective, by definition. Indeed, even what "facts" to include or not to include might bias the perception of information reliability. Ironically, it is precisely this subjective nature of opinions that causes us to seek out different points of views from others, including both friends and strangers. Therefore, in processing this curated data set, social search and recommendation systems must take care to understand each piece of information and how it might be valuable to users.

Third, we have to build ranking or recommender systems that help users decide what to read from the myriad of social information sources that are available. Searchers' skills in deciding whom and what to pay attention to and how to process facts and opinions from these social sources are critical to many decision-making and sense-making tasks. For example, when you call someone on the phone for information, one of the first steps is deciding whom to call. This is precisely the expertise modeling or question-routing problem in social question-and-answering (QA) systems.

Fourth, there are plenty of human factor issues in social information seeking. For example, in a social QA system, potential answerers might be "finicky": they don't want us to spam them; they don't like being interrupted; and they don't like it when we ask them overly simple questions. In other words, we have to deal with real human context and the associated social interaction.

Finally, we also have to socially engineer the growth of this system, so that early users get good enough experiences that they rave about the service and recommend it to other users. We want to build trust, and we want a network effect, such that, as each user joins the system, the whole system becomes even more useful to users that are already there.

In short, in thinking about how we are going to build better information seeking systems, we see how it is natural to think about the entire sense-making experience that includes social sources of information. The present manuscript is devoted to exactly this topic—broadening the scholarship around information seeking and sense-making to the social realm. There are multiple ways Dr. Shah has approached this question.

First, the book seeks to understand how we should curate social sources, situating the research here within past relevant works. For example, as discussed in a journal article, a collaborator and I used crowdsourcing survey techniques to understand social information seeking behavior [2] and what social sources are relied upon by users.

Second, the manuscript explores various ways in which socialness can be indirect and direct, with the most direct social information seeking activities as being entirely collaborative. Again, drawing from my own research before, we have found that social interactions were present and pervasive throughout the information seeking episode—before, during, and after the core search task [2]. Therefore, understanding the various social dimensions here is critical.

Third, the book catalogs and analyzes various tools and systems that have been built to support social information seeking and the methods researchers have employed to evaluate these systems to understand the degree to which the systems are successful and what user activities they support. For example, in evaluating a pioneering QA system called AnswerGarden, Mark Ackerman observed that users were often more satisfied when an answer came back quickly, even if the answer was somewhat less than perfect [1]. Given the amount of past work in this area, a comprehensive guide to evaluation approaches is sorely needed.

Finally, as parting words, let us not forget that users want one thing—getting their questions answered right now. Search engines have played that role for many years now. It can be argued that the greatest impact computers have had on the human endeavor is the Web search engine, whose development and refinement seems to be the epitome of computer science. That was before the Web truly became social. In the brave new social Web, search should and will be different, and reading this book will give you a sense of the direction where social search and information seeking is headed.

Los Altos Hill, CA, USA
March, 2017

Ed H. Chi
Sr. Staff Research Scientist
Google Research & Machine Intelligence

References

1. Ackerman, M.S.: Augmenting organizational memory: a field study of answer garden. ACM Trans. Inf. Syst. **16**(3), 203–224 (1998). http://doi.acm.org/10.1145/290159.290160
2. Evans, B.M., Chi, E.H.: An elaborated model of social search. Inf. Process. Manage. **46**(6), 656–678 (2010). http://dx.doi.org/10.1016/j.ipm.2009.10.012

Preface

We grew up learning in school that humans are social animals. More importantly, we have seen how we need social support (family, friends, colleagues) to accomplish many important tasks, including obtaining and using relevant information for various decision-making objectives. And yet, our favorite search engines are developed with individuals—rather than partners and groups—in mind. This could be because search engines are meant to be just a start of an information seeking activity, and not the end. Or it could be because we don't know how to create an effective search engine that incorporates the social and/or collaborative dimensions of our behavior.

Either way, studying the social aspect of information seeking is long overdue. Scholars have argued for decades that while Web search engines have been very effective in doing what they do, these systems have ignored the very fundamental aspect of human behavior—being social. While search engines have struggled to incorporate social/collaborative aspects to their search systems, people have been finding and utilizing methods and services to facilitate looking for, sharing, and making sense of information. They are increasingly seeking information through social channels such as social media services, social networking sites, and community-driven content providers. Examples of such behaviors include:

- Updating one's Facebook status to ask friends for advice
- Posting a question on a community-based question-answering service such as Yahoo! Answers
- Using Twitter to gather opinions through a poll

Social information seeking (SIS) is a field of research that involves studying situations, motivations, and methods involved in people's seeking and sharing of information in participatory online social sites, such as Yahoo! Answers, WikiAnswers, and Twitter, as well as building systems for supporting such activities.

Some may ask how SIS is different from collaborative information seeking (CIS), considering social and collaborative ties definitely have a lot in common. While this is true, they also have some important differences. A *real* collaboration is studied and understood with connections among the participants who work toward a common goal with explicitly expressed intentions in a mutually beneficial way.

Such connections have some level of inherent trust and a sense of shared ownership. To create a social tie, however, participants need neither a shared common goal nor a great deal of shared trust and knowledge to interact. In this way, SIS allows information seekers to expand their reach for seeking and sharing information.

My own journey has taken me through explorations of both SIS and CIS, almost at the same time. Until I started my PhD at the University of North Carolina (UNC) Chapel Hill, things were more straightforward for me with my work and interest in information retrieval (IR). But then I started looking at interactive IR and information seeking, specifically the situations where people seek information *with* and *through* other people. The former (*with*) defines CIS, whereas the latter (*through*) relates to SIS. For over a decade now, I have been exploring and writing for both CIS and SIS. I published the first full-length book on CIS with Springer in 2012, and so it is only fitting that I also publish the first full-length book on SIS with them. And that's what I present here. This volume is a culmination of more than a decade's work, dozens of studies and experiments, numerous conference and journal papers, a couple of PhD dissertations, and countless midnight candles burnt. The final product unfolds in the following manner.

First, we'll define and understand SIS in context. SIS sits at the intersection of the well-established and well-studied fields of information seeking/retrieval, social media, and social networking. It follows that here we will first look into issues of information seeking and social media/networking. Such research frames the first part of this book. This will give us the necessary foundation to then discuss how those aspects could intertwine in different ways to create methods, tools, and opportunities for supporting and leveraging SIS. Part II starts with the social dimension; primarily, we will examine SIS through question-answering activity. Part III brings the collaborative dimension of information seeking into the mix. After reviewing social information seeking and collaborative information seeking separately, it is interesting to note how often they overlap and connect. Therefore, we will provide a new context in which social and collaborative dimensions are considered together. We acknowledge that, to truly make a model of social and collaborative information seeking function, much more work needs to be done.

We finally come back to more concrete terms in Part IV of this book to consolidate what we know about how people have been studying SIS and related areas, what tools they have developed, and how they evaluate various methods and systems. It is important to complete this synthesis before launching into what might become the next big thing, so we conclude the book by laying out some important pointers for both theoretical and practical SIS work.

In the end, one should treat this book as a good starting point for exploring the next phase of information seeking/retrieval, specifically the one that will seamlessly incorporate social and collaborative dimensions.

There is a lot to be done for this next revolution in the fields of information retrieval, information seeking, and social media/networking. Let's get started.

New Brunswick, NJ, USA
February, 2017

Chirag Shah

Acknowledgments

A book like this does not happen with the efforts of a single person. And if this book shows anything, it is that we are social animals who use each other as support for difficult tasks. So I have taken help from many people over the years to make this book possible. I would like to thank all of the following people and organizations for their contributions to my research relating to this book. Without them, this work would not exist.

- My friends and colleagues Sanghee Oh (currently at Chungnam National University, South Korea) and Jung Sun Oh (currently at the University of Pittsburgh), who introduced me to the area of social/community-based question-answering as fellow PhD students at the University of North Carolina Chapel Hill. I wrote my first paper on this topic with them, which now seems like ages ago!
- My colleagues Dr. Marie Radford at Rutgers University and Dr. Lynn Connaway at OCLC for working with me on online/digital Q&A services, especially looking for hybrid solutions that connect virtual reference services run by libraries and peer-based, community-based/social Q&A services.
- My longtime collaborators Rob Capra at the University of North Carolina Chapel Hill and Preben Hansen at Stockholm University for helping me shape many of my ideas of collaborative information seeking over the years through co-organizing various workshops and other events with me. Some of their contributions are also reflected in the writing of Chap. 7.
- Several of my PhD students over the years for contributing to my understanding of various topics reported in this book as well as for working on different studies and experiments that produced new knowledge in the fields of collaborative information seeking, social information seeking, and interactive information retrieval. Specifically, I would like to recognize the contributions of Roberto Gonzalez-Ibanez, Erik Choi, Vanessa Kitzie, Long Le, and Manasa Rath. Parts of their papers and dissertations are sprinkled all over this book.
- My wonderful, diligent, and always responsive lab assistant Diana Floegel who not only helped me do a lot of editing and proofreading for this book, but also

contributed to many of the literature reviewing pieces. Without her, it would have been another year to have this book in your hands.

- The US Institute of Museum and Library Services (IMLS) for funding my work on social and collaborative information seeking under Cyber Synergy project (grant #LG-06-11-0342-11; 2011–2013), Early Career award (grant #RE-04-12-0105-12; 2012–2015), and award #LG-81-16-0025 (2016–2019) under the National Leadership Grant for project titled "Online Q&A in STEM Education: Curating the Wisdom of the Crowd."
- Brainly.com for providing not just funds for doing some of the work reported here, but also giving us access to their data and services to be able to run our experiments.
- My late father Rajendrakumar, mother Sneha, and sister Shweta, for their constant love, kindness, and support, even when they are all in different continents.
- And last, but not the least, my wife Lori. She has given me three beautiful children—Sophie, Zoe, and Sarah—but she takes care of four kids at home with myself included! Over the years, she has not only supported me both morally and emotionally but also been subjected to reading many drafts, parts of which are now in this book, and testing the early versions of my systems, including Coagmento that's described here. She is the invisible hand in all of my work, and it is no surprise that I couldn't have done this book (or stayed sane) without her.

Contents

Part III Collaborative Dimension of Information Seeking

Part IV Current State and Future Directions

List of Figures

List of Tables

Acronyms

ACM	Association for Computing Machinery
ACRL	Association of College and Research Libraries
ASIST	Association for Information Science and Technology
ASK	Anomalous States of Knowledge
ASP	Answer Satisfaction Prediction
CIB	Collaborative Information Behavior
CIR	Collaborative Information Retrieval
CIS	Collaborative Information Seeking
CLIR	Cross-Language Information Retrieval
CMC	Computer-Mediated Communication
CQA	Community Question-Answering
CSCW	Computer-Supported Cooperative Work
CTAR	Collaborative Technology Assisted Review
DAU	Daily Active User
EKR	Electronic Knowledge Repository
FRMB	Facebook Relationship Maintenance Behaviors
GUH	Group Unified History
HCI	Human-Computer Interaction
HIB	Human Information Behavior
IM	Instant Messaging
IPL	Internet Public Library
IR	Information Retrieval
ISC	Information Seek Cycle
ISCM	Information Seeking and Communication Model
ISCS	Internet Social Capital Scale
ISP	Information Search Process
LIS	Library and Information Science
LSM	Linguistic Style Matching
MAU	Monthly Active User
MISE	Multiple Information Seeking Episodes
MT	Machine Translation

NIST	National Institute of Standards and Technology
OC	Online Community
P2P	Peer-to-Peer
PDMS	Peer-to-Peer Data Management System
Q&A	Question-Answering
QR	Question-Routing
SCIS	Social and Collaborative Information Seeking
SDL	Structured Definition Language
SIGIR	Special Interest Group on Information Retrieval
SIS	Social Information Seeking
SLSS	Social Live Streaming Service
SNS	Social Networking Site
SQA	Social Question-Answering
TREC	Text REtrieval Conference
UGT	Uses and Gratification Theory
VR	Virtual Reference

Part I
Foundation

In the first part of this book, various foundational concepts are introduced. These include information seeking, social media, and social networking. But first, we start with an introduction to the primary topic of this book—social information seeking (SIS).

Chapter 1
Introduction

Abstract In this introductory chapter, we present the concept of social information seeking (SIS). SIS covers situations where people use their social connections to seek, share, and process information. The chapter provides several definitions that further explain and situate this notion. It then provides a brief overview of some of the activities and applications that employ SIS. The chapter introduces several concepts that relate to SIS, such as information seeking/retrieval/behavior, social media/networking, social search, question-answering, and collaborative information seeking (CIS). It uses the interconnections among these concepts to set the stage for studying and addressing various topics in SIS. The chapter concludes by describing the organization of the rest of the book.

1.1 Introduction

Social information seeking (SIS), sometimes referred to as *social search* or *social information retrieval*, is a relatively new area of study surrounding the seeking and acquiring of information from social spaces on the Internet. Examples include asking a question to a crowd on Yahoo! Answers[1] or Stack Overflow,[2] taking an informal poll about a dress you are thinking of wearing using Facebook,[3] and sharing recipes through Pinterest.[4]

As Evans and Chi [5] put it, SIS, or in their words, *social search*, is a term that is "used to describe search acts that make use of social interactions with others. These inter-actions may be explicit or implicit, co-located or remote, synchronous or asynchronous" [5, p. 2]. Social search, according to Chi [4], can be broken down into two different categories: social answering systems and social feedback systems. Social answering systems satisfy users' information needs with answers that are provided by other users. Personal social networks may be leveraged in these systems, and answers may be provided by people with varying levels of

[1] https://answers.yahoo.com.

[2] http://stackoverflow.com.

[3] https://www.facebook.com.

[4] https://www.pinterest.com.

C. Shah, *Social Information Seeking*, The Information Retrieval Series 38,
DOI 10.1007/978-3-319-56756-3_1

expertise. Yahoo! Answers and Facebook are both examples of social answering systems. Social feedback systems, on the other hand, rank results and information according to feedback from users, offering them to users in order of their ratings. Social bookmarking services fall under this category of social search systems. SIS covers a range of several different types of searches and services, each of which incorporates social interaction in some form.

Figure 1.1 depicts a set of services and applications, primarily within Web 2.0 framework, that promote and support SIS. This "promote and support" idea is important to consider here because few systems were created to explicitly cater to SIS. What we find, instead, is that people use their familiar social media and social

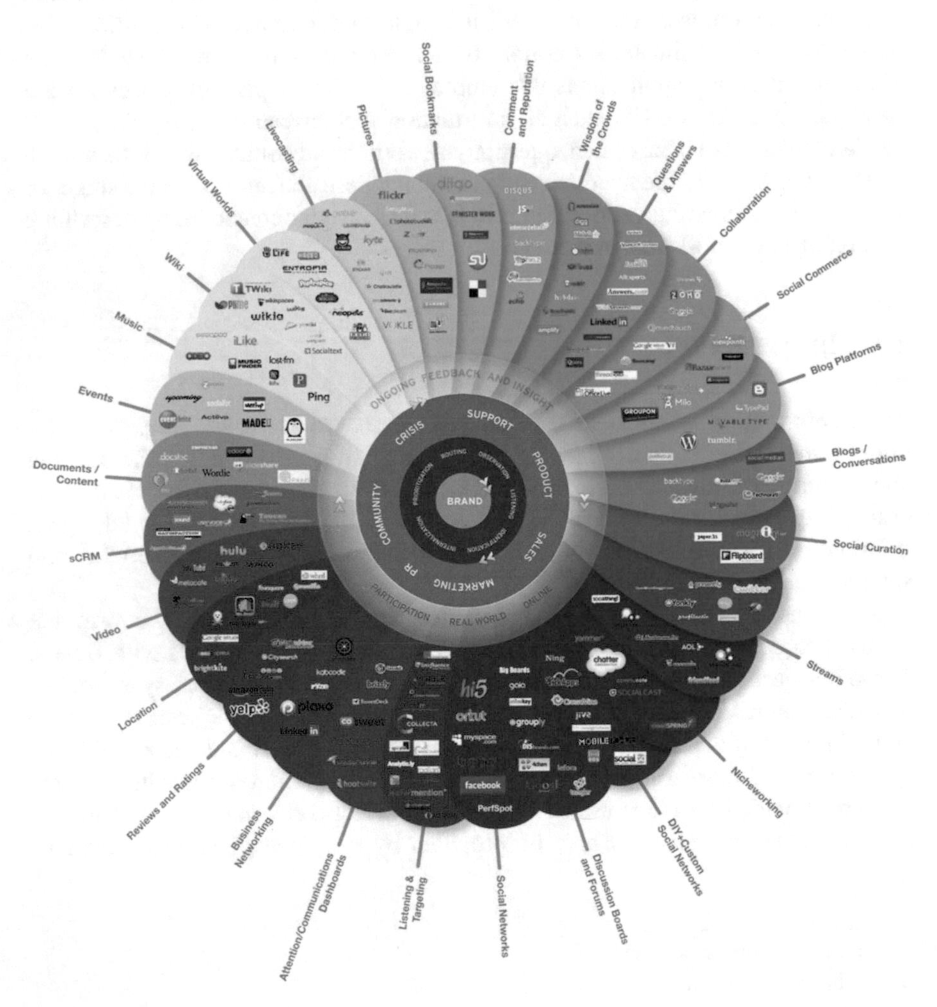

Fig. 1.1 Various social media/networking services that promote and support social information seeking. Source: WikiMedia, https://upload.wikimedia.org/wikipedia/commons/7/7c/Conversationprism.jpeg

networking platforms to carry out informational activities, thus engaging in SIS via common channels.

1.2 Defining and Situating SIS

We'll see later in this book that there may be a lack of common understanding or even consensus on the definition of SIS. But at this point, it's important that we at least lay down some groundwork and present some terminology. First, we'll form a definition of SIS; then we'll provide some context to situate it.

SIS describes the process through which users locate and share information in participatory online forums, such as social media platforms and question-answer Websites. According to Shah et al. [14], these sites "encourage and thrive on communities built around information exchange, introducing a social aspect to information seeking" (p. 205). Throughout pertinent literature, SIS can also be described as *social Q&A*, *social search*, or *social information retrieval.* In this book, we define social information seeking (SIS) as a field of research that involves studying situations, motivations, and methods for people seeking and sharing information in participatory online social sites, such as Yahoo! Answers, WikiAnswers,[5] and Twitter,[6] as well as designing, building, and evaluating systems for supporting such activities. From time to time, we will also find ourselves including "collaboration" as an aspect of these studies and systems because, as we will see in Chap. 7, it's often impossible to separate collaboration from a social system, and vice versa.

Let's try to understand SIS in light of related and more established domains of scholarly inquiry. Figure 1.2 provides a schematic view of this understanding.

Here, we can see that SIS is somewhere in the intersection of information seeking and social media/networking domains. However, since information seeking is a subset of information behavior and a superset of information retrieval (see Chap. 2), and since it becomes very difficult to talk about "social" without talking about "collaboration" (see Chap. 7), we have to consider those aspects in this big picture as well. Let's take a closer look.

SIS is but a piece of a much larger overall process. The domain falls under the broader topic of information seeking, which in turn is nested inside human information behavior. Information seeking, including SIS, is the behavior of seeking out specific information to fulfill some sort of information need [15]. The required information may be sought from any number of sources including libraries, print materials, Internet sources, and other people. Human information behavior encompasses information seeking, as well as all other information-related behaviors in which people engage. Such behaviors include both passively and actively seeking out information as well as using acquired information.

---

[5]http://www.answers.com.

[6]https://twitter.com.

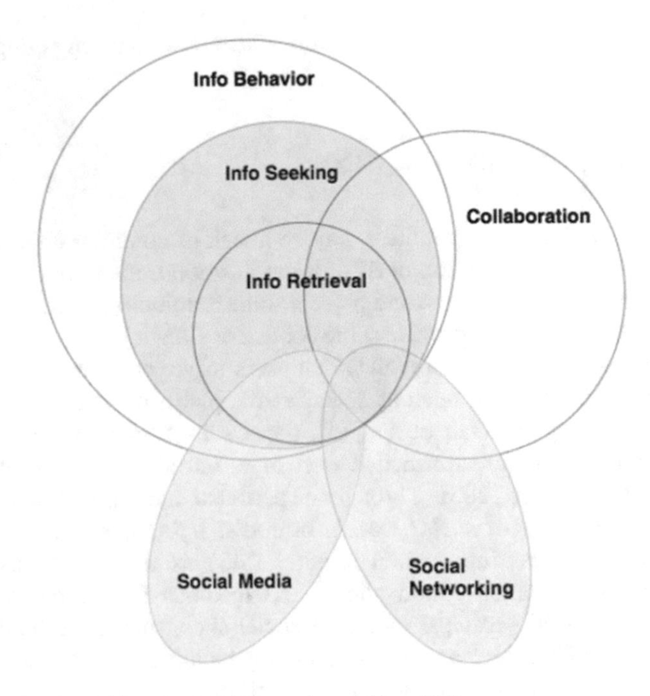

Fig. 1.2 A schematic view of social information seeking (SIS)

Explorations of SIS are also necessarily entwined with those of social media, as the strength of the former rests on the latter. As mentioned above, social media platforms such as Facebook, Twitter, message boards, and question-answer (Q&A) Websites are the tools with which SIS is performed. The importance of such platforms and systems lies in their flexibility. While search engines are designed for finding and providing information, they offer only objective information based on the query given, which is limiting. Social media, however, allows for questions to be asked in natural language, not in computer queries; the information need can be stated as a full question instead of reconfigured into a few keywords. Additionally, social media platforms leave room for subjective answers that are more difficult to come by through a search engine, such as opinions and recommendations. Further, they permit answers to be personalized or colored by the user and their social network's knowledge. Thus, answers can be tailored to the person asking the question [8].

One specific form that SIS can take is social/community Q&A, a community-based question-answer service. One user poses a question publicly, and those who are able and willing respond with answers. This, in the words of Shah et al. [14], "enables people to collaborate by sharing and distributing information among fellow users and by making the entire process and product publicly available" (p. 206). The information seeking process is made social by linking the seeker with those who can potentially satisfy their information need. Social Q&A is not only an example of SIS but also a component of collaborative information seeking. Related to SIS, collaborative information seeking is the idea that information seeking is often done jointly by multiple people filling multiple roles in the overall process [13]. In the case of social Q&A, and SIS more broadly, collaboration takes places between the person with the information need and those whom they contact through social information platforms, whether those people be strangers using the same Website or members of the asker's social network. These individuals fill different roles but ultimately join together to provide and acquire information and fulfill the information need.

1.3 SIS Activities and Applications

Let us now consider some of the practical applications and situations where we see SIS. Many of these should be familiar, and yet, we often don't think about them as SIS activities. By "activities," we mean acts and tasks that involve information seeking, sharing, and sense-making.

As the popularity of question-answer sites, social media, and other online social platforms has increased, so have the methods and practices used to study the information seeking exchanges that occur through these channels. Three broad categories of digital service include digital reference services, expert services, and social Q&A [11]. Specific studies within SIS research have examined the activities of both specific sites and specific user groups. For example, Adamic et al. [1] provide a comprehensive analysis of the knowledge exchange communities that form and thrive on Yahoo! Answers, while Savolainen [10] examines the interactions of travel planners across multiple platforms. Other areas of study involve virtual reference services, such as instant messaging interactions between librarians and library patrons, and *Ask-A* services powered by organizations other than libraries.

Throughout these studies, scholars generally seek to discover the motivations and methods employed by information seeking users. In their study of SIS on Facebook, for example, Wise et al. [16] contrast passive social browsing—such as scrolling through newsfeeds without specific information needs—with extractive social searching, in which Facebook users actively seek information from specific individuals or pages. And beyond site-specific findings, a few general theoretical frameworks are used by SIS researchers. O'Brien et al. [9], for example, use the "uses and gratification theory" (UGT) to examine how online users select information to share with others. Many scholars focus either on a platform's content or a conglomeration of users. Cha et al. [3] focus specifically on Twitter and the ways in which certain users are considered influential. Liu et al. [7], on the other hand, take a broader approach to SIS by studying how question-answer sites affect students' discussion, behaviors, and learning performance.

As an increasing number of information exchanges occur on platforms such as question-answer sites, social media sites, and virtual reference providers, research conducted in the SIS field becomes vital to understanding the motivations, methods, practices, and results that relate to social information seeking behavior. Scholars from various disciplines—including information science, psychology, and computer science—continue to study new and emerging SIS trends, which include the ways in which authority is established through social media interactions, the methods employed by users to elicit friendly and/or trusted responses, and how information seeking can satisfy social needs and learning agendas. Databases such as Academic Search Complete,[7] ScienceDirect,[8] SCOPUS,[9] and Library, Information Science & Technology Abstracts[10] index a wealth of materials on these subjects.

1.4 Relation to CIS and Previous Works

Given that there are several works on CIS, including my own books on the topic published by Springer, one wonders whether SIS is different enough from CIS to warrant a whole new book. Let me attempt to answer that—what may seem like just a rhetoric at this point.

There is a fundamental difference between a social and a collaborative tie. For a collaboration to take place, the participants need to have a certain level of familiarity and trust with one another. For a social connection, this is not a requirement. This may not sound like a huge difference in the way these notions are constructed, but it has significant implications. For instance, due to its requirements or expectations, a *true* collaboration is limited in its scope with respect to the size of the group and the nature of the project. It's highly unimaginable to see a thousand people working together to write a report on climate change with a joint goal of achieving one outcome of mutually beneficial nature. On the other hand, it is completely plausible (and happens often) that an individual asks his dozen friends through Facebook, his hundred followers through Twitter, and thousands or millions of strangers through an online forum to help with a report on climate change he is writing.

Collaboration requires a certain balance in roles, responsibilities, and benefits, whereas a social connection for working on information projects does not.

The C5 Model of collaboration that I presented in a book on CIS [12] and summarize in Chap. 6 of this book can help us see how strict the notion of collaboration could be. But once we start loosening the requirements for each of the five layers, we open up a whole new set of possibilities for people working with each other in small and big groups, producing and consuming information, and exchanging knowledge at an unprecedented scale and speed.

[7]https://www.ebscohost.com/academic/academic-search-complete.

[8]http://www.sciencedirect.com.

[9]https://www.scopus.com.

[10]https://www.ebscohost.com/academic/library-information-science-and-technology-abstracts.

This creates new opportunities and challenges. It now allows the well-established theories and practices of information seeking domain to mix with newer and more dynamic systems and services of social media. Through this amalgamation, we can study and support emerging forms of information behaviors that include people seeking and exchanging information through social media and crowdsourcing services. This phenomenon also raises new challenges to meet. For instance, learners (students and professionals) are increasingly using information generated by nonexperts without questioning its authenticity, validity, or quality. While this could be damaging at a personal level, the same behavior also causes large-scale societal problems such as those raised by "fake news" [2, 6].

The problems, challenges, and opportunities are quite different from what scholars (including myself) have covered while writing about CIS.

Of course, there are important overlaps with topics of CIS and computer-mediated communication (CMC), and wherever needed, these overlaps and differences are called out in this book. Chapter 6 provides an overview of CIS, primarily based on my previous book [12], but also adding and updating some material. Chapter 7 offers a unique overview of what combining SIS and CIS could look like. Since CMC is a topic on the periphery for this book, it is covered as an appendix.

1.5 Organization of This Book

In this chapter we introduced social information seeking (SIS) as an exciting and emerging domain of research and development. As we learned, there is much more to SIS than meets the eye. Specifically, we need to consider several interconnecting research domains and scholarly aspects. And that's how the rest of this book is organized.

The larger concept of information behavior covers all kinds of activities and contexts where people are interacting with information. This includes both active and passive interactions. In other words, when you *Google*[11] something, that's part of your information behavior, and so is the time when you accidentally saw a poster at a mall and discovered that the new Star Wars movie features your favorite Wookiee's comeback.[12] But then there are specific kinds of information interactions that involve realizing the need to find information, and actively looking for it. That's a subset of information behavior that we call information seeking. In Chap. 2, we will review many models and theories that discuss this concept using different contexts and populations. Many of these models believe that the act of seeking information starts when a person recognizes a gap in their knowledge. They also acknowledge that seeking information does not always lead to finding information.

---

[11]https://www.google.com.

[12]More on Wookiees can be discovered at this excellent *Wookieepedia* site: http://starwars.wikia.com/wiki/Wookiee.

There is a subset of information seeking, called information retrieval, where the assumption is that the information being sought exists and the challenge is to make sure it is retrieved. Therein lies a fundamental difference between information seeking and information retrieval: the former focuses on the person looking for information without assuming that the *right* kind of information exists, whereas the latter focuses on the system to make sure the information is found.

We will then turn our attention to the social side of human behavior. You'll find that this is not a new concept. Yes, we have always been social, even without Facebook or the Web. Being social and wanting to be a part of a community can perhaps be thought of as why and how we, the human species, survived and flourished over thousands of years. And now the advent of the Web, and specifically the Web 2.0, has allowed us to practice those aspects of our behavior at a speed and a scale not possible before. In Chap. 3, we will look at two important and connected domains of scholarly inquiry: social media and social networking. We will see that these services are more than just some novelty applications for teenagers. They are being used to not only share and discover information but also to produce, reproduce, and augment existing information. This, in a way, is democracy's next evolution, where anyone and everyone who can connect to the Web could participate in, contribute to, and shape our collective thinking.

Next, we will ask what happens if we combine those information seeking and social media/networking aspects of human behavior. And that's how we develop the second part of this book, which looks at the social dimension of information seeking. Chapter 4 will be dedicated to a very specific kind of method that people use while looking for information from their social/community-based ties. Not surprisingly, when people use others to seek information, they are not throwing out a bunch of keywords as they would with a search engine (and thank goodness for that!); they are instead asking questions. This particular chapter will categorize question-answering (Q&A) activities into online expert-based, community-driven, collaborative, and social spaces. There are several services that cater to one of these methods for Q&A. Interestingly, popular "social" platforms are often not designed with Q&A in mind. For example, Twitter is a microblogging service, but people use it for asking questions of their friends and followers.

We will expand our notion of how people explore and exploit their social connections to seek information beyond Q&A in Chap. 5, calling these behaviors social search. In addition to using social connections to look for information, this notion also includes searching within socially constructed information. As we review important theories, models, and practices, we will realize that we couldn't simply talk about people seeking information *through* other people without talking about how they do the same *with* other people. That latter case transitions us into the third part of this book.

The situation in which people seek information *with* other people is quite appealing since it incorporates another fundamental aspect of human nature: collaboration. In Chap. 6 we will see that there are many situations that either call for or could benefit from multiple people working together in seeking, sharing, and making sense of information. However, research in the fields of information seeking and information retrieval has disproportionately considered information seeking to be a solitary activity. What we see in Chap. 2 should be a proof that most, if not all, models of information seeking are designed around the image of a single person looking for information. To overcome this limitation, we will see how we could incorporate a collaborative dimension into information seeking by either extending existing models and methods to include that aspect or by building new methods from the ground up with collaboration in mind.

Of course, this dimension of "collaboration" is not that easy to separate from the "social" dimension of information seeking behavior. And that's why, in Chap. 7, we will look at both of those dimensions together in information seeking situations. One of the interesting things we will discover from this exercise is that often a multi-person activity starts with a social connection and then becomes collaborative, and vice versa. In other words, a collaborative project may end up exhibiting some social characteristics even though they were neither planned nor required.

Finally, in Chap. 8 we will revisit the idea of SIS in the context of all that is covered thus far (information seeking/retrieval/behavior, social media/networking, Q&A, social search, collaborative and social aspects of information seeking) and how that relates to research and practice. Specifically, we will see some of the most common research methodologies and evaluation strategies used for studying SIS users and systems. We will also see examples of main classes of applications that relate to SIS.

The book will finish with the conclusion presented in Chap. 9. In this chapter, we will summarize what we learned from all the preceding chapters, and then commence to synthesize those lessons. We'll accomplish this by presenting two different frameworks. After that, a list of theoretical and practical challenges and opportunities will be provided. This should help students, scholars, and anyone who wants to study and contribute to SIS and related areas.

It is important to note that almost every topic covered in this book could merit its own volume, but we are trying to present each in a single chapter. This means that we may not provide a comprehensive treatment of these topics. But we hope that the following chapters will present enough introductory materials with pointers toward further explorations for interested parties to pursue future inquiries.

References

1. Adamic, L.A., Zhang, J., Bakshy, E., Ackerman, M.S.: Knowledge sharing and yahoo answers. In: Proceedings of the 17th International Conference on World Wide Web - WWW '08, p. 665. ACM Press, New York (2008)
2. Allcott, H., Gentzkow, M.: Social Media and Fake News in the 2016 Election (No. w23089). Technical report, National Bureau of Economic Research (2017)
3. Cha, M., Gummadi, K.P., Haddadi, H., Benevenuto, F.: Measuring user influence in Twitter: the million follower fallacy. In: ICWSM 2010 - Proceedings of the 4th International AAI Conference on Weblogs and Social Media, pp. 10–17 (2010)
4. Chi, E.H.: Information seeking can be social. Computer **42**(3), 42–46 (2009)

5. Evans, B.M., Chi, E.H.: An elaborated model of social search. Inf. Process. Manage. **46**(6), 656–678 (2009)
6. Kahan, D.: The psychology of fake news. In: AAAS Annual Meeting (2017)
7. Liu, E.Z.-F., Cheng, S.S., Chen, S.Y., Chen, B.-I.: The impact of Q&A forums' level of elaboration on students' learning. Procedia - Soc. Behav. Sci. **64**, 604–608 (2012)
8. Morris, M.R., Teevan, J., Panovich, K.: What do people ask their social networks, and why? A survey study of status message Q&A behavior. In: Proceedings of ACM SIGCHI Conference on Human Factors in Computing Systems, Atlanta, GA (2010)
9. O'Brien, H.L., Freund, L., Westman, S.: What motivates the online news browser? News items selection in a social information seeking scenario. Inf. Res. **19**(3), Paper 634 (2014). Retrieved from http://InformationR.net/ir/19-3/paper634.html
10. Savolainen, R.: The use of rhetorical strategies in Q&A discussion. J. Doc. **70**(1), 93–118 (2014)
11. Shah, C.: Collaborative information seeking: a literature review. Advances in Librarianship **32**, 3–33 (2010)
12. Shah, C.: Collaborative Information Seeking: The Art and Science of Making the Whole Greater than the Sum of All. Information Retrieval Series. Springer, Berlin (2012)
13. Shah, C., Capra, R., Hansen, P.: Collaborative information seeking [Guest editors' introduction]. Computer **47**(3), 22–25 (2014)
14. Shah, C., Oh, J.S., Oh, S.: Research agenda for social Q&A. Libr. Inf. Sci. Res. **31**(4), 205–209 (2009)
15. Wilson, T.D.: Human information behavior. Inf. Sci. **3**(2), 49–55 (2000)
16. Wise, K., Alhabash, S., Park, H.: Emotional responses during social information seeking on Facebook. Cyberpsychol. Behav. Soc. Netw. **13**(5), 555–562 (2010)

Chapter 2
Information Seeking

Abstract This chapter introduces the concept of information seeking, along with various theoretical models and conceptual frameworks. The act of seeking information is seen as one that is fundamental to human behavior, and because of that, information seeking is conceptualized with respect to a person and their needs, irrespective of any system or the availability of any information. To put information seeking in perspective, it is shown as a subset of information behavior, which incorporates any and all kinds of interactions people have with information. On the other hand, information retrieval is seen as something more specific and system-oriented. A number of foundational models of information seeking are reviewed here, followed by a description of a set of models derived from those foundational works. These models consider the motivations behind seeking information, the nature of the information sought, and the context in which this process occurs. Several of these models also identify stages or steps of a typical information seeking process. The chapter finishes with a recognition that most times information seeking is studied considering an individual, disregarding social and/or collaborative aspects of information seeking.

2.1 Introduction

It is an understatement to say that we live in an Information Age. Information, however one defines it, has become a critical element of our survival and advancement. Ford [9] compares it to nourishment and argues that just as we have nutrition science and a food and drug administration, we ought to approach people's production and consumption of information with equitable curiosity and comprehensiveness.

Seeking information, however, is not a new form of behavior. From the very beginning of our existence, we have sought information on topics such as how to make a fire or how to find shelter from natural elements. In fact, one could claim that humans' natural curiosity and desire to satisfy that curiosity by obtaining new information make us who we are now: a knowledge society. Sure enough, Marchionini [19] defines information seeking as a process in which humans purposefully engage in an activity to change their state of knowledge.

C. Shah, *Social Information Seeking*, The Information Retrieval Series 38,
DOI 10.1007/978-3-319-56756-3_2

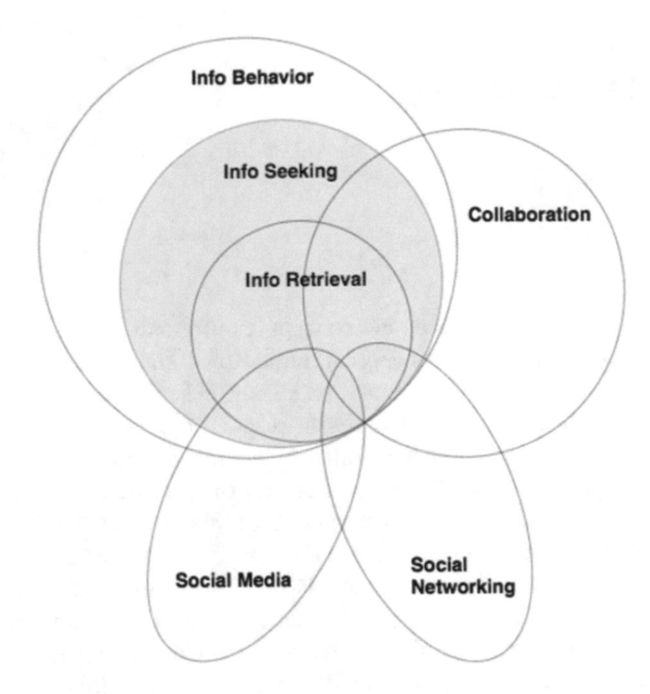

Fig. 2.1 A schematic view of information seeking and related concepts in context

Looking around, one can find a number of related concepts in the literature, including information behavior and information retrieval. So let's put things in perspective before we dive deeper. Figure 2.1 shows a conceptual link among these concepts.

As shown, information behavior is the most general and encompassing concept. It refers to all kinds of situations where people interact with information. And that's just about everywhere! Think about looking at your watch to find out what time it is. Think about picking up a book and skimming through it to decide if you want to purchase it. Think about the time when you looked up directions to a park, then checked the weather to determine if you needed an umbrella for your visit. From reading books to browsing online, and from asking for directions to making sense out of our phone bills, we are constantly interacting with information. In other words, information behavior covers a whole range of human behaviors and activities that involve information in some shape or form.

Information seeking, on the other hand, is a more specific kind of activity within that wide spectrum of behaviors. It refers to "a conscious effort to acquire information in response to a gap in [our] knowledge" [2, p. 5].

So what's in information behavior that's not in information seeking? In addition to scenarios in which individuals actively seek information, information behavior also covers situations where one is passively engaging in information interactions—such as that example of skimming through a book, or an incident of encountering new information without asking/looking for it. Information seeking, on the other hand, requires intentionality.[1]

And now we come to information retrieval (IR). It is a subset of information seeking behaviors and processes that deals with finding information through various tools and techniques. That may seem like information seeking, but there is an important difference. Information seeking makes no assumption about the information's existence; instead it refers to the process of looking for information. IR, on the other hand, assumes that there is specific information that one is looking for and focuses on methods for ensuring the retrieval of that information. Examples of these methods are searching, browsing, and filtering.

This process of information seeking goes beyond simply retrieving information; it is usually associated with higher-level cognitive processes, such as learning and problem solving [18]. Dervin and Nilan [5] provide a different framework for information seeking. They emphasize communication and the needs, characteristics, and actions of the information seeker as opposed to mere representation, storage, and retrieval of information. We talk about *seeking* the meaning of life; whether we *retrieve* it or not, that's a different question!

In this chapter, we won't be limited to information retrieval, and also won't go as high as information behavior. Information seeking will provide us a nice middle ground to talk about some important issues. Within the study of information seeking, several models have been proposed to understand and explain the information seeking process and information seeking behavior. These models may apply to specific domains, build on foundational concepts, fit within preexisting information seeking frameworks, or present original perspectives through which information seeking can be studied. And so, our discussion in this chapter will start with some of the foundational models, and then move to those models that are built on top of these foundational models.

2.2 Foundational Models

A number of information seeking researchers developed core theories of individuals' search processes. The following subsections introduce each model, many of which continue to provide foundational material for recent and emerging literature.

2.2.1 Dervin

Dervin [4] recognized that information seeking is a problem-solving technique, and the problem in question is a situation, a gap in one's knowledge, or a desire to

[1] Of course, scholars don't completely agree on this.

achieve a goal by using some information. Therefore, she presented a model with three phases of users facing and solving their information problems:

1. *Situation*. This phase establishes the context for the information need.
2. *Gap*. Users often find that, given a situation in this phase, there is a gap between what they understand and what they need to make sense of in their current circumstances.
3. *Use*. In this final phase, the gap is realized and manifested by questions or queries. The answers to those questions are put to use, thus allowing the user to move on to the next question.

Dervin's "situation-gap-use" model posits that information needs stem from a "situation" that creates a "gap" in a user's knowledge. This gap can be filled by a variety of tactics, or "uses." For example, Reinhard and Dervin [23] studied how novices made sense of four media technologies to analyze the complexity of media reception situations, how they converge and diverge, and how they involve multiple potential influences on media reception outcomes. They examined the situated processes involved in bridging gaps found in users' knowledge of new technology programs, such as virtual gaming and social worlds. The authors combined an experimental framework that controlled the parameters of engagement with qualitative interviewing methods to analyze users. Through their results, Reinhard and Dervin were able to study how participants engaged with new virtual worlds without reducing their analysis to merely the structural differences between platforms or the users' observable external characteristics. According to Dervin, information needs are best understood by examining the process that individuals employ to fill their respective knowledge gaps.

2.2.2 Belkin

While Dervin cared about understanding one's situation (past and present), Belkin [1] took a cognitive approach and proposed a model of information seeking that focused on information seekers' anomalous states of knowledge (ASK). This model stems from a user's knowledge gap (or "anomaly") and the need to fill it. Belkin developed this model based on his hypothesis that users of search systems are often unable to fully articulate their information needs. This leads them to miss vital components of their queries, and thus retrieve inaccurate or incomplete results. Belkin believed it was better for users to describe their anomalous states of knowledge than to formulate specific requests within a system.

In Belkin's study [1], the information seekers did not have a clear understanding of the problem they tried to solve nor the information needed to do so. Information seekers had to go through a stage of articulating their search request, and the search system helped to refine that request. Thus, the ASK model recognized that information retrieval is an iterative process, as users repeatedly returned to the IR system to satisfy their needs. ASK served as a theoretical basis for the design of interactive, user-centered information systems.

2.2.3 Ellis

Ellis [6], one of the pioneers in the early days of information seeking research, took a behavioral approach to study information retrieval system design. He broke information seeking patterns into six characteristics: starting, chaining, browsing, differentiating, monitoring, and extracting. The six stages can be defined as follows:

1. *Starting*. This characterizes the steps taken during an initial search for information, such as identifying potential sources.
2. *Chaining*. This characterizes the steps taken while following new directions established through those sources identified during starting. Backward chaining involves following references from an initial source and is a well-established research practice. Forward chaining follows sources that refer to an initial source.
3. *Browsing*. This characterizes the steps taken after sources have been located. It is semi-directed search activity.
4. *Differentiating*. This characterizes the steps taken after a sufficient amount of content has been gathered. Searchers select pertinent resources from their findings based on measures such as the subject and quality of information.
5. *Monitoring*. This characterizes search strategies that take place after initial inquiries. Users keep abreast of developments in their research area by following identified relevant sources, which differ from subject to subject.
6. *Extracting*. This characterizes retrospective searching, in which users systematically work through a resource to identify important information.

Ellis describes these stages in relation to retrieval system facilities and considers implementing an experimental system in a hypertext environment. Two additional stages of information seeking behavior—verifying and ending—were reported in Ellis et al. [8] as part of a model based on empirical research that has been tested in many domains, including a run in the context of an engineering company [7].

2.2.4 Wilson

Wilson [27] presented a model of information seeking processes that demonstrates how Ellis's work [6] could be incorporated into a general model of information behavior that applies to fields outside information science. This problem-solving model posits that the root of problematic information seeking behavior is the concept of "information need," which is subjective to each respective searcher and not directly accessible to an observer. The experience of an information need, then, can only be characterized by deductive observational reasoning or through user reports. Wilson [27] applies his theories on information seeking to the health-care industry, stating that its emotional impact serves as an activating mechanism that necessitates search strategies that fit within a stress/coping framework, as developed by Miller and Mangan [21]. Wilson's activating mechanism fills the "gap" between the "situation" and "use" that Dervin [4] identified.

Wilson's study identified three major intervening variables in the information seeking process: personal characteristics, which include emotional variables, educational variables, and demographic variables; social/interpersonal variables; and environmental variables, which can be divided into economic variables and source characteristics. Wilson's [27] model identifies four potential modes of information seeking:

1. *Passive attention.* Information seeking without intention, such as watching television.
2. *Passive search.* Occasions where one type of search results in information that happens to be relevant.
3. *Active search.* An individual actively seeks information.
4. *Ongoing search.* Active searching has established a framework of knowledge and/or ideas, but occasional continuing search is carried out to update or expand that framework.

2.2.5 Kuhlthau

Kuhlthau [14, 15] supplemented Ellis's work by attaching what she called information search process (ISP)—or associated feelings, thoughts, actions, and appropriate information tasks—to the stages of information seeking. ISP focuses on user traits such as thoughts, feelings, and actions rather than system-oriented information. The ISP model's six stages incorporate affective (feelings), cognitive (thoughts), and physical (actions) aspects exhibited by actual library users in a series of five field studies. Each stage also includes an appropriate task that will progress users to the next stage.

1. *Initiation.* Initiation occurs when a user becomes aware of their lack of knowledge or understanding. Uncertainty and apprehension are common, and thoughts focus on contemplating and comprehending the problem. Users must recognize the need for information, and may discuss possible topics and approaches.
2. *Selection.* Selection occurs when a user must identify their general topic to investigate or approach to pursue. Feelings of uncertainty give way to optimism, other users may be consulted, and thoughts center on weighing potential topics against constraining factors, such as personal interest and time.
3. *Exploration.* Exploration occurs when a user must investigate general information on a topic to increase their personal understanding. Thoughts center on becoming informed and oriented enough to articulate a point of view.

Communication between a user and a system may be awkward due to the user's inability to precisely express their information need. Feelings of confusion, uncertainty, and doubt arise.
4. *Formulation*. Formulation is the turning point in ISP. It occurs as users must form a focus for the information they encountered. Thoughts involve identifying and selecting ideas from which to form a focused perspective. This typically occurs gradually and brings an increased sense of confidence.
5. *Collection*. Collection characterizes the time in which interactions between the user and the system function most effectively and efficiently. The task involves gathering information related to the focused topic. Thoughts revolve around defining, extending, and supporting the focus, while actions involve selecting relevant information and making detailed notes. Confidence increases while uncertainty subsides.
6. *Presentation*. Presentation brings relief and satisfaction if the search has gone well, or disappointment if it has not. The user must complete their search and present or otherwise use their findings. Thoughts center around a personalized summation of the topic.

As Kuhlthau drew on Ellis's model to develop ISP, Wilson [28] presented a comparison of Ellis's and Kuhlthau's models, stating, "[...] [T]he two models are fundamentally opposed in the minds of the authors: Kuhlthau posits stages on the basis of her analysis of behaviour, while Ellis suggests that the sequences of behavioural characteristics may vary" (p. 256).

2.2.6 Westbrook

Using the work by Belkin, Dervin, Ellis, and Kuhlthau as reported above, Westbrook [26] proposed a model that redefined information seeking stages in order to reflect users' broad range of needs. Her set of actions includes needing, starting, working, deciding, and closing.

1. *Needing*. Westbrook compares needing to a hologram that a user walks around and through but may have difficulty verbalizing. Referencing Belkin, Kuhlthau, and Taylor, Westbrook views the action of needing as crucial, ambiguous, and evolutionary.
2. *Starting*. Though an initial start must be made, Westbrook believes there is no consensus among researchers regarding that start, however brief it may be. She believes it is the point at which a user moves beyond conceptualizing a need and determines a means to fulfill that need.
3. *Working*. Because the working process can constantly alter every aspect of an information need, it is the most complex and cyclical of Westbrook's stages. Every aspect may involve making a decision regarding the status of a need.
4. *Deciding*. Whether users locate their desired information or give up on their need, they will decide to discontinue their search at some point. Depending on the

decision, further action may or may not be required. Westbrook believes that her preceding literature missed this crucial step.

5. *Closing*. Closing may be the least common of the five actions and can take many forms. Academics may compose papers or presentations, while other users may have a personal need to wrap up an experience through a conversation with a librarian or friend.

In Westbrook's purview, these five actions encompass all preceding relevant research in user needs. User activities may include some or all of the stages in any order with any number of reiterations. In terms of system design, Westbrook calls for communications-based systems that help users inform themselves, create their own order, and cope with their own needs, as opposed to systems that collect, store, retrieve, and deliver one "right" answer.

2.2.7 Marchionini

Marchionini [20] presented another problem-solving approach to information seeking. His model seeks to understand search processes in an electronic environment in which information seeking depends on several interacting factors: information seeker, task, search system, domain, setting, and search outcomes. Marchionini sees the information seeker as the center of this process and believes that information seeking is composed of eight subprocesses which develop in parallel: (1) recognize and accept an information problem, (2) define and understand the problem, (3) choose a search system, (4) formulate a query, (5) execute search, (6) examine results, (7) extract information, and (8) reflect/iterate/stop.

1. *Recognize and accept an information problem.* This aligns with Dervin's "gap" and Belkin's "anomaly" and can be internally or externally motivated. Here, the user becomes aware of an information problem and, if deemed appropriate, accepts it and begins to define it for a search. This initiates problem definition but is largely ignored by system designers who narrowly view it as a user-specific process. Marchionini believes that systems that support interaction and engagement lead users to more readily accept their problems.
2. *Define and understand the problem.* This critical step remains active as long as the information seeking progresses. Most subsequent subprocesses transition back to this stage at some point. Cognitive processes identify key concepts and relationships that lead to a definition of the problem that is articulated as an information seeking task. This can be influenced by knowledge of the task domain and setting. The problem must be limited, labeled, and framed.
3. *Choose a search system.* This depends on the user's previous experience with their topic, scope of their information infrastructure, and expectations of an answer. The type of task and characteristics of various systems are taken into account. In practice, several systems are consulted throughout the process.

These are not only electronic; reference librarians, for example, are considered "systems."
4. *Formulate a query*. This involves matching the task with the chosen system. Typically, the first query string serves as an entry point into the system and is followed by browsing and/or query reformulations. *Semantic mapping* involves the user's own vocabulary's ability to generate content, while *action mapping* involves the strategies and tactics deemed best for fulfilling the task within the rules of a particular system.
5. *Execute search*. The physical actions needed to conduct an information search depend upon the user's mental model of a particular system. This stage is based on the semantic and action mappings that occur during query formulation. Electronic platforms have revolutionized execution, as they reduce the physical actions required for an information need's resolution.
6. *Examine results*. A system's response to a query must be analyzed by the user, who should assess progress toward completing their task by judging the quantity, type, format, and relevance of retrieved results. Expectations often shift throughout the process and are typically determined by the information need and the user's personal information structure.
7. *Extract information*. Assessments about relevance cause information to be extracted. If a document is deemed relevant, the user may immediately extract and save information or may continue to examine other results and later reexamine the document in light of new or different findings. Extracted information is manipulated and integrated into an information seeker's knowledge of their task's domain. A document's perceived relevance can be revised throughout the search process.
8. *Reflect/iterate/stop*. Typically, an initial retrieved set of documents serves as feedback for further query formations and executions. Users should monitor their progress and assess how well their tactics and retrieved information map onto their task. A stopping point may depend on external functions, such as a system's availability, or internal functions, such as motivation or ability.

The various frameworks and models presented in this section demonstrate the multifaceted nature of information seeking and information seeking behavior, as well as the rich research landscape that surrounds the subjects.

2.3 Models Built on Foundational Models

Rather than focus on specific domains, some theorists expand upon classic information seeking models to develop new or updated general theories. Considering the current rapid pace at which information is produced and disseminated through a near-infinite number of channels and sources, these modern theories shed important light on users' ability to satisfy their information needs. The following demonstrate how foundational models can apply to more modern contexts.

2.3.1 Expanded ISP

David et al. [3] proposed a multistep process built upon Kuhlthau's [14] information search process (ISP) that examines the process of information seeking in hyperlinked environments. Their model is ideally suited for information seeking situations in which goals are emergent. They developed a cyclical model to examine the relationships among perceived goal difficulty, goal success, and self-efficacy. The study examined the emergent properties of information seeking in hyperlinked environments using self-efficacy as a mediating mechanism and intrinsic motivation as a moderating factor.

The authors focused on a broad conception of information seeking behavior to develop a general framework that captured directed and semi-directed information seeking. Their model combines goal-setting theory (or the idea that human behavior is motivated by goals) with self-efficacy in information seeking, motivational factors, and—most fundamentally—the information seek cycle (ISC) initially proposed by Fredin and David [11]. ISC consists of three stages:

1. *Preparation*. When a user prepares to make choices from a menu of links in a hyperlinked system
2. *Exploration*. When a user navigates and explores their choices' results and processes the information
3. *Consolidation*. When a user evaluates the results against the goals they set during the preparation stage

After testing their model on 42 undergraduate students who were assigned a specific search task, researchers drew the following conclusions based on ISP and ISC:

1. Perceptions of goal difficulty carry forward from one stage to the next.
2. Goals perceived to be more difficult at the beginning of a cycle are less likely to be achieved.
3. Success did not significantly affect future cycles' information goals, but operated mainly through confidence.
4. While increased confidence within a cycle led users to believe the information goal would be easier, the previous cycle's lingering confidence seemed to encourage users to increase the difficulty of their goals.
5. Initial intrinsic motivation had a moderating effect on the link between success and confidence.

Ultimately, the study captured the dynamic shifts in goal constructs and related psychological processes involved in information seeking. But perhaps more significantly, it integrated other scholars' relevant theories and created an empirical test of the overarching framework of cyclical information seeking.

2.3.2 Information Seeking and Communication

Robson and Robinson [24] built on existing models of information seeking behavior to develop a model that encompassed both information seeking and communication. They hoped to identify key factors affecting communication and the use of information in order to create a practical model for both information providers and users.

The literature uncovered during this study demonstrated a divide between information seeking research concentrated in library and information science (LIS) and work done in the wider field of communication. While commonalities exist, LIS research focused on information and its user while communications research focused on the communicator and the communication process. The model proposed by Robson and Robinson [24] combined key elements from both fields to account for both an information seeker and a communicator or information provider.

In their review of information science research, Robson and Robinson [24] referred to Ellis, Kuhlthau, and Wilson. However, preexisting scholarship lacked any insight into communication as part of information behavior, and thus did not account for the following significant concepts:

1. Context
2. Demographics
3. Expertise
4. Psychological factors such as perception, self-efficacy, and cognitive dissonance

By combining information seeking research with concepts from communication, Robson's and Robinson's study developed a novel information seeking and communication model (ISCM). Both information users (including information seekers and those with information needs) and information providers or communicators (including authors, publishers, and Websites) operate within various and intersecting situational contexts that motivate information seeking behaviors and assessments. Interaction between searchers and communicators is necessary during this process. This fresh take on information seeking provides insight into searching behaviors and the importance of the utility and the credibility of information and its sources.

2.3.3 Mediated Information Retrieval

Using observational and longitudinal data collected in the United States and United Kingdom, Spink et al. [25] investigated the process of mediated information retrieval searching during human information seeking episodes to characterize aspects of that process, which included information seekers' changing situational contexts, information problems, uncertainty reduction, successive searching and cognitive styles, and cognitive and affective states.

Their research approach is embedded in a theoretical framework that draws on previous IR and human information behavior (HIB) studies. Drawing on Wilson and Belkin, Spink et al. [25] aimed to integrate both fields to further the development of future models that should account for Web and IR system design and evaluation. In particular, they examined interactive search episodes to study how shifts take place during and between searches over time. These shifts include changes in tactics, the definition of the information problem, strategies, terms, goal states, uncertainty, and feedback. Time, problem-solving processes, information seeking episodes, uncertainty, cognitive styles, interactive search sessions, and successive searching behaviors were also examined to investigate human information seeking and searching processes in mediated online searching environments. The authors related these variables to the work of other researchers such as Kuhlthau and Ellis.

The actual theoretical framework consists of a set of situated actions within interactive search episodes over a period of time that can be represented as human information seeking stages and successive searches. According to Spink et al. [25], these successive interactions can be integrated with Wilson's [28] theoretical framework to indicate steps along a problem-solving process. An analysis of these episodes could impact system design and design criteria through implications that concern graphic displays and interactivity of IR systems, which would facilitate research. Above all, this framework focuses on a larger picture that embraces information seeking and information searching and draws together major concepts (e.g., interaction and time) to integrate existing and future IR and information seeking models.

2.3.4 Emerging Concepts: Sense-Making and Multi-Session IR

First applied to information science by Dervin [4], sense-making draws on existing theories to consider how users attempt to make sense of uncertain situations. This could include how they interpret information to use for their own information-related decisions, and how they make sense of words in their own language. Qu and Furnas [22] advocated for a model-driven approach where existing user behavior models were used to inform the evaluation process. While their theory belongs to a family of formative, user-centered evaluation methods, it focused more on users' processes than specific system design. This allowed for a better understanding of the interaction between users and systems, as well as a discovery of the missing components in existing designs. Qu and Furnas [22] presented how a sense-making model informed a formative evaluation of a basic exploratory search system.

Zhang and Soergel [29] proposed a model that's framework analyzed and described cognitive processes and mechanisms involved in individual sense-making. They focused on changes to conceptual space and cognitive mechanisms used in achieving those changes. Their paper reviewed and extended existing sense-making models with ideas from learning and cognition. Sense-making models in human-computer interaction (HCI); cognitive system engineering; organizational communication; and LIS, learning theories, cognitive psychology, and task-based information seeking received special attention. The model resulting from that synthesis created a stronger basis for explaining sense-making behaviors and conceptual changes. It also illustrated the iterative process of sense-making.

Multi-session information seeking exemplifies another framework that expands upon older IR models, and can involve multistep information seeking processes, collaborative information seeking (CIS), and/or the systems that foster these interactions. Several theorists have developed models rooted in this concept.

Lee et al. [16] conducted a detailed walk-through of similarities between the "creative process" and the behavioral model of information seeking. They systematically analyzed and compared each stage in the "creative process" with "activities" in the behavior model of information seeking, and established links where similarities were found. Four common links were established: preparation, incubation, illumination, and verification. The researchers concluded that the type of information seeking task may have an impact on the extent to which an information seeker exhibits all stages of the model. In other words, depending on the type of task, the extent or way in which information seekers exhibit proposed stages in creative information seeking may be different.

Foster [10] offered a nonlinear model of information seeking behavior, which contrasted with earlier-stage models of information behavior and represented a potential cornerstone shift toward a new perspective for understanding user information behavior. The paper offered four main implications of the model as it applied to existing theories, required future research, and could develop information curricula. Central to these implications was the creation of a new nonlinear perspective from which user information seeking could be interpreted.

Lin and Belkin [17] proposed a model called multiple information seeking episodes (MISE), which consisted of four dimensions: problematic situation, information problem, information seeking process, and episodes. MISE explained successive search experiences for essentially the same information problem.

Kari and Savolainen's [12] theoretical paper proposed a contextual model of Web searching from an individual's perspective based on holistic reflection and earlier literature. The framework included various layers: lifeworlds, domains, situations, action, information action, information seeking, information sources, Internet, and Web. Together, they formed the dynamics of the entire creation. The researchers claim that the framework amounts to an exhaustive description of the context of Web information seeking, and that the theoretical construct can be taken advantage of when researching information seeking from practically any source.

Karunakaran et al. [13] offered collaborative information behavior (CIB) as an umbrella term to connote the collaborative aspects of information seeking, retrieval, and use. With findings from past studies conducted by their research team and other researchers, the authors provided the contours of a CIB model. They conceptualized CIB as comprised of a set of constitutive activities organized into three phrases: problem formulation, CIS, and information use. We will revisit this idea of CIB and CIS in Chap. 6.

2.4 Summary

Information seeking is one of the most fundamental attributes of human behavior. It's a combination of human curiosity and consciousness. These particular attributes have allowed us to invent life-sustaining tools and techniques, discover methods for survival and progress, and advance from Stone Age to Information Age. In this chapter, we reviewed information seeking as a concept primarily studied in the fields of information science and IR. We saw that information seeking is a subset of information behavior, but more general than IR. But just like many other theoretical concepts, you can be forgiven for mixing one term with another. Scholars who do fabulous work in IR may also be making significant contributions to information seeking and vice versa. And so, unsurprisingly, the models and methods we reviewed in this chapter had overlaps among information behavior, information seeking, and IR. We learned that most of the models recognize the need for seeking information—whether it's called *need*, *gap*, or *anomalous state of knowledge*. Most of them also identify phases or stages in one's information seeking process, and almost all of them start and end with a human. After all, information seeking is about focusing on a person rather than the system/resources.

What is often striking to some scholars is that all of these models assume an individual information seeker. But in reality, we find many situations in which people are seeking information *through* and/or *with* other people, the former being a social information seeking situation and the latter being a collaborative information seeking scenario. In other words, while the models described in this chapter do a fine job of explaining individual information seeking processes, they tell us little to nothing about those social and collaborative situations. At best, they try adding social and collaborative steps as a new layer or a factor of information seeking. But that's quite ad hoc, and those who greatly care about social and collaborative aspects of information seeking, including myself, argue that we need to study such situations in a more holistic way and not as an afterthought. And so we will revisit these two concepts in the later chapters when we talk about social Q&A, social search, and collaborative information seeking, as well as their combination as social and collaborative information seeking.

References

1. Belkin, N.: Anomalous states of knowledge as a basis for information retrieval. Can. J. Inf. Sci. **5**, 133–143 (1980)
2. Case, D.O., Given, L.M.: Looking for Information: A Survey of Research on Information Seeking, Needs, and Behavior, 4th edn. Emerald Group Publishing Limited, Amsterdam (2016)
3. David, P., Song, M., Hayes, A., Fredin, E.S.: A cyclic model of information seeking in hyperlinked environments: the role of goals, self-efficacy, and intrinsic motivation. Int. J. Hum.-Comput. Stud. **65**(2), 170–182 (2007)
4. Dervin, B.: Useful theory for librarianship: Communication, not information. Drexel Libr. Q. **13**, 16–32 (1997)

5. Dervin, B., Nilan, M.: Information needs and uses. In: Annual Review of Information Science and Technology, vol. 21, pp. 3–33. Knowledge Industry Publications, White Plains (1986)
6. Ellis, D.: A behavioral approach to information retrieval system design. J. Doc. **45**(3), 171–212 (1989)
7. Ellis, D., Haugan, M.: Modelling the information seeking patterns of engineers and research scientists in an industrial environment. J. Doc. **53**(4), 384–403 (1997)
8. Ellis, D., Cox, D., Hall, K.: A comparison of the information seeking patterns of researchers in the physical and social sciences. J. Doc. **49**(4), 356–369 (1993)
9. Ford, N.: Introduction to Information Behaviour. Facet Publishing, London (2015)
10. Foster, A.: A nonlinear model of information-seeking behavior. J. Am. Soc. Inf. Sci. Technol. **55**(3), 228–237 (2004)
11. Fredin, E.S., David, P.: Browsing and the hypermedia interaction cycle: a model of self-efficacy and goal dynamics. J. Mass Commun. Q. **75**(1), 35–54 (1998)
12. Kari, J., Savolainen, R.: Towards a contextual model of information seeking on the Web. New Rev. Inf. Behav. Res. **4**(1), 155–175 (2003)
13. Karunakaran, A., Reddy, M.C., Spence, P.R.: Toward a model of collaborative information behavior in organizations. J. Am. Soc. Inf. Sci. Technol. **64**(12), 2437–2451 (2013)
14. Kuhlthau, C.C.: Inside the search process: information seeking from the user's perspective. J. Am. Soc. Inf. Sci. **42**(5), 361–371 (1991)
15. Kuhlthau, C.C.: Seeking Meaning: A Process Approach to Library and Information Services. Ablex Publishing, Norwood (1994)
16. Lee, S.-S., Theng, Y.-L., Goh, D.H.-L.: Creative information seeking Part I: a conceptual framework. ASLIB Proc. **57**(5), 460–475 (2005)
17. Lin, S.-J., Belkin, N.: Validation of a model of information seeking over multiple search sessions. J. Am. Soc. Inf. Sci. Technol. **56**(4), 393–415 (2005)
18. Marchionini, G.: Information-seeking strategies of novices using a full-text electronic encyclopedia. J. Am. Soc. Inf. Sci. **40**(1), 54–66 (1989)
19. Marchionini, G.: Information Seeking in Electronic Environments. Cambridge University Press, Cambridge (1995)
20. Marchionini, G.: Information Seeking in Electronic Environments. Cambridge Series on Human-Computer Interaction. Cambridge University Press, Cambridge (1995)
21. Miller, S.M., Mangan, C.E.: Interacting effects of information and coping style in adapting to gynecologic stress: should the doctor tell all? J. Pers. Soc. Psychol. **45**(1), 223–36 (1983)
22. Qu, Y., Furnas, G.W.: Model-driven formative evaluation of exploratory search: a study under a sensemaking framework. Inf. Process. Manage. **44**(2), 534–555 (2008)
23. Reinhard, C.D., Dervin, B.: Comparing situated sense-making processes in virtual worlds: application of Dervin's sense-making methodology to media reception situations. Convergence: Int. J. Res. New Media Technol. **18**(1), 27–48 (2012)
24. Robson, A., Robinson, L.: Building on models of information behaviour: linking information seeking and communication. J. Doc. **69**(2), 169–193 (2013)
25. Spink, A., Wilson, T.D., Ford, N., Foster, A., Ellis, D.: Information-seeking and mediated searching. Part 1. Theoretical framework and research design. J. Am. Soc. Inf. Sci. Technol. **53**(9), 695–703 (2002)
26. Westbrook, L.: User needs: a synthesis and analysis of current theories for the practitioner. RQ **32**(4), 541–549 (1993)
27. Wilson, T.D.: Information behavior: an interdisciplinary perspective. Inf. Process. Manage. **33**(4), 551–572 (1997)
28. Wilson, T.D.: Models in information behaviour research. J. Doc. **55**(3), 249–270 (1999)
29. Zhang, P.Y., Soergel, D.: Towards a comprehensive model of the cognitive process and mechanisms of individual sensemaking. J. Assoc. Inf. Sci. Technol. **65**(9), 1733–1756 (2014)

Chapter 3
Social Media and Social Networking

Abstract Information can travel at the speed of light, and social media and social networking services make it possible to actually deliver that information at lightning speed to and for billions of people around the planet. This chapter introduces these two concepts, along with various services that facilitate them and a number of issues stemming from their introduction and use. The chapter first describes how social media and social networking services and systems are defined and studied. In doing so, it points out how being social—something that is fundamental to humankind—has taken shape in the online world. The chapter then dives deeper into some of the issues introduced by and studied within the context of social media/networking. These include privacy, identity construction, impression making, communication, social capital, knowledge sharing, access, and digital inequality.

3.1 Introduction

Some time in 2011, there was an earthquake that moderately shook the Northeast United States. Its epicenter was around Washington, DC, and the shockwaves propagated through a large part of the East Coast. While the quake did not produce any substantial damage to people or properties, it was intriguing that, before Bostonians physically felt the tremors, they learned about this event through tweets from the DC area. This is truly an example of information traveling at the speed of light—certainly at a speed faster than an earthquake!

If this was written a decade ago, we would be talking about how amazing this phenomenon is—information dissemination through a microblogging site in a manner not previously conceivable. But we live in an era where such instances are a commonplace. The power of the participatory Web, often called the Web 2.0, is realized and practiced by almost everyone connected to the Internet. While it's not a physically different entity, Web 2.0 reflects a revolutionary mentality in Web users. This new platform, which includes user-driven services and user-generated content, affords us the ability to not only seek and consume information but also to produce and manipulate it. In this chapter, we will see how this new information behavior is manifested through social media and networking services.

C. Shah, *Social Information Seeking*, The Information Retrieval Series 38,
DOI 10.1007/978-3-319-56756-3_3

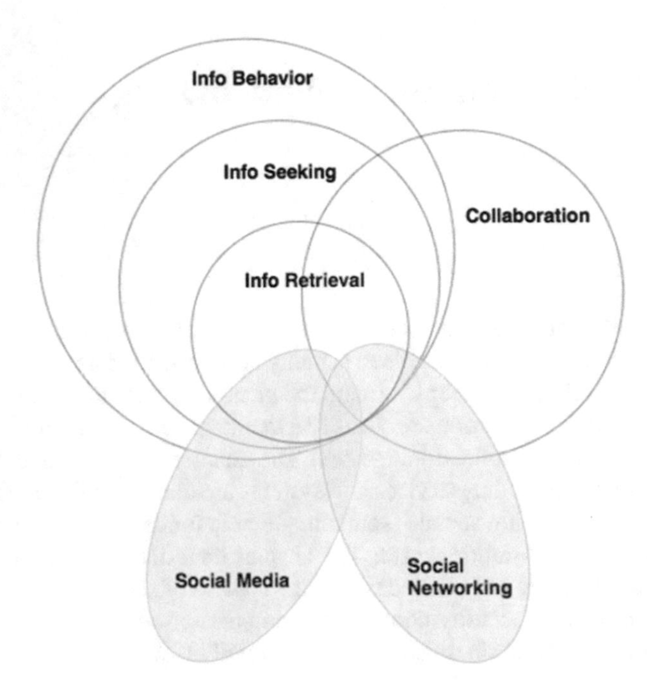

Fig. 3.1 A schematic view of social media and social networking in the context of other related concepts

The chapter will start with a section on social media and a section on social networking, even though at times it's hard to separate them. Then we will dive deeper into some of the core issues relating to social media/networking, including privacy, identity construction, communication and knowledge sharing, and social capital. The big picture of all our related concepts, along with social media and social networking, is shown in Fig. 3.1.

3.2 Social Media

Various sources have tried to concretely define social media. Social media encompasses "forms of electronic communication (as Websites for social networking and microblogging) through which users create online communities to share information, ideas, personal messages, and other content (as videos)" (Merriam-Webster). Or, "Social media refers to websites like Facebook, Twitter, LinkedIn,[1]

[1]https://www.linkedin.com.

Instagram,[2] MySpace,[3] YouTube,[4] and the like, sites where individuals create, share, or exchange information and ideas in a virtual community and network" [16, p. 135]. Still, others point out that social media can be used by businesses to attract more consumers for their specific products or services: "Consumers are utilizing platforms—such as content sharing sites, blogs, social networking, and wikis—to create, modify, share, and discuss Internet content" [26]. One thing we can all agree on: a *lot* of people use social media.

As of September 2016, the online social networking application Facebook registered more than 1.18 billion daily active users on average [12]. 1.09 billion daily active users access the site via mobile devices, while 1.79 billion users access the site monthly and 1.66 billion users access the site monthly via mobile [12]. Facebook reports that approximately 84.9% of daily active users are outside the United States or Canada [12].

Facebook currently leads the way as the most popular social networking platform, followed by WhatsApp[5] and Facebook Messenger. In general, social media usage has grown exponentially in the past 10 years. In 2006, 7% of the United States population used one or more social networking sites (SNSs). Now, in 2016, 65% engage via social media, and 76% of American Internet users participate in social networking [7].

Social media users range from teenagers to adults; members of Generation X (35–44 years old) are increasingly joining the number of users, spectators, and critics of social media [25, p. 59]. As of 2014, the over-65 demographic was driving social media growth, while the 50–63 age cohort had stalled. Instagram and Tumblr[6] are most popular with younger age groups, but most forms of social media now reach users of all ages and genders [7].

And we don't only see diversity in demographics when it comes to social media; there are also differences in how social media users engage with their chosen platforms. "Social media is fueled by information, just as the Internet and other digital media before it, but the information on social media is different from other media in that we are not just consumers of the information on it, but are also active producers of information within it" [38, p. 34]. Social media users generally tend to seek information that is in accordance with their interests, needs, or existing attitudes. They tend to avoid information that contradicts their viewpoints and often employ selective exposure, in which they consciously or unconsciously avoid or reject contradictory information. "Hence, people often stay within their own comfort zones in regard to information seeking and information sharing, rather than venture into zones that involve a lot of sense-making" [38, p. 37].

---

[2]https://www.instagram.com.

[3]https://myspace.com.

[4]https://www.youtube.com.

[5]https://www.whatsapp.com.

[6]https://www.tumblr.com.

Many researchers have attempted to answer one basic, central question concerning social media: why do people participate? Studies have found numerous reasons behind users' participation in social media, many of which support observations of diverse information seeking behaviors. For instance, in a study conducted by Kim et al. [27], researchers examined a variety of social media platforms used as information sources to support various purposes. Leist [31] found that online communities are used for "providing and receiving social support when confronted with a difficult life situation, regardless of geographical location or time" (pp. 1–2). People also use social media as a form of validation and reassurance. According to Maslow's Hierarchy of Needs, everything we do revolves around a need we are seeking to satisfy. Once our basic physiological needs such as food, shelter, and water are satisfied, we then need to satisfy our needs for love, belonging, esteem, and self-actualization. Through social media usage, users can meet new people, establish and build relationships with others, express their creativity, and build self-confidence through their interactions. However, a study done by Derek Ruth and Jürgen Pfeffer found that social media is not the most accurate measure of human behavior, since users can misrepresent who they are online [35]. Through their respective examinations of social media, researchers mine a plethora of information.

3.3 Social Networking

SNSs include Facebook, Twitter, Tumblr, Instagram, LinkedIn, YouTube, Yelp, and hundreds of other platforms that attract millions of users, many of whom have integrated SNS use into their daily practices [5, p. 210]. SNSs support a wide range of interests and activities. Despite commonalities found among key technological features, the cultures that emerge around SNSs are varied. boyd[7] and Ellison [5] isolate three key features of SNSs: they allow individuals to (1) construct a public or semipublic profile within a bound system, (2) articulate a list of other users with whom they can connect, and (3) "view and traverse their list of connections and those made by others within the system" (p. 211). Social networking sites began to appear around 1997 and have since grown in global popularity. Duggin and Smith state that, in 2013, 73% of adults online used some sort of SNS (as cited in [16, p. 135]). As of December 2014, Facebook spanned 80 languages [13].

The countless interactions that occur via SNSs comprise an important component of social media. According to Narayan [38], "social media platforms have become tangible and real places where we gather in intended and unintended ways" (p. 33). Social media has altered the concept of "cyberspace" through its transformation of abstract information spaces into concrete places visited in everyday lives and public spheres. Through social media, users are able to construct their identities, play to real and perceived audiences, engage in knowledge sharing activities, and perform

[7]No, this is not a typo. This is how dannah boyd spells her name!

other tasks that involve interacting with both technology and fellow SNS users. When defining social networking, Kietzmann et al. [26] identify seven functional building blocks: identity, conversations, sharing, presence, relationships, reputation, and groups. The rich information landscape forged by social networking/media has gained a great deal of scholarly and critical attention. Current trends examine identity construction, communication tactics, social capital, knowledge sharing activities, and issues of access.

3.4 Privacy

Social media's growing popularity has given new urgency to individuals' right to privacy. Though users may dole out personal information that ranges from movie preferences to social security numbers, Purdy [41] points out that all data is stored or disseminated without the knowledge of individuals involved. While an estimated 99% of that data may never be analyzed, it remains available.

Two major areas of concern exist between social media and privacy: government behavior and children's safety. The law dealing most specifically with online privacy in the United States is the Electronic Communications and Privacy Act of 1986, which was passed long before social media became pervasive [41]. Although many social media users are aware of privacy concerns, they continue to post personal and/or sensitive information to friends and followers, all of which can easily become available to the public depending on privacy settings. Additionally, law enforcement agencies commonly request information from major social media outlets. Facebook, Twitter, LinkedIn, and Dropbox have all developed their own regulations for responding to such requests [41]. After data released by whistle-blower Edward Snowden concerning the Verizon metadata program combined with panic over the NSA's violation of online privacy rights via the PRISM surveillance program, a number of laws were introduced to protect digital privacy at the state level. According to Richards [42], a survey of current privacy laws finds them insufficient given the current cyber-landscape.

Children's online privacy is of particular concern. Purdy [41] contends that children and teenagers—who make up a significant portion of social media users—are less likely to be concerned about privacy than older users. The plethora of information that can be gathered from their posts, including addresses and other location indicators, can easily put children in harm's way. Many parents may not be tech-savvy enough to guide their children through an online privacy lesson. A clinical report compiled by the American Academy of Pediatrics [40] discusses youths' exposure to social media and concludes that cyberbullying, "Facebook depression" (in which young people exhibit signs of depression after spending an extended period interacting online rather than face-to-face), sexting, and exposure to inappropriate content are all potential ramifications of online social networking. Internet safety education is a must for young social media users.

Acquisti et al. [1] summarized and connected various streams of empirical research on privacy behavior. They identified three themes that influence how humans behave in the face of privacy concerns:

1. Uncertainty about the consequences of privacy-related behavior and their own preferences over those consequences
2. The context dependency of people's concern (or lack thereof) about privacy, which can vary and change over time and/or based on cultural norms and an illusion of anonymity
3. The degree to which privacy concerns are manipulable by commercial and governmental bodies

In her analysis of these concerns, Johnstone [24] contends that the processes result in "privacy tradeoffs" in which people uncharacteristically disclose personal information that may ultimately be contrary to their and others' best interests.

Beyond everyday social media users and at-risk children, many studies on privacy and social media focus on specific professional groups and how they can navigate various privacy-related challenges. Health-care professionals, for example, publish a great deal of information concerning social media usage. The Alaska Nurses Association [39] permits its members to participate in online social networking, but cautions against including any patient details in their posts and interactions. This protects patients' right to privacy and prevents nurses from breaking their professional, legal, and ethical obligations. Library scholars also focus on social media and its potential effects. Their works generally promote the notion that librarians must continue to champion privacy rights in the face of social media's many controversies and loopholes. For example, Lamdan [30] argues that because social media has become a major source of information and a hub for information seeking, librarians must shape and spread social media policies that protect users' privacy and allow them to seek and share information without limits.

3.5 Identity Construction and Making Impressions

Many studies of social media and SNSs focus on users' ability to both establish their identities and make impressions via their respective profiles and activities. Donath [8] states, "in the world of the virtual community, identity is [. . .] ambiguous. Many of the basic cues about personality and social role we are accustomed to in the physical world are absent" (n.p.). Studying UseNet, Donath [8] asserts that virtual identities can be deceptive and are often based upon an account name, the content and connotation of posts, and social cues such as signatures. Deception can apply to social categories, impersonations, concealed attributes, and "trolls," or those who attempt to pass as legitimate participants in a group [8]. Hancock [23] also tackles digital deception by examining identity-based forms of online deception and the lies that are often present in everyday digital communications.

Gonzales and Hancock [20] examine how computer-mediated self-presentations can alter identities. Using a linguistic analysis, they found that presenting oneself in a mediated context "engenders a sense of public being" that could manipulate an audience [20, p. 179]. They also believe that the Internet serves as an outlet for self-construction, which can inform user behavior.

In terms of the impression a user can make through social media, Utz [43] conducted an experiment to determine how self-generated information combines with friend-generated information and the sheer number of friends a user possesses to influence perceived popularity, communal orientation, and social attractiveness. Her hypothesis operated based on the "warranting principle," or the idea that "perceivers' judgments about a target rely more heavily on information which the targets themselves cannot manipulate than on self-deceptions" [45, p. 229]. Walther et al. [45] used the warranting principle to discuss the effects of social comments on impression formation. They found that there may be domains of impressions for which warranting is heuristically useful—such as physical attractiveness—and others where it is not, such as attributions of introversion and extroversion [45, p. 247]. It would seem, however, that interactions via social media have an important effect on one's social media identity and presence. These interactions revolve around various methods of communication.

3.6 Communication via Social Media Platforms

Many scholars focus on the ways in which communication and expression occur on social media platforms. One area of interest concerns how social media interactions align with face-to-face interactions via communication styles and tactics. In a study conducted among Facebook users, Kramer et al. [28] found that emotional states could be transferred to others via emotional contagion. Previously, emotional contagion—which leads people to experience the same emotions as those they are interacting with without their knowledge—was thought to only apply to in-person situations, but Kramer, Guillory, and Hancock's study suggests that social media interactions can contain many nuances previously assumed to apply only to nonverbal cues. These findings also suggest that massive-scale contagion via social networks is possible.

In their study of Twitter users, Marwick and boyd [36] identify an important difference between social networking and face-to-face communication. They focus on a Twitter user's "imagined audience" and posit that, because social media users do not have a concrete understanding of their reach, they "take cues from the social media environment to imagine the community" (p. 115). In doing so, social media users often frame their posts around imagined audiences that are entirely different from those who actually read and interact with their posted content. These users engage in strategic self-commodification to appeal to their target and/or perceived followings. Bernstein et al. [4] found that social media users consistently underestimate their audience size for their postings, guessing that their audience is only 27% of its actual size. In a related study, Yee and Bailenson [47] examined self-representation in virtual environments, such as SNSs. They discovered the "Proteus Effect," in which those who represented themselves as confident and/or conventionally attractive engaged in a higher rate of self-disclosure and self-assuredness throughout their interpersonal interactions. While Yee and Bailenson [47] focused mainly on cordial interactions, they admit that their findings also have implications for hostile online communication (p. 274).

In a cornerstone study of computer-mediated communication, Walther [44] contended that "media"—which can be applied to today's conception of social media—could facilitate communication that surpasses typical face-to-face interpersonal information sharing. Walther [44] coined the term "hyperpersonal" to describe this phenomenon and stated that receivers, senders, channels, and feedback elements all contribute to enhanced computer-mediated interpersonal communications. "Hyperpersonal" interactions may be related to current social media phenomena, including offensive postings, "Twitter wars," and other abrasive and/or revealing social networking activities.

In the realm of communication via social media platforms, some scholars focus on specific types of exchanges. Gil de Zuniga and Valenzuela [18], for example, studied engaged citizenship and found that citizen communication that took place within large online networks fostered weak interpersonal ties, which led to invigorated civic participation (p. 415).

3.7 Social Capital

Closely related to communication tactics is the idea of "social capital," which a user can accrue through effective social networking. Appel et al. [3] define individual social capital as "the sum of the resources embedded in social structure, or the potential to access resources in social networks for some purposeful action" (p. 399). Social capital contains two distinct measures: bonding and bridging. Bonding refers to resources accessible through one's homogeneous and trusted social network, whereas bridging refers to resources accessible through heterogeneous networks that involve weaker social ties [3]. Various methods have been employed to measure social capital, including analyses of trust levels, participation in voluntary associations, and other levels of engagement. Williams's [46] Internet Social Capital Scale (ISCS) is one way in which these constructs are combined into a metric tool. Appel et al. [3] argue that the ISCS is ineffective due to its conflation of social capital with related concepts, such as social support and attachment. They advocate for alternative measures that rely strictly on the discrete concept of social capital.

Researchers have employed various methods to quantify SNS users' social capital. Ellison et al. [10] studied social capital in the context of Facebook users' "connection strategies," or relational communication activities (p. 873). They found that users derived social capital benefits, such as emotional support and exposure to diverse ideas, through information seeking behaviors rather than connection strategies that focused on close friends or strangers. In a later study, Ellison et al. [11] examined the relationship between bridging social capital and Facebook Relationship Maintenance Behaviors (FRMB), or behaviors that "assess the extent to which subjects report they engage in activities that signal attention to and purposefully cultivate relationships on the site" (p. 864). Ellison et al. [11] found significant positive relationships between measures of bridging social capital and users' total number of friends and their engagement in FRMB. Kwon and Adler [29] provide a comprehensive overview of social capitals' evolution and cross-disciplinary acceptance as a valid field of study.

3.8 Knowledge Sharing

Social media and social networking can facilitate a variety of knowledge sharing practices. These interactions can be both formal and informal and may or may not be in relation to organized business and managerial practices. Gibbs et al. [17] assert, "Social media tools such as blogs, social network sites (SNSs), wikis and microblogging are proliferating in organizations and providing new sites of collaboration, coordination, and community" (p. 102). Social media enables organizations to participate in knowledge sharing by helping people locate expertise and relevant content, engage in sense-making about other employees, access new people and perspectives, and increase contact among virtual employees [17, p. 102]. Gibbs et al. [17] specifically focus on the ways in which social media platforms can strategically limit information sharing in order to maximize individual and organization-wide productivity and positive attitudes. In their review of enterprise social media practices within organizations, Leonardi et al. [32] provide a comprehensive understanding of communicative activities and work accomplishments through social media platforms.

Faraj et al. [14] report their investigation about knowledge collaboration in online communities (OCs), which include social media platforms and SNSs. They posit that OCs facilitate an unparalleled scale and scope of communication. Specifically, they examine the fluidity inherent in OCs, which engenders a dynamic flow of resources that results in positive and negative consequences. They identify five tensions (passion, time, socially ambiguous identities, social disembodiment of ideas, and temporary convergence) that, when met with certain generative responses, sustain knowledge collaboration through OCs [14]. In a later study, Faraj et al. [15] expand upon this research and create a framework that explores the antecedents of leadership in online communities focused on knowledge work. Fleck and Johnson-Migalski [16] specifically analyze information and knowledge sharing that occur between Adlerian mental health providers and their patient community, and conclude that social media use can educate and reduce clients' isolation if companies are willing to embrace its impact.

Knowledge sharing and classification via Web-based collaborative tagging systems comprise another area of study. Golder and Huberman [19] define collaborative tagging as "the process by which many users add metadata in the form of keywords to shared content" (p. 198). They assert that tagging can be traced through stable patterns that expedite knowledge sharing through imitation. In a more recent study, Mican and Tomai [37] reiterated these findings, and added that social tagging systems contain various semantic structures that can be integrated with recommendation systems, and thus used to identify experts and trustworthy content.

In a linguistic study of group information seeking, Gonzales et al. [21] found that linguistic style matching (LSM)—an algorithm for calculating verbal mimicry based on an automated textual analysis of function of words—could predict the cohesiveness of groups in both face-to-face and computer-mediated interactions. Thus, verbal mimicry can predict underlying social dynamics that may affect information seeking and sharing on SNSs. In another study that compares face-to-face information seeking and sharing with computer-mediated learning, Lester and King [33] found that students in virtual classroom settings were able to learn just as much as their traditional counterparts.

Zimmer [48] raises a different, but important, issue in his research on social media usage and knowledge gathering. His approach states that researchers who mine SNSs for data are subject to ethical concerns, including consent, properly identifying and respecting privacy, data anonymization prior to release, and the relative expertise of institutional review boards. Lewis et al. [34] also discuss social network analysis, though they use Facebook data to demonstrate the potential to improve network research through social media platforms, particularly because SNSs demonstrate users' cultural preferences.

3.9 Access and Digital Inequality

Of course, social media's ability to facilitate knowledge sharing is contingent upon potential users' ability to access and utilize its features. And at this point, it's important to consider how the world is divided up when it comes to access to digital information (see Fig. 3.2).

Hampton [22] argues against those that believe that users with more privilege and resources reap the most benefits from Internet services. Examining community-level interactions, Hampton [22] states, "The literature on digital inequality [...] has overlooked change within the context where social and civic inequalities are reproduced. The Internet reduces the transaction costs of communication, and this, in turn, undermines contextual constraints on social and civic involvement" (p. 2). Communication and knowledge sharing via social media may actually reduce knowledge gaps. Related to social media's potentially inclusive effects, Allan [2], when studying women in the Sahara, points out that social media "can preserve diverse women's voices, whose perspectives are too often invisible in mainstream news media" (p. 704). Current trends seem to focus on how social media can provide access to marginalized groups, rather than how it could further inhibit disadvantaged populations.

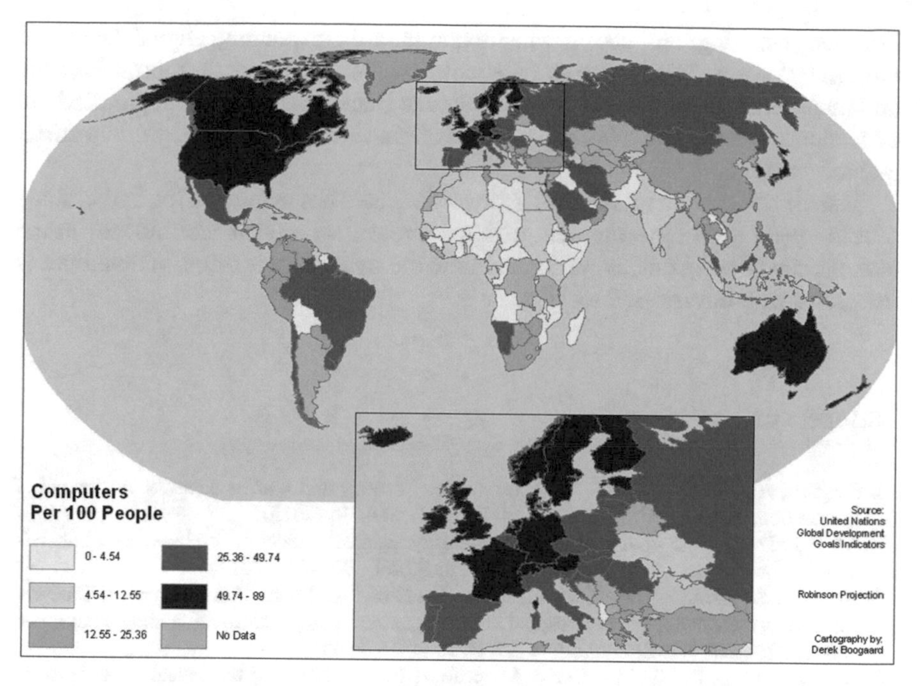

Fig. 3.2 The global digital divide. Source: WikiMedia, https://upload.wikimedia.org/wikipedia/commons/b/bd/Global_Digital_Divide1.png

Another major area of access-related study concerns social media users' ages. Buckingham's [6] *Youth, Identity, and Digital Media* contains essays that tackle the generational divide in social networking, as well as the advantages and disadvantages granted to young people through their social media literacy. Dutot [9] used the digital gap that exists between generations to study individuals' willingness to adopt social media. Findings suggested that age influences optimism, innovativeness, and perceived usefulness toward the adoption of social media [9].

3.10 Summary

This chapter provided an introduction to social media and social networking concepts, services, and issues. Those born in this century may not even know of the time when these services did not exist, and millennials may not be able to imagine their lives without being connected to and through social media/networking. But relatively speaking, social media and social networking sites (SNSs) are new areas of study that have deep implications for how individuals, interest groups, and corporations communicate with both known contacts and perceived audiences. Thus far, scholars have focused on identity formation, communication, social capital, knowledge sharing, and access when examining the expanding digital landscape created by various SNSs, such as Facebook, Twitter, Instagram, Tumblr, LinkedIn, and more. Emerging scholarly trends may take shape around marketing initiatives, educational potential, and social media's role in relaying emergency notifications and information.

In some respect, the social media/networking field has matured a lot, and in some other respect, maybe we are just getting started! Let's revisit that thought in the next section of this book as we look at how the social aspect of our online lives is integrated with information seeking.

References

1. Acquisti, A., Brandimarte, L., Loewenstein, G.: Privacy and human behavior in the age of information. Science (New York, NY) **347**(6221), 509–514 (2015)
2. Allan, J.: Privilege, marginalization, and solidarity: women's voices online in Western Sahara's struggle for independence. Feminist Media Stud. **14**(4), 704–708 (2014)
3. Appel, L., Dadlani, P., Dwyer, M., Hampton, K., Kitzie, V., Matni, Z.A., Moore, P., Teodoro, R.: Testing the validity of social capital measures in the study of information and communication technologies. Inf. Commun. Soc. **17**(4), 398–416 (2014)
4. Bernstein, M.S., Bakshy, E., Burke, M., Karrer, B.: Quantifying the invisible audience in social networks. In: Proceedings of the SIGCHI Conference on Human Factors in Computing Systems - CHI '13, p. 21. ACM Press, New York, NY (2013)
5. boyd, D.M., Ellison, N.B.: Social network sites: definition, history, and scholarship. J. Comput.-Mediat. Commun. **13**(1), 210–230 (2007)
6. Buckingham, D. (ed.): Youth, Identity, and Digital Media. MIT Press, Cambridge, MA (2008)
7. Chaffey, D.: Global social media research summary 2016. Smart Insights: Social Media Marketing (2016)
8. Donath, J.S.: Identity and deception in the virtual community. In: Kollock, M., Smith, P. (eds.) Communities in Cyberspace, Chap. 2, pp. 27–57. Routledge, London (1998)
9. Dutot, V.: Adoption of social media using technology acceptance model. Int. J. Technol. Hum. Interact. **10**(4), 18–35 (2014)
10. Ellison, N.B., Steinfield, C., Lampe, C.: Connection strategies: social capital implications of Facebook-enabled communication practices. New Media Soc. **13**(6), 873–892 (2011)
11. Ellison, N.B., Vitak, J., Gray, R., Lampe, C.: Cultivating social resources on social network sites: Facebook relationship maintenance behaviors and their role in social capital processes. J. Comput.-Mediat. Commun. **19**(4), 855–870 (2014)
12. Facebook Inc.: Company info: Facebook newsroom (2016)
13. Facebook Inc.: Company profile. Technical Report, Facebook, Inc., Menlo Park, CA (2016)
14. Faraj, S., Jarvenpaa, S.L., Majchrzak, A.: Knowledge collaboration in Online communities. Organ. Sci. **22**(5), 1224–1239 (2011)
15. Faraj, S., Kudaravalli, S., Wasko, M.: Leading collaboration in online communities. MIS Q. Manage. Inf. Syst. **39**(2), 393–412 (2015)
16. Fleck, J., Johnson-Migalski, L.: The impact of social media on personal and professional lives: an Adlerian perspective. J. Individ. Psychol. **71**(2), 135–142 (2015)
17. Gibbs, J.L., Rozaidi, N.A., Eisenber, J.: Overcoming the 'ideology of openness': probing the affordances of social media for organizational knowledge sharing. J. Comput.-Mediat. Commun. **19**(1), 102–120 (2013)
18. Gil de Zuniga, H., Valenzuela, S.: The mediating path to a stronger citizenship: online and offline networks, weak ties, and civic engagement. Commun. Res. **38**(3), 397–421 (2011)

19. Golder, S.A.: Usage patterns of collaborative tagging systems. J. Inf. Sci. **32**(2), 198–208 (2006)
20. Gonzales, A.L., Hancock, J.T.: Identity shift in computer-mediated environments. Media Psychol. **11**(2), 167–185 (2008)
21. Gonzales, A.L., Hancock, J.T., Pennebaker, J.W.: Language style matching as a predictor of social dynamics in small groups. Commun. Res. **37**, 3–19 (2010)
22. Hampton, K.N.: Internet use and the concentration of disadvantage: glocalization and the urban underclass. Am. Behav. Sci. **53**(8), 1111–1132 (2010)
23. Hancock, J.T.: Digital deception: why, when and how people lie online. In: Oxford Handbook of Internet Psychology. Oxford University Press, Oxford (2012)
24. Johnstone, M.J.: Privacy, professionalism and social media. Aust. Nurs. Midwifery J. **23**(7), 23 (2016)
25. Kaplan, A.M., Haenlein, M.: Users of the world, unite! The challenges and opportunities of social media. Bus. Horiz. **53**(1), 59–68 (2010)
26. Kietzmann, J.H., Hermkens, K., McCarthy, I.P., Silvestre, B.S.: Social media? Get serious! understanding the functional building blocks of social media. Bus. Horiz. **54**(3), 241–251 (2011)
27. Kim, K.-S., Joanna Sin, S.-C., Tsai, T.-I.: Individual differences in social media use for information seeking. J. Acad. Librariansh. **40**(2), 171–178 (2014)
28. Kramer, A.D.I., Guillory, J.E., Hancock, J.T.: Experimental evidence of massive-scale emotional contagion through social networks. Proc. Natl. Acad. Sci. **111**(24), 8788–8790 (2014)
29. Kwon, S.-W., Adler, P.S.: Social capital: maturation of a field of research. Acad. Manage. Rev. **39**(4), 412–422 (2014)
30. Lamdan, S.S.: Social media privacy: a rallying cry to librarians. Libr. Q. **85**(3), 261–277 (2015)
31. Leist, A.K.: Social media use of older adults: a mini-review. Gerontology **59**(4), 378–384 (2013)
32. Leonardi, P.M., Huysman, M., Steinfield, C.: Enterprise social media: definition, history, and prospects for the study of social technologies in organizations. J. Comput.-Mediat. Commun. **19**(1), 1–19 (2013)
33. Lester, P.M., King, C.M.: Analog vs. digital instruction and learning: teaching within first and second life environments. J. Comput.-Mediat. Commun. **14**(3), 457–483 (2009)
34. Lewis, K., Kaufman, J., Gonzalez, M., Wimmer, A., Christakis, N.: Tastes, ties, and time: a new social network dataset using Facebook.com. Soc. Netw. **30**(4), 330–342 (2008)
35. Malik, M.M., Pfeffer, J.: A macroscopic analysis of news content in Twitter. Digital J. **4**(8), 955–979 (2016)
36. Marwick, A.E., boyd, D.: I tweet honestly, I tweet passionately: Twitter users, context collapse, and the imagined audience. New Media Soc. **13**(1), 114–133 (2011)
37. Mican, D., Tomai, N.: Extracting usage patterns and the analysis of tag connection dynamics within collaborative tagging systems. Inf. Econ. **17**(1/2013), 99–112 (2013)
38. Narayan, B.: From everyday information behaviors to clickable solidarity in a place called social media. Inf. Econ. J. **5**(3), 32–53 (2013)
39. National Council of State Boards of Nursing.: A nurses' guide to social media. Alaska Nurse **67**(3), 12–15 (2016)
40. O'Keeffe, G.S., Clarke-Pearson, K., Council on Communications and Media: The impact of social media on children, adolescents, and families. Pediatrics **127**(4), 800–804 (2011)
41. Purdy, E.R.: Online privacy (2013)
42. Richards, R.D.: Compulsory process in cyberspace: rethinking privacy in the social networking age. Harv. J. Law Public Policy **36**(2), 519–548 (2013)
43. Utz, S.: Show me your friends and I will tell you what type of person you are: how one's profile, number of friends, and type of friends influence impression formation on social network sites. J. Comput.-Mediat. Commun. **15**(2), 314–335 (2010)
44. Walther, J.B.: Computer-mediated communication: impersonal, interpersonal, and hyperpersonal interaction. Commun. Res. **23**, 3–43 (1996)

45. Walther, J.B., Van Der Heide, B., Hamel, L., Shulman, H.: Self-generated versus other-generated statements and impressions in computer-mediated communication: a test of warranting theory using Facebook. Commun. Res. **36**, 229–253 (2009)
46. Williams, D.: On and off the 'Net: scales for social capital in an online era. J. Comput.-Mediat. Commun. **11**(2), 593–628, (2006)
47. Yee, N., Bailenson, J.: The Proteus effect: the effect of transformed self-representation on behavior. Hum. Commun. Res. **33**(3), 271–290 (2007)
48. Zimmer, M.: "But the data is already public": on the ethics of research in Facebook. Ethics Inf. Technol. **12**(4), 313–325 (2010)

Part II
Social Dimension of Information Seeking

Having seen what individual information seeking looks like, and covering some groundwork on social media/networking, now we will see how social dimension of one's behavior is integrated in their information seeking activities through crowdsourcing and social media services. This part covers these two aspects—information seeking through crowdsourcing with online Q&A and social sources—in the following two chapters.

Chapter 4
Online Question-Answering (Q&A)

Abstract Using online communities or crowds to satisfy information needs is becoming more common. This chapter reviews various ways in which people seek information from others by asking questions through online services. These services, referred to here as online Q&A, are categorized as expert-based, community-based, collaborative, and social. A comparative analysis, along with examples, is presented to show how these services differ in meaningful ways. Going beyond the types of online Q&A, we'll discuss their content and users. The discussion on content is divided into questions and answers. The description of users is based on asking and answering behaviors, as well as some views on balancing those two actions. Finally, the chapter introduces several special classes of users in online Q&A services and what they could mean for a given Q&A platform's success and survivability.

4.1 Introduction

It is in human nature to ask questions. This natural behavior allows us to express our curiosity and advance our understanding. While we have been asking all sorts of questions for thousands of years, from "what's the meaning of life" to "where's the beef," it is only in recent history that we have started using electronic mediums, specifically the Internet, to ask our questions.

This began with online forums and newsgroups and has continued today with the Web and Web 2.0. Modern online Q&A refers to people asking and answering questions through various platforms and services. Some of these are specifically designed for supporting Q&A, and others can be repurposed to allow users to express their Q&A needs.

An important aspect of online Q&A is its social dimension, since in most cases people are asking questions of other people—experts or novices, known or unknown—rather than an automated system. And that's why it's impossible to cover SIS comprehensively without talking about online Q&A. So here we go again with our familiar figure depicting various related concepts in Fig. 4.1. Here, online Q&A can be found in the intersection of information retrieval, social media, social networking, and collaboration.

C. Shah, *Social Information Seeking*, The Information Retrieval Series 38,
DOI 10.1007/978-3-319-56756-3_4

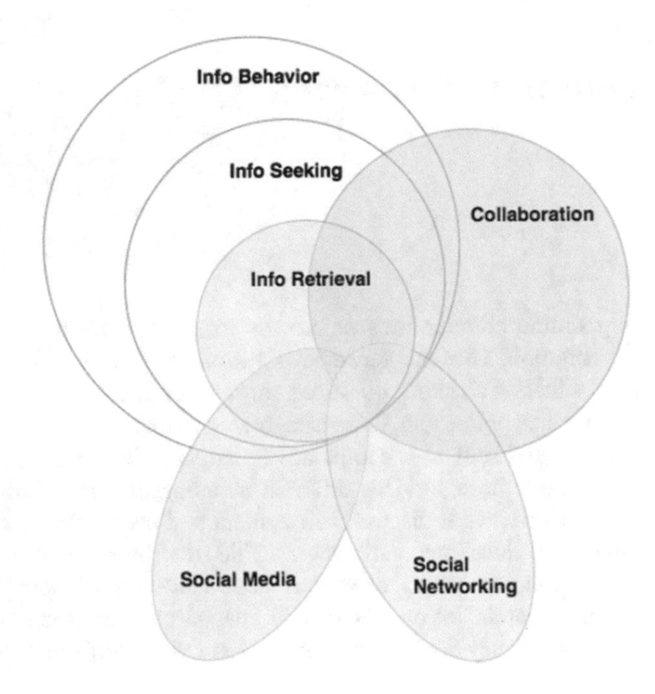

Fig. 4.1 A schematic view of related concepts that contextualize online Q&A

In this chapter we will talk about various kinds of online Q&A services. We will compare and contrast them, and discuss some of the elements of questioning and answering through them. In addition to the content (questions, answers, comments), we will also look at the users of these services. Specifically, we will talk about special classes of users in an online Q&A platform and their impacts on that community's SIS behaviors.

4.2 Types of Online Q&A

Let's consider a broader view of Q&A services as shown in Fig. 4.2. These services can be divided into face-to-face and online. A traditional face-to-face Q&A example is reference service in a library. Here, an information seeker goes to a reference desk and asks questions of a reference librarian. The librarian may then have a conversation, often referred to as a reference interview [48, 55], with the asker to understand their needs and provide a customized answer. Unfortunately, many of these reference services have been recently struggling as more and more people turn to online resources for their information needs.

Turning our attention to online Q&A services, we can categorize them into machine-driven and human-driven platforms. The former is a type of Q&A service

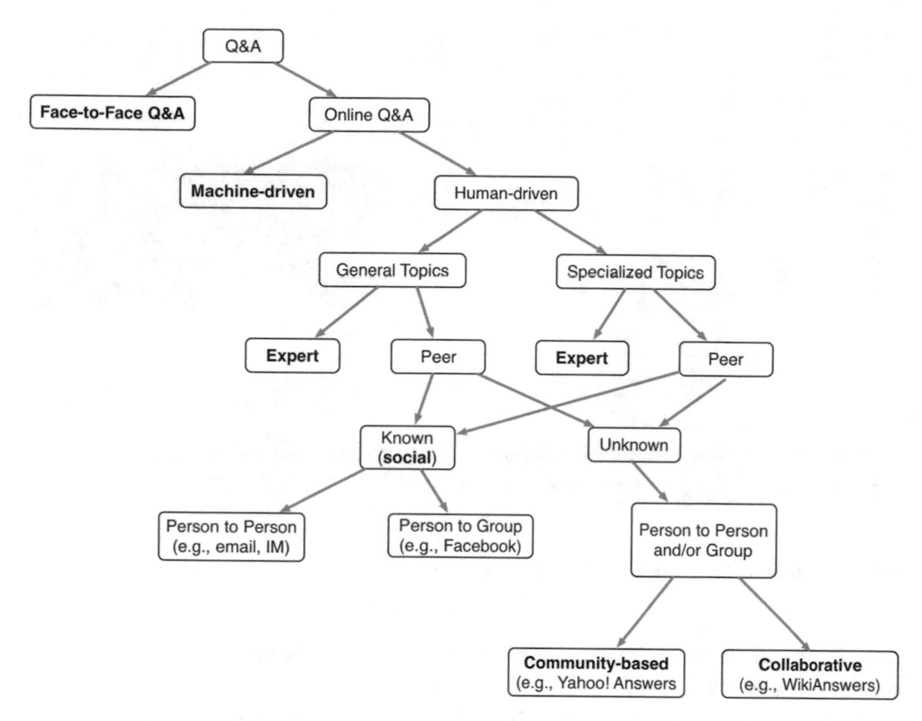

Fig. 4.2 A taxonomy of Q&A

where potential answers to a question are derived by first retrieving relevant documents and then extracting specific passages from those documents that may contain answers. The IR community has spent a lot of effort over several decades on automatic Q&A systems. For many years the Text REtrieval Conference (TREC) run by the US National Institute of Standards and Technology (NIST) had a track on Q&A, and there were streams of papers published in the World Wide Web (WWW), Special Interest Group in Information Retrieval (SIGIR), Conference on Information and Knowledge Management (CIKM), and other related communities. Ask.com[1] (originally AskJeeves.com) is a good example of a commercial system with machine-driven Q&A.

While the traditional approaches to machine-driven Q&A may have stepped out of the spotlight, search engines have been optimizing—often using heuristics and otherwise machine-learning techniques—ways to extract answers from a query (even if it wasn't posed as a question). Knowledge graph, or a variation of it, is such an example offered by most commercial search engines. In the example shown in Fig. 4.3, for query/question "who was marie curie," in addition to the famous ten blue links, Google gives us a specifically extracted and formatted "answer" on the right. But this appearance of Google answering our question is, well, just an

[1] www.ask.com.

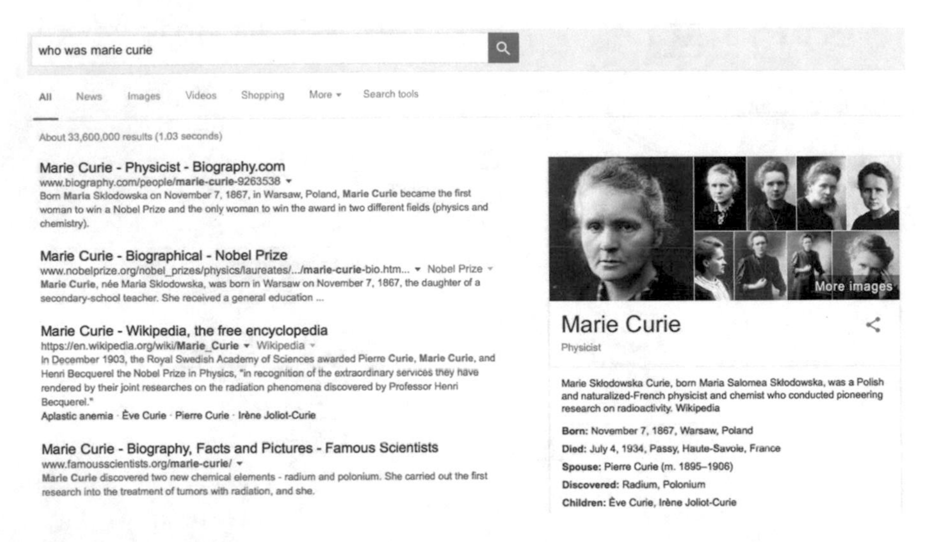

Fig. 4.3 An example of knowledge graph with Google

appearance. If you run "marie curie," a typical keywords-based query, you would get the same result.

This is not to say that Google is merely doing something very basic. There are many built-in rules that it must follow to emulate a Q&A transaction. Try another query—"what did marie curie discover"—and you will get something like Fig. 4.4.

Now let's search for "what's the capital of Mongolia?" or even just "capital of Mongolia" with Bing, and chances are that we'll see something like Fig. 4.5. Here, the answer is extracted and presented before the traditional list of relevant documents.

If that seemed like an easy example, try "how to get gum out of hair?" (Fig. 4.6). Again, the search engine (in this case, Google) has extracted and presented an answer right before all other results.

But this approach has its limitations. What if someone asked, "does this outfit make me look weird?" This would be a tricky question for a search engine (or for most humans!). What the asker is looking for here is not a general fact or ideas, but a specific opinion for a personal situation. And that's where we turn to the other branch of online Q&A: human-driven.

Human-driven online Q&A services provide outlets for information retrieval where the user's information need is articulated by natural language questions posed to a community whose members can answer the question or even offer feedback on the given responses, resulting in a personalized set of answers generated via the collective wisdom of many [8]. Since the early 2000s, online Q&A services have become popular on the Web and, according to a Hitwise report, there was an 889% increase in visits to online Q&A services between 2006 and 2008 within the United States [69].

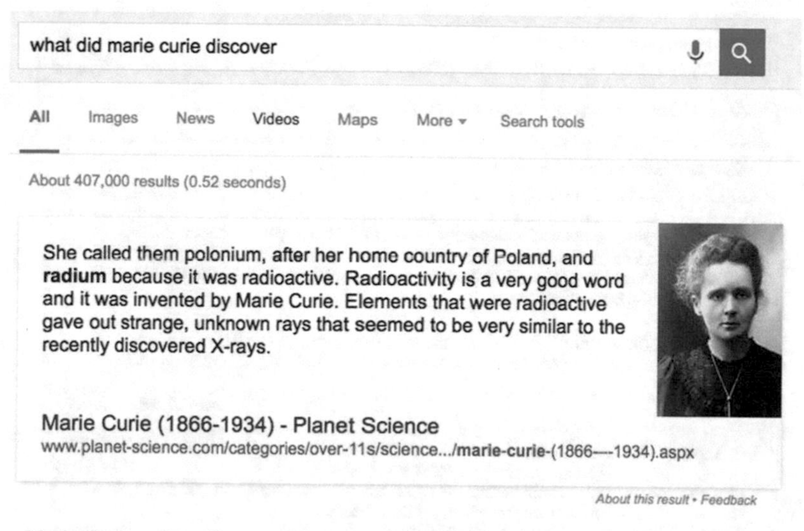

Fig. 4.4 An example of answer extraction by Google

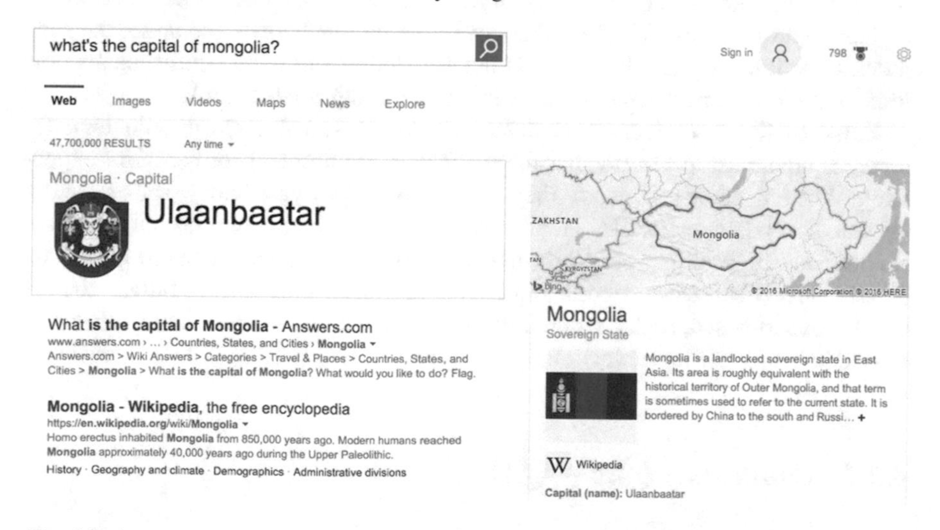

Fig. 4.5 An example of a search engine automatic extraction of factual answers (Bing)

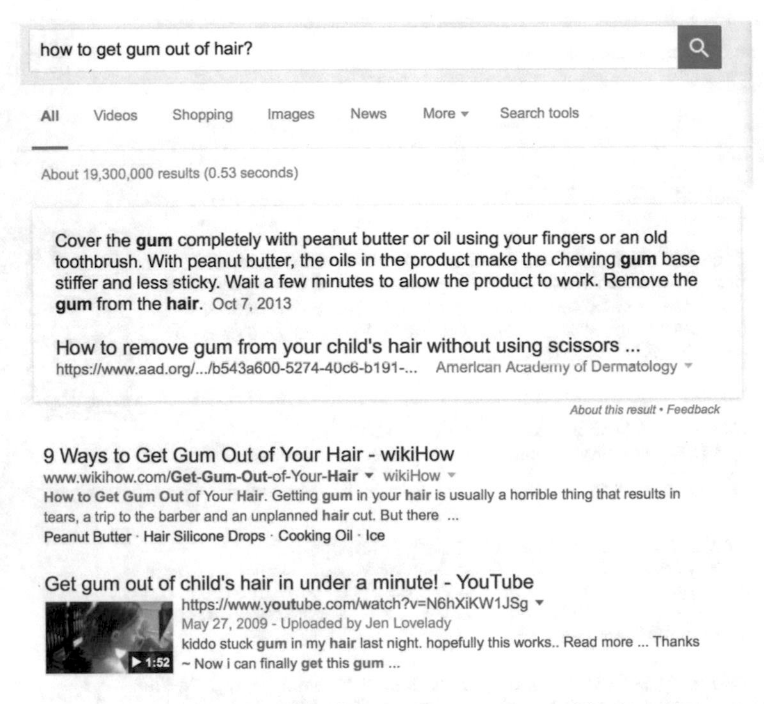

Fig. 4.6 A search engine (here, Google) extracting an answer to a method question

Such services can be divided into two categories: general-purpose (or horizontal) services and specialized (or vertical) services. A service such as Yahoo! Answers is a general-purpose Q&A platform that covers pretty much any topic under the sun. Stack Overflow, on the other hand, is not for finding out if that outfit makes you look weird; it is a specialized service for programming-related Q&A.

Some of these services—horizontal or vertical—involve Q&A with experts, whereas others use peers (regular users with no requirement for a certain expertise). When it comes to peers, they could be people you know (social Q&A) or you don't know. For the latter case, the answers to your questions could be provided by multiple people in that community (community-based Q&A) or collaboratively constructed (collaborative Q&A). These four types of human-driven Q&A—expert-based, social, community-based, and collaborative—are further discussed in the following subsections.

4.2.1 Community Q&A (CQA)

A community-based online Q&A service, sometimes referred to as a knowledge exchange community [1], constitutes a user-driven environment where people searching for personalized answers post various types of questions to the Q&A

community. A community-based online Q&A service consists of three components: (1) a mechanism for information seekers to submit questions in natural language, (2) answerers or responders who actively submit answers to questions, and (3) a community built around this exchange [62]. Most community-based Q&A services also archive question-answer pairs and make them publicly available to allow people to search these pairs, therefore avoiding duplication of previously asked questions and answers, which saves time and effort for users [8].

An example of a CQA service is Yahoo! Answers, launched by Yahoo! in 2005, which has become by far the largest English-language-based online Q&A site. According to Leibenluft [35], more than 120 million users have joined Yahoo! Answers, and they've generated approximately 400 million answers to posed questions. Figure 4.7 shows an example of a question and associated answers. While a question may receive multiple answers, some questions also go unanswered [64]. Even if a question gets a few or several answers, it may take a while to get an answer that satisfies the asker [57]. Of course, someone answering a given question at a later

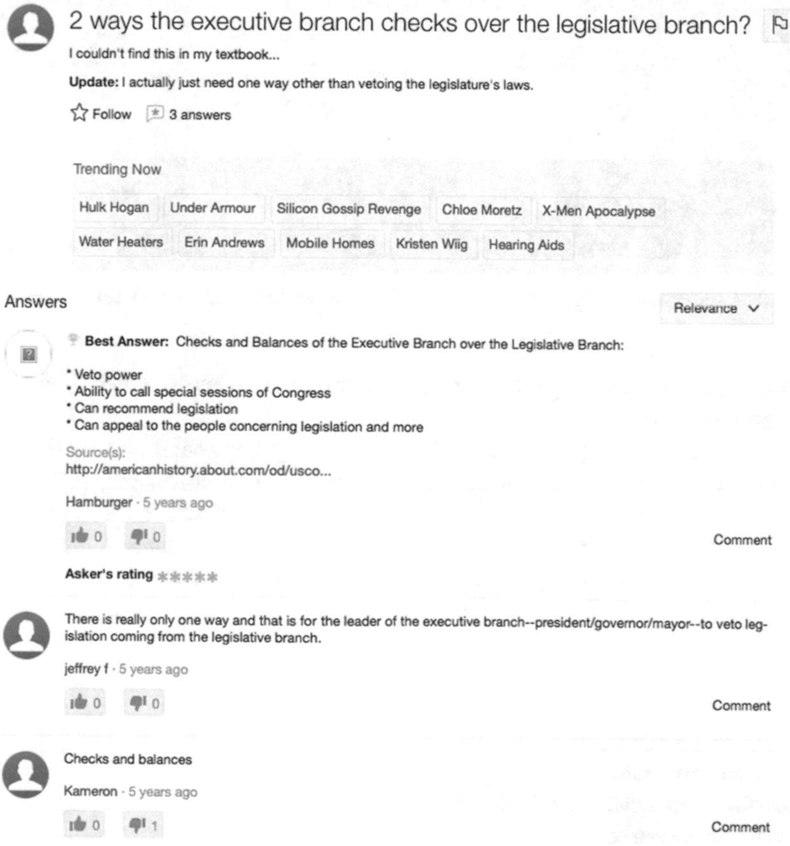

Fig. 4.7 A screenshot of the Yahoo! Answers Website, showing how a question may receive multiple answers from multiple people in the community

Fig. 4.8 A screenshot of the Brainly Website, which specializes in homework-related Q&A

time also has the advantage of seeing all the previous answers, which likely makes their answer stronger.

In addition to Yahoo! Answers, there are many horizontal and vertical CQA services we use today. Examples include Naver[2] in South Korea, Askville[3] by Amazon,[4] and Answerbag,[5] one of the first services to appear in the United States that was shut down in 2015. Specialized/vertical CQA include Stack Overflow for programming-related questions and Brainly[6] (Fig. 4.8) for homework-related questions.

[2] http://www.naver.com.

[3] http://askville.amazon.com, which is now defunct.

[4] https://www.amazon.com.

[5] http://www.answerbag.com.

[6] http://brainly.com.

4.2.2 Collaborative Q&A

As we saw in the Yahoo! Answers example of online CQA, multiple people can give multiple answers to a given question. But their answering activities are not truly independent. One could see all the previous answers before posting their own, thus hopefully improving upon what's already posted. What if all of these answerers collaborated and constructed one really good answer instead of several independent responses?

In some cases, people are expressing different, and often conflicting, ideas and opinions, so it may not be possible or appropriate to put them together in some way. But there are questions (e.g., factual, and even some advice seeking questions) that could benefit from cocreated answers. That's where collaborative Q&A comes in.

Unlike a community-based Q&A service where every question-answer pair is separately located in an archived thread list, collaborative Q&A services facilitate the ability to edit and improve the phrasing of a question and/or its answer over time via user collaboration. Examples of collaborative Q&A services are WikiAnswers and Wikipedia Reference Desk,[7] which allow users to rephrase existing questions and answers in order to best address the information needs of both the asker and other community members interested in the same or similar topics. Like a community-based online Q&A service, WikiAnswers also displays a list of similar questions that have already been asked on the site in order to assist in fulfilling an asker's information need [7].

Figure 4.9 shows an example of answering activities on a question in WikiAnswers. Here, as you can see, several people at different times contributed to constructing a single answer for the posted question.

4.2.3 Expert-Based Q&A

As in the first two Q&A services, an expert-based Q&A service allows users to ask questions and receive direct responses from others. However, in these services, answers are provided by a group of experts rather than an open community. Another factor that differentiates these types of sites from the other models is that many expert-based services include pricing systems, collectively referred to as a price-based knowledge market [11], that allow the asker to specify the range of payment an answerer receives based on perceived value (i.e., Google Answers'[8] payments ranged from $2 to $200 with a nonrefundable listing fee of $0.50). However, other expert-based Q&A models such as AllExperts[9] allow an expert to voluntarily join

[7]https://en.wikipedia.org/wiki/Wikipedia:Reference_desk.

[8]http://answers.google.com/answers.

[9]http://www.allexperts.com.

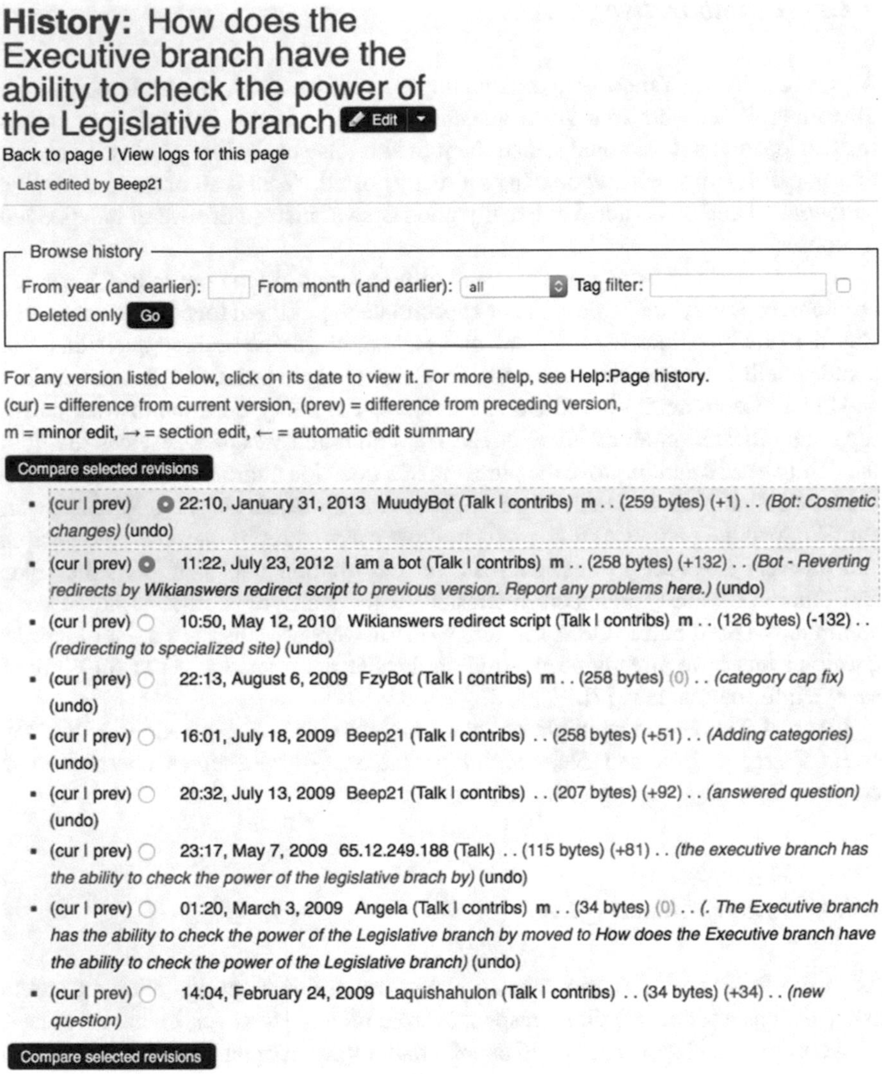

History: How does the Executive branch have the ability to check the power of the Legislative branch Edit

Back to page | View logs for this page

Last edited by Beep21

Browse history

From year (and earlier): From month (and earlier): all Tag filter:

Deleted only Go

For any version listed below, click on its date to view it. For more help, see Help:Page history.
(cur) = difference from current version, (prev) = difference from preceding version,
m = minor edit, → = section edit, ← = automatic edit summary

Compare selected revisions

- (cur | prev) 22:10, January 31, 2013 MuudyBot (Talk | contribs) m . . (259 bytes) (+1) . . *(Bot: Cosmetic changes)* (undo)
- (cur | prev) 11:22, July 23, 2012 I am a bot (Talk | contribs) m . . (258 bytes) (+132) . . *(Bot - Reverting redirects by Wikianswers redirect script to previous version. Report any problems here.)* (undo)
- (cur | prev) 10:50, May 12, 2010 Wikianswers redirect script (Talk | contribs) m . . (126 bytes) (-132) . . *(redirecting to specialized site)* (undo)
- (cur | prev) 22:13, August 6, 2009 FzyBot (Talk | contribs) m . . (258 bytes) (0) . . *(category cap fix)* (undo)
- (cur | prev) 16:01, July 18, 2009 Beep21 (Talk | contribs) . . (258 bytes) (+51) . . *(Adding categories)* (undo)
- (cur | prev) 20:32, July 13, 2009 Beep21 (Talk | contribs) . . (207 bytes) (+92) . . *(answered question)* (undo)
- (cur | prev) 23:17, May 7, 2009 65.12.249.188 (Talk) . . (115 bytes) (+81) . . *(the executive branch has the ability to check the power of the legislative brach by)* (undo)
- (cur | prev) 01:20, March 3, 2009 Angela (Talk | contribs) m . . (34 bytes) (0) . . *(. The Executive branch has the ability to check the power of the Legislative branch by moved to How does the Executive branch have the ability to check the power of the Legislative branch)* (undo)
- (cur | prev) 14:04, February 24, 2009 Laquishahulon (Talk | contribs) . . (34 bytes) (+34) . . *(new question)*

Compare selected revisions

Fig. 4.9 A screenshot of the WikiAnswers Website, showing how an answer to a question could be collaboratively constructed by the community

the system and provide answers to questions based on their self-identified expertise without fees. The Internet Public Library (IPL),[10] an asynchronous digital reference service [52], can also be characterized as an expert-based Q&A service since an

[10]http://ipl.org.

Civil Engineering/**Favorable and unfavourable actions**

Expert: Babak Esmailzadeh Hakimi - 5/21/2016

Question
If a wind load(lateral) ,Representative certificate permanent action(vertical) and an imposed load(vertical) acts on a bracing, can wind load be taken as a favourable action??
Please tell me if you know
Thank you

Answer

Dear Danu

There is no absolute favorite action. The lateral load can make a favorite situation for some members while it makes an unfavorite situation for others. For example a vertical loading make the bracings be suppressed under compression stresses. The lateral loading makes one of the diagonals to behave in tension which is somhow favorite and add the compression in the other diagonal which is not wanted. Then there is no strict favorite action.

Regards
BEH

Fig. 4.10 A screenshot of the AllExperts Website, showing an answer provided by an expert

expert, in this case a reference librarian, interacts with users to resolve information needs (Fig. 4.10).

Another example is a service run by several libraries, called *Ask a Librarian*. Often, this is a chat-based system where one could directly interact with a librarian just as they would at a physical reference desk. Even the Library of Congress has such a service.[11]

It is worth noting that many of these services have struggled to stay alive, and several have already shut down. Google Answers closed in 2005 after existing for a very short time.[12] IPL, on the other hand, stayed alive for a long time thanks to the library community's (faculty and students at library schools, and librarians) efforts. There was even an attempt to bring it to the Web 2.0 era with the introduction of IPL 2.0, but eventually it was terminated in June 2015. The Website is still available, but without any support for asking a question of a librarian.

This is not to imply that expert-based Q&A systems have an inherent problem, but these examples do indicate a need for a different approach. We need a Q&A model that creates more sustainable services.

A few academic attempts have been made in the recent years to address just that. One proposes to create a hybrid model that incorporates an expert-based Q&A service such as virtual reference (VR) and crowd-based or social Q&A [65]. Another great example of a hybrid system is IM-an-Expert [72]. In this service

[11]https://www.loc.gov/rr/askalib.

[12]See [61] for a commentary and analysis on what may have gone wrong with Google Answers.

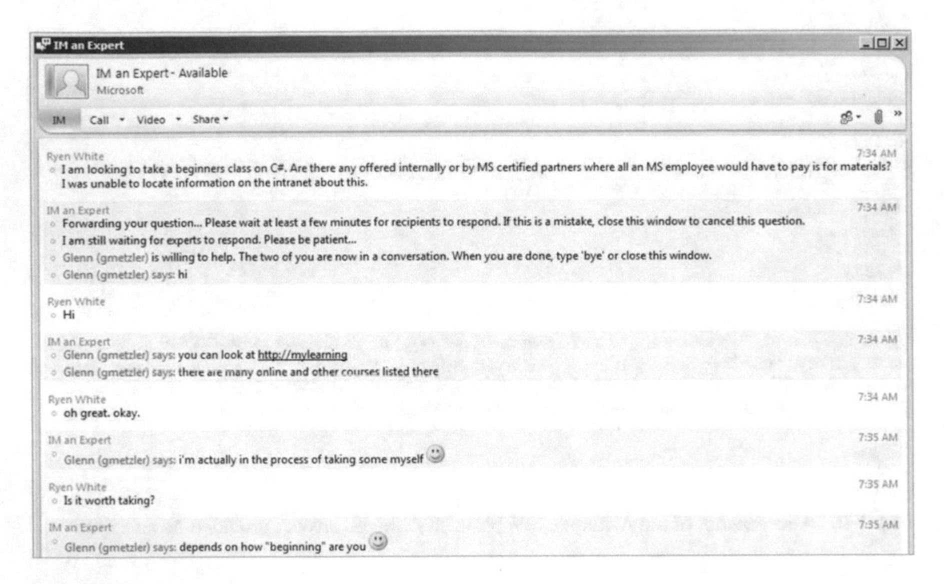

Fig. 4.11 A Q&A session with IM-an-Expert

(see Fig. 4.11), a person submits a question to the system, which then matches the question to potential experts who could do online chat with the asker to provide answers, opinions, or advice.

A slightly different model for expert-based Q&A can be seen with Quora,[13] where unlike Google Answers, the experts are developed through their services to the community rather than handpicked or hired. The result is high-quality content generated and managed through curation, albeit at the expense of scale.

4.2.4 Social Q&A (SQA)

Social Q&A provides users with the opportunity to ask questions to friends or acquaintances within SNSs or social search engines [28]. According to Paul et al. [49], the question-answering interactions within social networking sites (e.g., Facebook, Twitter, etc.) are gaining increased popularity because these sites let people leverage the expertise of a network of friends, as well as engage in the collective knowledge of their social network community.

[13]https://www.quora.com.

Fig. 4.12 An example of social Q&A on Twitter

Fig. 4.13 Another example of social Q&A on Twitter

Arguably, social Q&A services share many of the same characteristics as community-based services, such as a repository of questions and answers for sharing knowledge within a Quora community [70], but with a few key differences. For example, Honeycutt and Herring [27] found that Twitter users utilize the service to solicit highly personalized information. According to Morris et al.'s [42] study of users who post questions to social networking sites, askers typically trust their answerers since they come from their personal network. In addition, the information received is personalized based on an answerer's knowledge of the asker.

Figures 4.12, 4.13, and 4.14 present a few examples of how people are using social media services to ask questions. Now, can you imagine running these questions as Web search queries?!

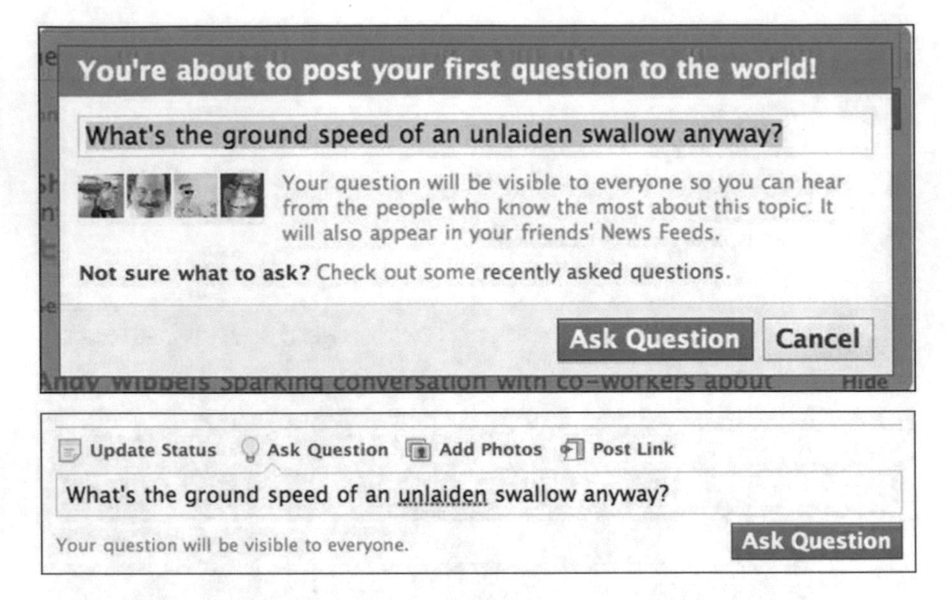

Fig. 4.14 An example of social Q&A on Facebook

4.3 Comparing Various Q&A Models

By now, most characteristics of various Q&A models, and more importantly, their differences, should be clear. Just in case, Table 4.1 provides a summary.

Rather than asking which one is the best, it is important to consider the strengths and weaknesses of each of these models/services. Each are able meet certain kinds of needs and situations. There is some recent work by Choi et al. [12, 13] that investigates where people go to ask various kinds of questions. To discover this information, the authors divided questions into four types: (1) information seeking questions, (2) advice seeking questions, (3) opinion seeking questions, and (4) social questions. Using these types as a framework, they collected samples of questions from four different Q&A services that cater to each category. Finally, they classified the questions based on the four types. The results are in Table 4.2.

Examples of the four question types include:

- *Information seeking*. How many sports and events are in the Olympics?
- *Advice seeking*. How can we take payday loan on Christmas?
- *Opinion seeking*. Coke or Pepsi?
- *Social*. Why are some people so negative when you are being positive?

As we can see from Table 4.2, each kind of Q&A service exhibits different characteristics regarding its questions' content. Expert-based Q&A services, not surprisingly, tend to overwhelmingly contain more factual questions than social inquiries. Social Q&A services, on the other hand, have a much larger pool of social questions.

Table 4.1 Comparison of various Q&A models

	Social	Community based	Collaborative	Expert-based
Who can ask?	Anyone	Anyone	Anyone	Anyone (nonexpert)
Who can answer?	Anyone from one's social group	Anyone in the community	Anyone in the community	Designated experts
Nature of the connection	Social, weak or strong	Stranger, weak	Stranger, weak	Stranger, weak
Nature of the community	Friends, followers	Crowd	Crowd	Crowd with identified experts
Pros	Highly personalized, trustworthy	Fast, abundant	More refined answers	High quality
Cons	Small scale with unknown agendas	Content by unknown entities for content generators	Higher learning curve	Expensive, limited scale
Examples	Facebook, Twitter	Yahoo! Answers, Stack Overflow	WikiAnswers, Wikipedia Reference Desk	Google Answers, Quora

Table 4.2 Question types across various Q&A services

Q&A model	Information seeking	Advice seeking	Opinion seeking	Social
Community (Yahoo! Answers)	35 (7%)	204 (40.8%)	250 (50%)	10 (2%)
Collaborative (WikiAnswers)	253 (50.6%)	192 (38.4%)	55 (11%)	0 (0%)
Expert (IPL)	436 (87.2%)	34 (6.8%)	30 (6%)	0 (0%)
Social (Twitter)	86 (17.2%)	170 (34%)	26 (5.2%)	218 (43.6%)

In the next section, we will expand our views on content within Q&A services, going beyond questions and question types.

4.4 Content in Online Q&A

There are two primary entities to consider when talking about online Q&A: content and users. In this section we will talk about content. Within content, there are two obvious types: questions and answers. Of course, the users of an online Q&A service may also generate other kinds of content such as comments and assessments (likes, ratings), but we will weave the discussion of those into our description of content and users.

4.4.1 *Questions*

Questions are where it all begins. They serve as not only the starting point of the Q&A process but also the driver of what happens next—who answers, how they answer, how well they answer, etc.

It is assumed that good questions bring good answers [63]. It follows that many investigations in the literature have focused on understanding question quality and difficulty.

Studies of question quality in online Q&A look at both textual and non-textual features. Examples of such works include Agichtein et al.'s [3] assessment of answer and question quality, as well as the relationship between answers and questions, within Yahoo! Answers. Textual features found to have a significant influence on the authors' model used in this work include punctuation density, number of words per sentence, number of unique words, and entropy. Bian et al. [9] and Li et al. [37] also found that non-textual features, such as an asker's profile, influence question quality.

Yang et al. [76] used findings to inform the development of a system that flags questions for revision; however, the authors focused on unanswered questions, which are not synonymous with question quality. Even if a question receives an answer, there is no indication that the answerer understood the asker's information need. Alternatively, a question that clearly states the asker's information need might not receive an answer based on variable factors, such as the time of day the question was posted (a non-textual feature Yang et al. [76] used in their prediction model).

A rich body of literature has focused on developing a taxonomy for questions asked within digital reference services (see [5, 19, 21, 26, 31, 56, 66]). Numminen and Vakkari [44] argued that Sears [56] developed the most comprehensive taxonomy, which "covered the greatest range of various types of questions and included the most detailed subdivision of questions" [44, p. 1251]. Sears's [56] taxonomy divided reference questions into three categories: (1) ready reference questions, (2) specified search questions, and (3) research questions.

Similar research has been performed within other online Q&A sites. For example, Harper et al. [24] developed two distinct question types in order to investigate the archival value of online Q&A sites (Ask MetaFilter, Answerbag, Yahoo! Answers): (1) informational questions that are more likely to gather information and (2) conversational questions that stimulate discussion to solicit opinions from others. Another study by Harper et al. [25] utilized a rhetorical framework to classify questions using the same online Q&A sites as the previous study [24]. The framework has three major categories: (1) deliberative (advice, identification), (2) epideictic (approval, quality), and (3) forensic (prescriptive, factual). The study found that factual (31%) questions are most frequently asked, followed by identification (28%), advice (11%), and prescriptive (11%).

As reported in the previous section, a recent study by Choi et al. [14] also focused on frequency distributions for question type among four different online Q&A services, each representative of a type of Q&A site identified above. The study developed four different question types using previous research by Harper et al. [25]: (1) information seeking questions, (2) advice seeking questions, (3) opinion seeking questions, and (4) non-information seeking questions (self-expression).

Recent studies have also paid attention to how a question is formulated and how this impacts quality within online Q&A environments. For example, Shah et al. [63] examined why fact-finding questions from Yahoo! Answers failed or did not receive an answer. A typology was developed in order to determine reasons for why a question might fail, and the results indicated that the most significant proportion of failed questions were too complex and/or overly broad (34%), followed by those that lacked information (14%), had multiple related questions (13%), and were ambiguous (10%). Choi et al. [15] performed a similar study but focused on fact-finding questions that both did and did not receive an answer. They subsequently developed a model that predicts question quality (good or bad) using a question's textual features for training and non-textual features as evaluated by human assessors for testing.

The results from a study by Shah et al. [64] revealed that six significant textual attributes contribute to the model with the highest percentage of accuracy: (1) interrogative words used at the beginning of a question; (2) the number of unique words in the question, which is an indicator that the information within the question is more specific; (3) the clarity score representing the complexity of the question; (4) the presence of content that provides additional information in order to give the reader a better understanding of what the asker is looking for; (5) the number of question marks, which signifies how many questions the user asks; and (6) the presence of taboo words, which indicates whether the question is socially appropriate.

4.4.2 *Answers*

Let's now switch our attention to answers, which is where the majority of content-related studies for online Q&A are done because:

1. Typically, answers contain more content (e.g., there are more of them and they are longer) than what's available in questions.[14] We found that on average one question on Yahoo! Answers had six answers [60].
2. Answers are where the circle of Q&A finishes. Without quick and quality answers, the whole Q&A service could collapse.

Given the access to a large database of human relevance judgments approximated by Best Answer ratings and the need to moderate the variable quality of content exchanged within these sites, many information retrieval researchers have attempted

[14] I say *typically* because there are failed or failing Q&A services such as Google Answers where the balance of questions-answers tips against answers [61].

to determine the relationship between various features generated from within Yahoo! Answers and human judgments [4, 54]. While the aggregated quality of the total content within CQA has been deemed reasonable, Su et al. [67] discovered that within individual cases, answer quality is highly variable; 17–45% of the answers provided to questions posed by the authors were correct as opposed to 65–95% of questions rated as Best Answers within a large-scale sample. This indicates that user satisfaction may increase if a system is able to process a question, locate similarly worded archived questions within its database, and retrieve already-posted high-quality answers.

Researchers addressing this problem have typically created classifiers—which identify various aspects of answer quality—by using Best Answer ratings as an indication of answerer satisfaction (e.g., [38]). The literature includes several approaches to identifying Best Answers. Liu et al. [38] generalized these approaches into an Asker Satisfaction Prediction (ASP) framework, which includes textual and semantic features of questions and answers, history of answer satisfaction by category, and past activity of askers and answerers [3, 6, 29, 32, 38, 60]. Other studies have attempted to both add classification features and use other evaluative baselines for answer quality using human-based assessments. Examples of the former include typologies for question type labeled by human assessors where findings indicate that the distribution of Best Answers significantly varies among these types [24, 38], and examples of the latter include using human assessments as baselines for answer quality [3, 60]. These classifiers often employ either regression-based or probabilistic-based analyses including support vector machines and Bayesian networks [3, 38]. There have also been attempts to classify questions based on their types—such as advisory, factual, or opinion-based—in order to recommend an appropriate Q&A service (e.g., [14]).

Adamic et al. [2] performed a large-scale analysis of Yahoo! Answers, with 8.4 million answers, 1.1 million questions, and 700,000 distinct users. They found that a user tends to provide more Best Answer ratings when their participation rate (e.g., asking, answering, evaluating) is lower [2]. This suggests that users who interact more within Yahoo! Answers might evaluate answers differently than those who do not take advantage of the community-based elements of the site, a finding also present in studies of other online Q&A communities, such as the UseNet community. In contrast to these findings, Agichtein et al. [3] found that Yahoo! Answers users tend to adopt multiple roles (e.g., asking and answering questions) and are thus more difficult to classify based on their participatory practices. The authors attribute this to the site's incentive mechanisms, which do not allow a user to ask questions until they accrue points by providing answers and/or evaluating content. This feature of the Yahoo! Answers service might also account for the noted imbalance between resolved answers—or answers that receive a Best Answer rating—and total answers [2].

Agichtein et al.'s [3] study performed one of the first large-scale experiments combining content-based features and network-based features in order to identify quality answers as ranked by human coders within Yahoo! Answers using the ASP framework with 71 features. Findings indicate that models trained on each set of features from the framework perform at a substandard level, but the combination of features leads to adequate classification performance, suggesting that each set of features provides independent information that makes a unique contribution to the overall model.

4.5 Users in Online Q&A

Now we turn our attention to the people who generate the content we've just discussed. We can divide online Q&A users into two primary classes: askers and answerers. Of course, these are not necessarily mutually exclusive. The same people can both ask and answer questions, and as we will see in a later subsection here, for a peer-based online Q&A service to be sustainable, there needs to be an appropriate balance of asking and answering behaviors within that community of users.

4.5.1 Askers

Online Q&A involves two central types of users: askers—or those who submit a question to a particular site—and answerers, or those who provide answers to askers' questions. Choi and Shah [13] point out that despite online Q&A's growth, little is known about what motivates users to ask questions in these environments. Recently, however, some research focuses specifically on askers to uncover various facets of querying behavior, which could provide a general framework for conceptualizing different contexts and situations of information needs in online Q&A.

Some work examines general information seeking behavior that can apply to askers in online Q&A settings. Wilson [74], for example, pointed out that physical, affective, and cognitive needs, as well as an information seeker's social role and environment, motivate questioning behavior. Later, Wilson asserted that information seeking behavior may occur when an individual feels "a consequence of a need" [75, p. 251]. Wilson [75] contends that such a user would satisfy their desire by making demands on formal or informal information sources or services, which may or may not be successful.

A small body of work focuses on askers' motivations within online Q&A platforms. Using NCknows, a chat-based digital reference service, Pomerantz and Luo [51] investigated why users ask questions in order to determine the effectiveness of chat reference service in meeting library users' information needs. Their study, which combined traditional evaluation of users' satisfaction toward the reference encounter with details of their information use and motivation for using a chat reference service, isolated six categories of motivation: (1) to answer a work-related question, (2) to answer a question from their personal lives, (3) to conduct a known-item search, (4) to answer a question about the library itself, (5) to help others look for information, and (6) "others." This study was limited, however, because it surveyed a limited population.

Other studies focused on subject-specific queries to gain insight into the motivation behind askers' participation in SIS. Lee, Downie, and Cunningham [20] studied users looking for music-related information on Yahoo! Answers and Google Answers and found that identifying either artist or work was their most frequent motivation. When analyzing how everyday life contexts affect motivations for health-related information seeking, Zhang [77] identified three potential factors: cognitive motivation, emotional motivation, and social motivation. Morris et al. [41] looked specifically at SNSs to determine the types of questions asked and motivations for posting questions to social media rather than other platforms, such as search engines. They found that users trusted their social networks and believed SNSs performed better than search engines in addressing subjective questions.

Choi and Shah [13] conducted the most comprehensive study of askers' motivations to date. To investigate, they conducted a sequential mixed-method analysis that employed an Internet-based survey, diary method, and interviews among users of Yahoo! Answers and WikiAnswers. Findings revealed that cognitive needs—which include finding relevant information in immediate surroundings, seeking advice or opinions for decision-making, and learning via self-education—were the most significant motivation, but other motivational factors also played an important role depending on askers' contexts and situations. These other factors included (1) affective needs, or social and emotional support; (2) personal integrative needs, or finding support for or insight into one's own life; (3) social integrative needs, or identifying with others and gaining a sense of belonging or social interaction; and (4) tension-free needs, or filling time with fun or an emotional release. These recently acquired findings could develop better question-answering processes in online Q&A environments and gain insight into the broader understanding of online information seeking behaviors.

4.5.2 Answerers

Another body of social information seeking research focuses on answerers' behaviors. A variety of motivations drive question answerers within community-based online Q&A services. Oh [45] investigated Web 2.0 environments that focus on health-related information. Specifically, he examined common behavior among answerers who respond to questions asked by anonymous users on Yahoo! Answers. An online questionnaire proposed ten motivational factors: enjoyment, efficacy, learning, personal gain, altruism, community interest, social engagement, empathy, reputation, and reciprocity. Altruism was ranked the most influential, while personal gain was ranked the least. Enjoyment and efficacy were more influential than other social motivations, such as reputation or reciprocity, though different user groups (based on demographics, expertise, etc.) demonstrated some variations. Though his study focused on health-related information seeking, it can be applied to other domains and contexts.

Nam et al. [43] also emphasized altruism in their study of Knowledge-iN users, though they found learning and competency were significant. Rafaeli et al. [53], on the other hand, examined Google Answers's knowledge sharing market and found that economic and social incentives were important. Moore and Serva [40] analyzed member motivation for contributing to various types of virtual communities and found that social engagement was a significant factor. According to their research, answerers contribute to Q&A sites to satisfy their desire to belong to a social group and connect with others. This factor can be referred to as a motivation of belonging.

Kankanhalli et al. [30] examined employees' willingness to contribute answers and information to electronic knowledge repositories (EKRs). They used social exchange theory to create a cost/benefit analysis of EKR contributions, as well as social capital theory to account for various contextual factors that affect participation. After surveying a number of public sector organizations, they found that knowledge self-efficacy and enjoyment in helping others were the most significant motivational factors. These so-called intrinsic benefits were not contingent upon contextual factors; however, other "extrinsic benefits," such as reciprocity and recognition, were affected by contextual elements. These elements included generalized trust, pro-sharing norms, and identification. Though this study's largest implications apply to organization-wide knowledge management practices, its findings also lend insight into answerers' intrinsic and extrinsic motivations.

Harper et al. [23] developed a framework of question answerers' intrinsic and extrinsic motivations, which included perceptions of values, interactions, online social cognition, information ownership, reciprocity, gratitude, access to technology, generalized exchange, reputation, status, norms commonality, payment, and social/cultural capital. Panovich et al. [47] examined question-answering behavior on SNSs. According to the researchers, SNSs provide many opportunities to study online information seeking behavior due to their widespread use. Their work related answering behaviors to "tie strength," a friendship-measuring method from sociology. They found that tie strength applies to friends' answering behaviors. In particular, they claimed that stronger ties (i.e., closer friendships) provided a subtle increase in information that more significantly contributed to participants' overall knowledge and was less likely to have been seen before.

Bronstein et al. [10] also examined SNS contributions to determine why certain users choose to share information while others remain lurkers, a term we will discuss later in this chapter. They administered a survey to gauge the relationship between online participation and a series of variables that included anonymity, social value orientation, motivations, participation in offline activities, the Internet's political influence, and users' personality traits. Results suggested that frequent contributors have a host of factors in common: they identify themselves; report higher levels of offline extroversion, openness, and activity; and express interest in the topic to which they are responding. According to this study, personality traits factor in with the motivations behind answering behavior.

Oh [45] provides a litany of possible alternative motivational factors that warrant further attention: self-enjoyment, personal satisfaction, self-efficacy, self-competence, learning, access to information, community attachment, community advancement, gift-giving culture, financial incentives, and product development are avenues for future research.

4.5.3 *Balance of Askers-Answerers*

Since Q&A services' askers and answerers are both humans whose time, effort, and level of participation may be limited, it is important for a Q&A service to seek a good balance of users. If there are many people who want to answer and not enough people asking questions (doesn't often happen), we may waste the potential of those answerers. On the other hand, if there are many more askers than answerers (does happen), then answers may be slow to come or even not come at all.

Of course, unless we are talking about expert-based Q&A services, these askers and answerers are not usually different groups; the same participants can both ask and answer a question. Still, having a good balance of these behaviors is paramount. Let's look at a case study that examines what that balance looks like and what happens to services that don't achieve a good balance. Spoiler alert: Google Answers shuts down!

Shah et al. [61] looked at users' participation patterns in Yahoo! Answers and Google Answers. Of course, Google Answers was an expert-based Q&A system, so a special class of users was responsible for answering while everyone else could ask questions. But despite the platform's strictures, the authors still mined valuable data from the balance between its demonstrated asking and answering behaviors.

Now, Yahoo! Answers users earn and spend points based on their activities (e.g., asking a question costs 5 points; answering a question earns 10 points). And as they earn points, they can move up a level, with there being seven total levels. It's kind of like playing a game.

As illustrated in Fig. 4.15, Yahoo! Answers' upper-level users are much higher on the "Points" axis compared to those in lower levels.[15] This correlation is simply based on the definition of levels. What is more interesting to note is that there are other patterns as well. Users in higher levels seem to be answering many questions, but not necessarily posing that many more questions, as compared to those at lower levels.[16] We will examine this issue later in this section.

[15]Levels 1, 4, and 7 were chosen simply to keep the display uncluttered for this figure.

[16]This scatter plot may seem misleading as there appear to be many more points for higher levels than for lower levels. This is due to the fact that a majority of points at lower levels fall at the same spot, whereas points at higher levels are more distributed.

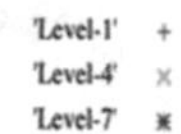

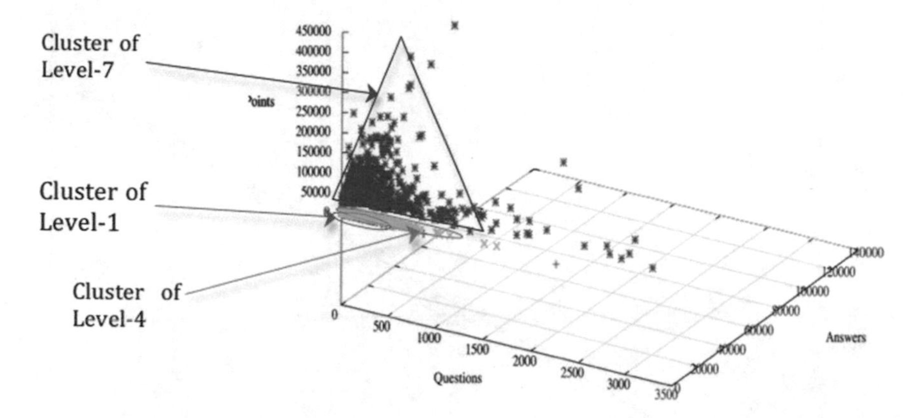

Fig. 4.15 Distribution of users in different levels according to the number of questions, number of answers, and the points in Yahoo! Answers

Let us now look at user participation in terms of consumer and contributor behavior at each level. Users at higher levels exhibit greater participation by contributing more than those at lower levels. This pattern can be inferred by the very definition of levels in Yahoo! Answers. A user achieves a given level based on points earned. While there are several factors that lead to earning or losing points, providing answers and having those answers selected as the best are the two major factors that lead to the acquisition of points. In other words, in spite of a complex formula for determining levels of user participation, the one factor that can solely reflect these levels is the number of answers contributed by a given user.

A plot of users in levels 1, 4, and 7 is depicted in Fig. 4.16. We can clearly see from this plot that lower-level users are basically consumers rather than contributors. There are a few outliers exhibiting some stronger consumers or contributors. Yahoo! Answers identifies top contributors in each of its 25 categories based on the number of questions a user has answered in that category. The collection used here had 55,005 users and 1677 top contributors.[17]

Shah et al. [61] found that while Yahoo! Answers users exhibit a *healthy* behavior, things were quite different for Google Answers users. Google hired only 535 answerers to assist a significantly higher number of askers.[18] And so many of

[17]There is some similarity in Yahoo! Answers's definition of top contributor and our usage of contributor. However, "contributor" here is defined as a characteristic of a user based on the number of questions that individual has answered.

[18]In fact, the potential pool of askers was the whole world, but the service never got to be that popular.

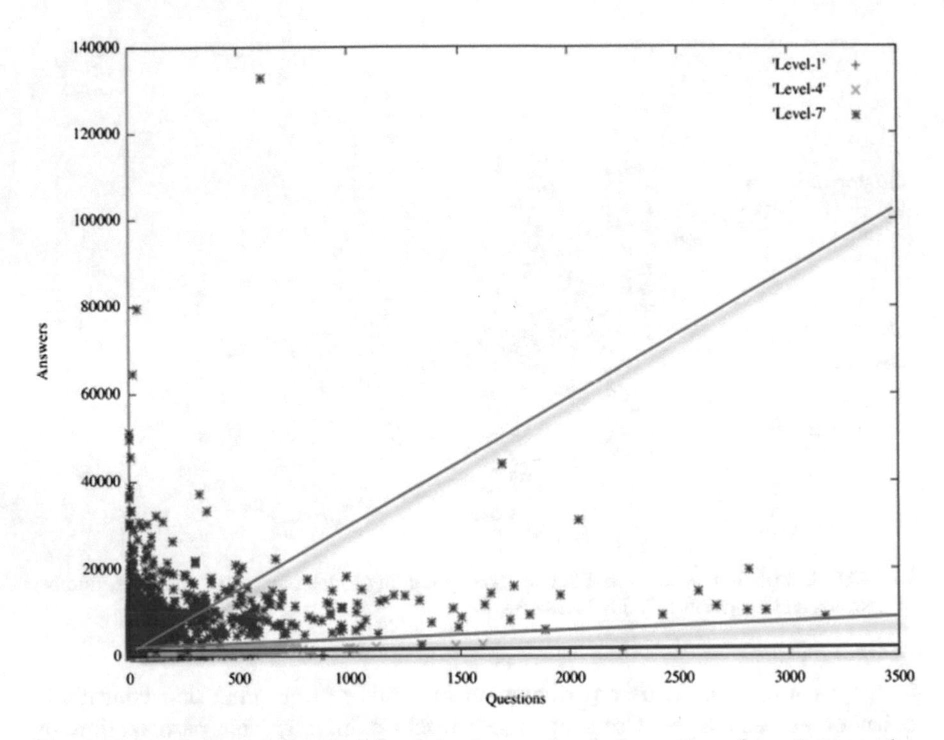

Fig. 4.16 Distribution of users in different levels according to the number of questions, number of answers, and the points in Yahoo! Answers

the questions went unanswered, fostering dissatisfaction among askers and turning them away from the service. After a brief debut, Google shut down its Answers service in 2006.

4.5.4 Special Users

While askers and answerers classify two general types of online Q&A users, not all participants are the same, or equally *important*. There are subsets of users in any community that are of more interest to service providers, advertisers, and scholars. These "special" users are grouped based on unique behaviors that characterize their specific actions within a Q&A service. Here we consider some of those classes of users in an effort to introduce the reader to the rewards that can be gained from identifying special users. We'll explore rising stars, struggling users, and potential answerers.

Rising stars are those users who consistently provide quality posts and earn a respected reputation from other community members. They are central to Q&A sites because they attract traffic from Internet users and subsequently drive sites' development. White et al. [73] contend that a community's size is a large component of its overall effectiveness, meaning rising stars are crucial components of an online Q&A service. White and Richardson [71] studied synchronous social question-answering, which involves a real-time dialog between askers and answerers. They found that an answerer's expertise significantly impacted both the quality and trajectory of a dialog. From these findings, they suggested that synchronous social Q&A systems should consider the relative expertise of candidate answers with respect to askers. Daud et al. [17] tackled the difficult task of finding rising stars in academic networks. They developed StarRank, a new computational method based on PageRank, to determine users' influence. Similarly, Li et al. [36] attempted to locate rising stars in publication networks using PubRank, also modeled after PageRank. They considered factors such as authors' interactions, track records, and chronological development. See [33] for more details on identifying rising stars in Q&A sites.

Struggling users are active community members who experience difficulty with providing quality answers. Their posts may experience a high deletion rate. Unlike "lurkers," who Gong et al. [22] define as Q&A users who inexplicably maintain minimal social connections, struggling users make an effort to participate in online communities. Sun et al. [68] compiled a literature review of online lurkers and concluded that several factors—including environmental, personal, relational, and security situations—influence lurking behavior. These individuals may be coaxed out by major global events. Struggling users, however, engage with sites' day-to-day content. They may, as Dervin [18] contends, misunderstand the context surrounding their topic, or even their chosen platform's larger social focus. Their answers can be incomplete, inaccurate, or inappropriate. Efforts, such as that proposed by O'Neill's [46] analysis of ChaCha[19] and other then-emerging answering systems, should be made to assist these users with their information seeking or answering tasks. Interactions with other users, instructional guides, classification systems, and other information seeking strategies may help struggling users to improve their actions before they leave a Q&A site. See [34] for more details on identifying struggling users in Q&A sites.

Potential answerers include users who could efficiently and effectively answer an asker's question, and thus reduce waiting time and develop quality answers within a particular site. Pelleg et al. [50] recently found that automatic quality assessment significantly improves users' experiences as compared to community feedback, which can be delayed and time-consuming. White, Richardson, and Liu [39] emphasize the importance of the ratio of answered to unanswered questions in a Q&A service. Identifying potential answerers would improve this ratio and thus serves as a paramount objective in SIS research. Shah and Pomerantz

[19] http://www.chacha.com.

[60] studied answer quality in Q&A and developed a method to automatically predict answer quality in Yahoo! Answers. Unfortunately, this method manually extracted thirteen answer features and was very expensive. Shah and Kitzie [59] asserted that answer effectiveness is most influenced by relevance, quality, and sanctification. Li et al. [37] developed a question-routing system within community question-answering to estimate answerer expertise for routing questions to potential answerers. Their results achieved higher accuracies of routing questions with lower computational costs.

It is important to note that throughout a user's "lifetime" (or period of use) on a Q&A site, they may evolve or otherwise shift into different roles. Danescu-Niculescu-Mizil et al. [16] studied lifetimes and found that users are initially receptive to online communities until they slowly become disillusioned with the language gap (e.g., jargon, expertise) between themselves and other members. Other factors influence the trajectory of users' participation, including their desire to learn, whether their information need was satisfied, and external factors such as career changes or relocation.

4.6 Summary

This chapter recognized that questioning is one of the fundamental behaviors of a human being when it comes to seeking information. Over the last few decades, due to amazing advancements made by the search engine industry, we have all grown accustomed to throwing out a bunch of keywords when we want to find something. But when it comes to seeking information from others, thankfully, we still use questions.

Online social and crowdsourcing services make it easy for people to seek information from others by posting questions. While some of these sites were created specifically for question-answering (Q&A), some others are being used for Q&A without that specific design. Examples of the former are Yahoo! Answers and Stack Overflow, whereas Twitter and Facebook fall under the latter category of services.

We saw in this chapter that there are four major categories of Q&A services: community-based, expert-based, collaborative, and social. We also saw how the nature of questions posted on each of these platforms varies. In the end, it's up to the information seeker to practice their freedom to explore and choose whatever works for them. It's not uncommon for people to seek information through multiple unconventional media and methods.

References

1. Adamic, L.A., Zhang, J., Bakshy, E., Ackerman, M.S.: Knowledge sharing and yahoo answers. In: Proceedings of the 17th International Conference on World Wide Web - WWW '08, p. 665. ACM Press, New York, NY (2008)
2. Adamic, L.A., Zhang, J., Bakshy, E., Ackerman, M.S.: Knowledge sharing and yahoo answers: everyone knows something. In: Proceedings of the 17th International Conference on World Wide Web, vol. 4, pp. 665–674. ACM, New York (2008)
3. Agichtein, E., Castillo, C., Donato, D., Gionis, A., Mishne, G.: Finding high-quality content in social media. In: Proceedings of the International Conference on Web Search and Web Data Mining - WSDM '08, pp. 183–194. ACM Press, New York, NY (2008)
4. Agichtein, E., Liu, Y., Bian, J.: Modeling information-seeker satisfaction in community question answering. ACM Trans. Knowl. Discov. Data **3**(2), 1–27 (2009)
5. Arnold, J., Kaske, N.K.: Evaluating the quality of a chat service. portal Libr. Acad. **5**(2), 177–193 (2005)
6. Belkin, N.J., Oddy, R.N., Brooks, H.M.: Ask for information retrieval: Part I. Background and theory. J. Doc. **38**(2), 61–71 (1982)
7. Bernhard, D., Gurevych, I.: Answering learners' questions by retrieving question paraphrases from social Q&A sites. In: Proceedings of the Third Workshop on Innovative Use of NLP for Building Educational Applications, June 2008, pp. 44–52
8. Bian, J., Liu, Y., Agichtein, E., Zha, H.: Finding the right facts in the crowd. In: WWW '08. ACM Press, New York, NY (2008)
9. Bian, J., Liu, Y., Agichtein, E., Zha, H.: Finding the right facts in the crowd. In: Proceedings of the 17th International Conference on World Wide Web - WWW '08, pp. 467–476. ACM Press, New York (2008)
10. Bronstein, J., Gazit, T., Perez, O., Bar-Ilan, J., Aharony, N., Amichai-Hamburger, Y.: An examination of the factors contributing to participation in online social platforms. Aslib J. Inf. Manage. **68**(6), 793–818 (2016)
11. Chen, Y., Ho, T.H., Kim, Y.M.: Knowledge market design: a field experiment at Google Answers. J. Public Econ. Theory **12**(4), 641–664 (2010)
12. Choi, E., Shah, C.: Asking for more than an answer: what do askers expect in online Q&A services? J. Inf. Sci. **42**(2), 0165551516645530 (2016)
13. Choi, E., Shah, C.: User motivations for asking questions in online Q&A services. J. Assoc. Inf. Sci. Technol. **67**(5), 1182–1197 (2016)
14. Choi, E., Kitzie, V., Shah, C.: Developing a typology of online Q&A models and recommending the right model for each question type. In: Proceedings of the ASIST Annual Meeting, vol. 49(1), pp. 1–4 (2012)
15. Choi, E., Kitzie, V., Shah, C.: 10 points for the best answer-baiting for explicating knowledge contributions within online Q&A. In: Proceedings of the ASIST Annual Meeting, vol. 50. Wiley, New York (2013)
16. Danescu-Niculescu-Mizil, C., West, R., Jurafsky, D., Leskovec, J., Potts, C.: No country for old members: user lifecycle and linguistic change in online communities. In: WWW 2013-Proceedings of the 22nd International Conference on World Wide Web, pp. 307–317 (2013)
17. Daud, A., Abbasi, R., Muhammad, F.: Finding rising stars in social networks. In: Meng, W., Feng, L., Bressan, S., Winiwarter, W., Song, W. (eds.) Database Systems for Advanced Applications, pp. 13–24. Springer, Wuhan (2013)
18. Dervin, B.: Given a context by any other name: methodological tools for taming the unruly beast. In: Dervin, B., Foreman-Wernet, L., Lauterbach, E. (eds.) Sense-Making Methodology Reader: Selected Writings of Brenda Dervin, Chap. 7, pp. 111–132. Hampton Press, Cresskill (2003)
19. Desai, C.M.: Instant messaging reference: how does it compare? Electron. Libr. **21**(1), 21–30 (2003)

20. Downie, J.S., Cunningham, S.J.: Challenges in cross-cultural/multilingual music information seeking. In: Proceedings of the 6th International Conference on Music Information Retrieval (ISMIR), pp. 1–7 (2005)
21. Garnsey, R.R., Powell, B.A.: Electronic mail reference services in the public library. Ref. User Serv. Q. **39**(3), 245–254 (2000)
22. Gong, W., Lim, E.P., Zhu, F.: Characterizing silent users in social media communities. In: Proceedings of the 9th International Conference on Web and Social Media, ICWSM 2015, pp. 140–149 (2015)
23. Harper, F.M., Raban, D., Rafaeli, S., Konstan, J.A.: Predictors of Answer Quality in Online Q&A Sites. ACM Press, New York, NY (2008)
24. Harper, F.M., Moy, D., Konstan, J.A.: Facts or friends?: distinguishing informational and conversational questions in social Q&A sites. In: Proceedings of the 27th International Conference on Human Factors in Computing Systems, pp. 759–768. ACM, New York (2009)
25. Harper, F.M., Weinberg, J., Logie, J., Konstan, J.A.: Question types in social Q&A sites. First Monday **15**(7) (2010)
26. Hodges, R.A.: Assessing digital reference. Libri, vol. 52(3) (2002)
27. Honeycutt, C., Herring, S.C.: Beyond microblogging: conversation and collaboration via twitter. In: Proceedings of the 42nd Annual Hawaii International Conference on System Sciences, HICSS (2009)
28. Horowitz, D., Kamvar, S.D.: The anatomy of a large-scale social search engine. In: Proceedings of the 19th International Conference on World Wide Web, pp. 431–440 (2010)
29. Jeon, J., Croft, W.B., Lee, J.H., Park, S.: A framework to predict the quality of answers with non-textual features. In: Proceedings of the 29th Annual International ACM SIGIR Conference on Research and Development in Information Retrieval - SIGIR '06 (2006)
30. Kankanhalli, A., Tan, B.C.Y., Wei, K.: Contributing knowledge to electronic knowledge repositories: an empirical investigation. MIS Q. **29**(1), 113–143 (2005)
31. Kibbee, J., Ward, D., Ma, W.: Virtual service, real data: results of a pilot study. Ref. Serv. Rev. **30**(1), 25–36 (2002)
32. Kitzie, V., Choi, E., Shah, C.: Analyzing question quality through intersubjectivity: World views and objective assessments of questions on social question-answering. Proc. Am. Soc. Inf. Sci. Technol. **50**(1), 1–10 (2013)
33. Le, L.T., Shah, C.: Retrieving Rising Stars in Focused Community Question-Answering, pp. 25–36. Springer, Berlin (2016)
34. Le, L., Shah, C., Choi, E.: Bad users or bad content? breaking the vicious cycle by finding struggling students in community question-answering. In: Proceedings of ACM CHIIR 2017 Conference, Oslo (2017)
35. Leibenluft, J.: A librarian's worst nightmare: Yahoo Answers, where 120 million users can be wrong. Slate (2007)
36. Li, X.-L., Foo, C.S., Tew, K.L., Ng, S.-K.: Searching for rising stars in bibliography networks, pp. 288–292 (2009)
37. Li, B., King, I., Lyu, M.R.: Question routing in community question answering: putting category in its place. CIKM'11, pp. 2041–2044 (2011)
38. Liu, Y., Bian, J., Agichtein, E.: Predicting information seeker satisfaction in community question answering. In: Proceedings of the 31st Annual International ACM SIGIR Conference on Research and Development in Information Retrieval - SIGIR '08, Section 2, p. 483 (2008)
39. Liu, Q., Agichtein, E., Dror, G., Gabrilovich, E., Maarek, Y., Pelleg, D., Szpektor, I.: Predicting web searcher satisfaction with existing community-based answers. In: Proceedings of the 34th International ACM SIGIR Conference on Research and Development in Information - SIGIR '11, p. 415. ACM Press, New York, NY (2011)
40. Moore, T.D., Serva, M.A.: Understanding member motivation for contributing to different types of virtual communities. In: Proceedings of the 2007 ACM SIGMIS CPR Conference on 2007 Computer Personnel Doctoral Consortium and Research Conference The Global Information Technology Workforce - SIGMIS-CPR '07, p. 153. ACM Press, New York, NY (2007)

41. Morris, M.R., Teevan, J., Panovich, K.: What do people ask their social networks, and why? A survey study of status message Q & A behavior. In: CHI 10, pp. 1739–1748 (2010)
42. Morris, M.R., Teevan, J., Panovich, K.: What do people ask their social networks, and why? A survey study of status message Q&A behavior. In: Proceedings of ACM SIGCHI Conference on Human Factors in Computing Systems, Atlanta, GA (2010)
43. Nam, K.K., Ackerman, M.S., Adamic, L.A.: Questions in, knowledge in?: a study of Naver's question answering community. In: SIGCHI Conference on Human Factors in Computing Systems, pp. 779–788. ACM Press, New York (2009)
44. Numminen, P., Vakkari, P.: Question types in public libraries' digital reference service in Finland: comparing 1999 and 2006. J. Am. Soc. Inf. Sci. Technol. **60**(6), 1249–1257 (2009)
45. Oh, S.: The characteristics and motivations of health answerers for sharing information, knowledge, and experiences in online environments. J. Am. Soc. Inf. Sci. Technol. **63**(3), 543–557 (2012)
46. O'Neill, N.: Cha Cha, Yahoo !, and Amazon: new answer services emerge. Searcher **15**(4), 7–11 (2007)
47. Panovich, K., Miller, R., Karger, D.: Tie strength in question & answer on social network sites. In: Proceedings of the ACM 2012 Conference on Computer Supported Cooperative Work, pp. 1057–1066 (2012)
48. Parus, D.J.: The reference interview: communication and the patron. Katharine Sharp Review (2) (1996)
49. Paul, S.A., Hong, L., Chi, E.H.: Is Twitter a good place for asking questions? A characterization study. In: AAAI Conference on Weblogs and Social Media, pp. 1–4 (2011)
50. Pelleg, D., Rokhlenko, O., Szpektor, I., Agichtein, E., Guy, I.: When the crowd is not enough: improving user experience with social media through automatic quality analysis. In: Proceedings of the 19th ACM Conference on Computer-Supported Cooperative Work & Social Computing - CSCW '16, pp. 1078–1088. ACM Press, New York, NY (2016)
51. Pomerantz, J., Luo, L.: Motivations and uses: evaluating virtual reference service from the users' perspective. Libr. Inf. Sci. Res. **28**(3), 350–373 (2006)
52. Pomerantz, J., Nicholson, S., Belanger, Y., Lankes, R.D.: The current state of digital reference: validation of a general digital reference model through a survey of digital reference services. Inf. Process. Manage. **40**(2), 347–363 (2004)
53. Rafaeli, S., Raban, D.R., Ravid, G.: How social motivation enhances economic activity and incentives in the knowledge sharing market. Int. J. Knowl. Learn. **3**(1), 1–11 (2007)
54. Rosenbaum, H., Shachaf, P.: A structuration approach to online communities of practice: the case of Q&A communities. J. Am. Soc. Inf. Sci. Technol. **61**(9), 1933–1944 (2010)
55. Ross, C.S., Nilsen, K., Radford, M.: Conducting the Reference Interview: a How-to-Do-it Manual for Librarians, 2nd edn. Neal-Schuman Publishers, New York, NY, (2009)
56. Sears, J.: Chat reference service: an analysis of one semester's data. Issues Sci. Technol. Librarians. **32**, 92001 (2001)
57. Shah, C.: Measuring effectiveness and user satisfaction in Yahoo! Answers. First Monday **16** 2–7 February 2011 (2011)
58. Shah, C., Gonzalez-Ibanez, R.: Spatial context in collaborative information seeking. J. Inf. Sci. **38**(4), 333–349 (2012)
59. Shah, C., Kitzie, V.: Social Q&A and virtual reference-comparing apples and oranges with the help of experts and users. J. Am. Soc. Inf. Sci. Technol. **63**(10), 2020–2036 (2012)
60. Shah, C., Pomerantz, J.: Evaluating and predicting answer quality in community QA. In: Proceeding of the 33rd International ACM SIGIR Conference on Research and Development in Information Retrieval - SIGIR '10, p. 411. ACM Press, New York, NY (2010)
61. Shah, C., Oh, J.S., Oh, S.: Exploring characteristics and effects of user participation in online social Q&A sites. First Monday **13**(9) (2008)
62. Shah, C., Oh, S., Oh, J.S.: Research agenda for social Q&A. Libr. Inf. Sci. Res. **31**(4), 205–209 (2009)

63. Shah, C., Radford, M.L., Connaway, L.S., Choi, E., Kitzie, V.: "How much change do you get from 40$?" - analyzing and addressing failed questions on social Q&A. In: Proceedings of the ASIST Annual Meeting, vol. 49(1) (2012)
64. Shah, C., Kitzie, V., Choi, E.: Questioning the question – addressing the answerability of questions in community question-answering. In: 2014 47th Hawaii International Conference on System Sciences, pp. 1386–1395. IEEE, New York (2014)
65. Shah, C., Radford, M.L., Connaway, L.S.: Collaboration and synergy in hybrid Q&A: participatory design method and results. Libr. Inf. Sci. Res. **37**(2), 92–99 (2015)
66. Smyth, J.: Virtual reference transcript analysis: a few models. Searcher **11**(3), 26–30 (2003)
67. Su, Q., Pavlov, D., Chow, J.-H., Baker, W.C.: Internet-scale collection of human-reviewed data. In: Proceedings of the 16th International Conference on World Wide Web - WWW '07, p. 231. ACM Press, New York, NY (2007)
68. Sun, N., Rau, P.-L.P., Ma, L.: Understanding lurkers in online communities: a literature review. Comput. Hum. Behav. **38**, 110–117 (2014)
69. Tatham, M.: U.S. visits to question and answer websites increased 118 percent year over-year Yahoo! Answers receives 74 percent of all U.S. visits (2008)
70. Wadhwa, V.: Why I don't buy the Quora hype (2011)
71. White, R.W., Richardson, M.: Effects of expertise differences in synchronous social Q&A. In: Proceedings of the 35th International ACM SIGIR Conference on Research and Development in Information Retrieval - SIGIR '12, p. 1055. ACM Press, New York, NY (2012)
72. White, R.W., Richardson, M., Liu, Y.: Effects of community size and contact rate in synchronous social Q&A. In: Proceedings of the 2011 Annual Conference on Human Factors in Computing Systems - CHI '11, pp. 2837–2846 (2011)
73. White, R.W., Richardson, M., Liu, Y.: Effects of community size and contact rate in synchronous social q&a. In: Proceedings of the 2011 Annual Conference on Human Factors in Computing Systems - CHI '11, p. 2837. ACM Press, New York (2011)
74. Wilson, T.D.: On user studies and information needs. J. Doc. **37**(1), 3–15 (1981)
75. Wilson, T.D.: Models in information behaviour research. J. Doc. **55**(3), 249–270 (1999)
76. Yang, L., Bao, S., Lin, Q., Wu, X., Han, D., Su, Z., Yu, Y.: Analyzing and predicting not-answered questions in community-based question answering services. In: Proceedings of the Twenty-Fifth AAAI Conference on Artificial Intelligence, pp. 1273–1278 (2011)
77. Zhang, Y.: Contextualizing consumer health information searching: an analysis of questions in a social Q&A community. In: Proceedings of the 1st ACM International Health, pp. 210–219 (2010)

Chapter 5
Social Search

Abstract This chapter introduces the intersection of information seeking/searching and social media/networking. This intersection is called social search, and it references two concepts: people looking for information that is socially constructed and people using social connections to look for information. While some of the aspects of social search overlap with social Q&A, or in general Q&A services, there are important differences. The present chapter dwells on those differences and the uniqueness of social search by way of subtopics such as social annotations, social navigation, and co-browsing. The chapter also introduces several pertinent theories and models for social search. There are discussions on the technology for providing and facilitating social search, as well as related topics such as collaborative search.

5.1 Introduction

As we have seen multiple times in this book, people are increasingly looking for information through their social connections. Searching has gone social in different ways for quite some time. In a sense, we have come full circle in terms of our search habits. As many scholars identified decades ago, information seeking/searching is social [32]. Or at least it's meant to be social. That's how we succeeded for a long time—asking around through our social ties when we had information needs. And then at some point we started storing that information in tablets, scrolls, books, and finally digital devices, making it possible to bypass talking to a person and instead go straight to the information.

To add to that, the Internet, and more specifically the Web, brought us a host of fantastic tools that made it possible to not even leave our house to look for information. And so while searching for information was conceived to be a social activity, thanks to amazing search engines, databases, and other services that were all designed for individual access, somewhere we lost that social touch.

C. Shah, *Social Information Seeking*, The Information Retrieval Series 38,
DOI 10.1007/978-3-319-56756-3_5

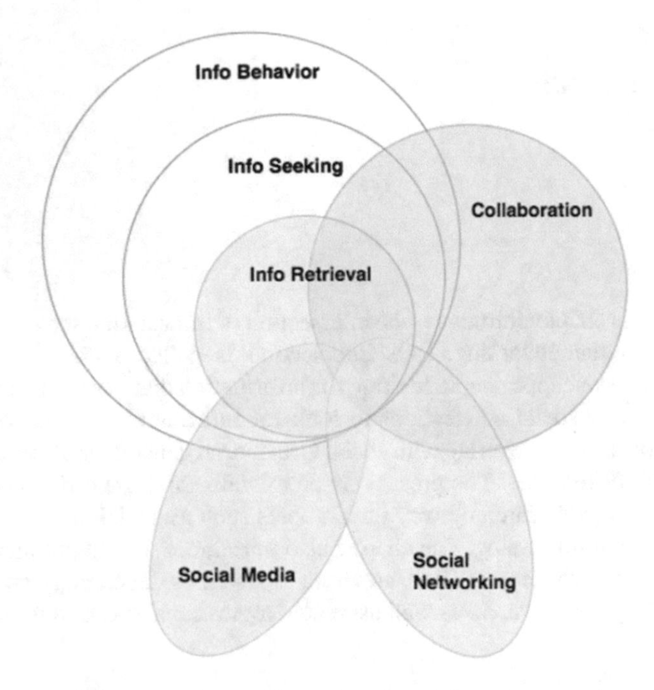

Fig. 5.1 Contextualizing social search with the help of related concepts—social media/networking, collaboration, and information retrieval

Fast forward to the twenty-first century and we have something called the Web 2.0, which is essentially a set of services and methods for not just accessing but also producing and sharing information with others. And so we are coming back full circle to exploiting our social connections to search for information (Fig. 5.1). In this chapter, we will see different ways this social search phenomenon is exhibited and studied.

5.2 Defining Social Search

Let's start with some examples of social search. We actually saw a couple of them in the previous chapter when we talked about social Q&A. But search is more than just Q&A. Our most common method for searching is still through keywords, so it's expected that we have a way to search through our social information using keywords.

Such an example is shown in Fig. 5.2, which comes from Google Social Search. There is nothing very fancy here. This particular search engine is simply using Google's search algorithm on data specifically generated in various social media sources such as Facebook, Twitter, and Pinterest.

Fig. 5.2 A screenshot of Google Social Search

Of course, there are some scholarly works that directly address social search. For instance, Evans and Chi [12] discussed how social interactions could help individuals who search together. They explicitly called this *social search*. Social ties that lead to social search can be extended to stronger ties leading to collaborative search.

Let us talk about how ties in information seeking environments—such as transforming weaker ties into stronger ones to encourage possible collaboration—have also been used in several other places. For instance, there are co-browsing applications that let visitors of the same Web page be aware of each other to encourage interactive information seeking [9].

Sometimes stronger ties are formed not for collaborative purposes, but to possibly filter information. Most collaborative filtering systems depend on converting weaker ties (e.g., users of the same system who are interested in similar objects) to stronger ties (e.g., users who are connected based on their behavior and able to influence each other). For instance, a Netflix[1] user can have social (weaker) ties with their friends on Netflix's network, but when Netflix's collaborative filtering system starts making recommendations based on their social network, and when the users in that network start using those recommendations and/or start interacting with their peers based on their similar interests, the weaker ties of that social network become stronger and more specific.

In summary, a social network typically exhibits weaker ties among the participants based on their interactions, intentions, and objectives. A collaborative network, on the other hand, shows stronger ties. A social tie can be useful and converted to a collaborative tie. The reverse can happen too. Often, participants without social ties are put in a collaborative project. While working on such a project, the participants may develop a social tie. Based on this, we know that one tie (social or collaborative) does not subsume the other; they both can complement each other.

Though social search is not always explicitly defined in information seeking literature, it describes the process in which individuals seek to satisfy an information need through their social connections. Such connections could include Facebook friends, email networks, and other social media networks that encourage the exchange of information through social interactions. According to Evans and Chi [13], social search has been applied in the Web 2.0 field to describe searches that:

1. Utilize social and expertise networks
2. Are done in shared social workspaces
3. Involve social data mining or collective intelligence processes to improve the search process

A number of models examine various aspects of social search in detail.

5.3 Social Search Theories

From the onset of sophisticated Internet social networks, information scientists have researched the various factors that motivate and affect social searchers and the development of their chosen systems.

5.3.1 An Early Model

Watts and Dodds [33] present early social search theories. They believe social networks are valuable due to their "searchability," or allowance of ordinary people to direct messages through personalized networks of acquaintances in order to reach

[1] https://www.netflix.com.

a specific person. This quantifiable model offers an explanation of social network searchability in terms of recognizable personal identities, or sets of characteristics measured along a number of social dimensions. The model is based on six contentions of social networks:

1. Individuals in social networks are endowed with both network ties and identities, or sets of characteristics attributed to themselves and others based off social group dynamics.
2. Individuals break the world down into cognitively measurable groups, which include various networks of social connections.
3. Group membership defines identity and is also the primary basis for social interaction and acquaintanceship.
4. Individuals hierarchically partition the world in multiple, independent categories.
5. Individuals construct measures of "social distance" that capture closeness within a group.
6. Given only local information about a network, individuals forward a message to a single person.

This model can, in theory, be applied to any data structure in which elements exhibit quantifiable characteristics of the researchers' notion of identity. Additionally, similarity between two elements can be judged along multiple dimensions.

5.3.2 Information-Driven Motivation

Borgatti and Cross [4] examine the motivations behind users' decision to seek information from other people. They propose a formal information seeking model in which the probability that a person would seek information from another person is a function of: (1) knowing what that person knows, (2) valuing what that person knows, (3) being able to gain timely access to that person's thinking, and (4) believing that seeking information from that person would not have a high cost. They also believe that knowledge, access, and cost variables mediate the relationship between physical proximity and information seeking. Results from two studies strongly support both theories, with the exception of the mediation cost concept.

Amershi and Morris [2] believe that social search can improve cumbersome information seeking practices, such as collaborative search habits that occur in shared computer settings, or those settings in which individuals conduct a collaborative search using only one device. After conducting interviews with teachers, librarians, and developing world researchers, they discovered the many limitations of collaborative endeavors. In order to improve colocated collaborative Web search, they introduced CoSearch, a social search technique in which collaborative Web search is improved through the use of multiple readily available devices. They concluded that CoSearch enabled distributed control and division of labor, and thus reduced frustrations associated with shared computer work while preserving the positive aspects of communication and collaboration during information retrieval.

According to McDonnell and Shiri [25], social search can enhance Web searching. They believe that social search has a substantial role to play in Web search due to its ability to enhance information seeking through synchronous collaboration. They present a taxonomy of social search that includes several dimensions on which the activity can be categorized:

1. *Synchronous vs. asynchronous collaboration*. Synchronous collaboration refers to social search activities that take place in real time, whereas asynchronous collaboration refers to users who do not interact in real time.
2. *Implicit vs. explicit collaboration*. Implicit collaboration refers to systems, such as social bookmarking systems, in which collaboration emerges from an analysis of the behavior of users who do not interact with each other. Explicit collaboration occurs when users have an explicit assumption that, via a particular system, their questions will be answered by someone in their social network.
3. *Finding people vs. finding information (search target)*. Some researchers exclusively define social search as a search for people, but most focus on a user's goal to find information resources.
4. *Search vs. discovery (finding)*. "Search" refers to the traditional information retrieval model, whereas "discovery" refers to practices that may allow users to discover new sites that cannot be found via search.
5. *Sense-making vs. content selection in results*. Another dimension of social search lies in the degree to which a system relies on social media to either select content or make sense of search results.

After identifying these five dimensions, McDonnell and Shiri [25] propose a user-centered model of social search, stating that a great deal of previous research narrowly focuses on methods that users cannot directly manipulate or influence.

5.3.3 Cognitive Motivation

Evans et al. [14] believe that social search can have cognitive benefits as well as informational benefits. Using a talk-aloud protocol and video, they explored the actions of eight subjects as they completed two "Google-hard" search tasks. Tasks alternated between social condition—or those in which participants could only use social resources—and nonsocial condition, in which participants could use normal Web-based information sources. The study found that asking questions on social networking sites and targeting friends one-on-one both resulted in increased information processing. Social networking sites garnered more answers to a question, while one-on-one interactions produced more thorough answers. Researchers concluded that technological and cultural affordances of different social information media could provide complementary cognitive benefits to searchers. The work suggests that online tools could be better integrated to support this process.

Evans and Chi [11] draw attention to core concepts within social search. Their study illuminates the idea that, though search engine researchers often view searching as a solitary activity, social interactions play an important role throughout the search process. They reach this conclusion via a critical incident survey of over 150 users of Amazon's Mechanical Turk[2] service. Their study integrates models of sense-making and information seeking behavior to present a canonical social model of users' activity before, during, and after search.

In a second study, Evans and Chi [13] surveyed another 150 users and focused on difficulties encountered during searches. Social interactions ranged from highly coordinated with shared goals to loosely coordinated with sought advice, but all suggested similar conclusions to those reached during their initial study. They found that users have a strong social inclination throughout the search process and thus interact with others for a variety of reasons. According to their data, self-motivated searchers, users conducting informational searches, and users with failed or difficult queries demonstrated the highest degrees of social search. Their finding that users interact before, during, and after search processes paves the way for system design suggestions that specifically pertain to each stage in a search process. These tools would take natural, nuanced search behaviors into account.

5.3.4 *Collaborative Search*

Often related to social search is collaborative search, as shown in two of the earlier studies reported by Evans and Chi [11, 13] on topics of collaborative search environments and practices. According to Morris et al. [28], collaborative search is a social search where users share an information need and work together to fulfill that need. Morris [27] examined collaborative Web search practices through a study of 204 knowledge workers at a large technology company. Findings indicated that a large proportion of users engaged in searches that included collaborative activities. Based off these results, it was concluded that Web search interfaces should be designed with tools for sharing. Twidale et al. [32] made an early plea for collaborative Web systems, stating that collaboration is vital to online information retrieval and thus necessitates a shift away from single-user system interfaces. Their study specifically examined digital libraries and introduced the Ariadne system, which provides computerized support for collaboration between browsers.

Golovchinsky et al. [18] provide an in-depth picture of collaborative information seeking as social search. They classify systems for computer-supported collaboration for information seeking along four dimensions:

1. *Intent—Explicit vs. Implicit*. Explicit information seeking classifies scenarios in which collaborators search for information based on a declared understanding

[2]https://www.mturk.com/mturk/welcome.

of their mutual information need, which may evolve over time. Implicit intent pertains to collaborative filtering systems that infer users' similar information needs based on their actions or opinions.
2. *Depth of mediation*. Depth of mediation describes the level at which collaboration occurs in the system. This can be user interface or search engine back end. Mediation affects a system's awareness of its users' contributions and how it uses those contributions to influence searches.
3. *Concurrency*. Searchers can collaborate synchronously (e.g., in real time), or asynchronously, where previous searches influence later searches.
4. *Location*. Collaborators can work in the same place at the same time, which allows them to communicate in a variety of ways beyond the computer. They can also be distributed, which may increase the chances for collaboration but decrease possible communication channels.

Golovchinsky et al. [18] also classify various user roles in a collaborative human-computer system. These include:

1. *Peer*. The most common situation involving existing (non-mediated) tools during which all collaborators use the same interfaces to control the system and coordinate their activities.
2. *Domain A expert/domain B expert*. A variation of the peer role in which collaborators use the same interfaces but possess different domain knowledge. Mediation can help users recognize documents relevant to both sets of expertise.
3. *Search expert/search novice or domain expert/domain novice*. Often, collaborators will possess varying degrees of expertise or familiarity with a domain and with search tools.
4. *Search expert/domain expert*. These roles introduce true asymmetries between team members' contributions. The search expert knows the system but can only make rudimentary suggestions based on information provided by the domain expert. The domain expert has a better understanding of the information need and, subsequently, more evaluative power. When mediated, this dynamic can be quite successful.
5. *Prospector/miner*. Unlike other roles, these focus on searchers' activities during the search. One collaborator can search broadly (prospector), while the other searches deeply (miner).

Other role combinations are possible, and not all are pairs. Regardless, this research suggests that most complex tasks improve with collaboration, and existing tools must be better designed to support these tasks. Golovchinsky et al. [18] believe that dimensions of collaboration and roles can foster a design framework for systems that support explicit collaboration. We will talk about collaboration more in the next section of this book.

5.4 Social Search Technology

Morris et al. [28] believe that the recent and rapid rise in social networking tools and practices has allowed users to expand upon their preexisting propensity to turn to social contacts with their questions. They surveyed 624 people to discover what types of questions are asked and answered via social networking platforms. They explored relationships between answer speed and answer quality, properties of participants' questions (e.g., type, topic, and phrasing), and properties of participants themselves (e.g., age, gender, and social network use habits).

Horowitz and Kamvar [22] developed Aardvark, an actual social search engine. The system allowed users to ask a question via email, instant message, text message, or voice. It then routed the question to a person within that user's social network who was deemed most likely to be able to answer it. The challenge lied in finding a qualified answerer, rather than in finding satisfactory documents. Unlike traditional search engines, trust was based on authority rather than intimacy. This new kind of search engine presented an alternative to preexisting platforms and search strategies. Google acquired Aardvark in 2010 and shut it down a year later.

Other researchers have examined specific kinds of social search technology, such as peer-to-peer (P2P) systems. Condie et al. [8] postulate that P2P systems, such as Gnutella, have potential for large-scale, robust information sharing but cannot meet said potential because they match users to randomly selected peers within their network. They present a new protocol that forms adaptive, self-organizing topologies for data sharing within P2P networks. This would allow a user to directly connect to peers that would provide the most satisfactory content. It would also prevent certain attacks, reward active peers, and punish malicious peers and free riders.

In a later study of P2P systems, Faye et al. [15] acknowledge a significant challenge to building schema-based P2P systems: locating peers that are relevant with respect to a given query. They propose a new semantic routing mechanism in the context of the SenPeer P2P Data Management System (PDMS). A distributed data structure, or expertise table, is maintained by super-peers that describe data at neighboring peers. The table is combined with matching techniques to create a semantic overlay network, which exploits semantic links for efficient query propagation toward peers that may have relevant data. Based on criteria such as precision, recall, and number of messages, this semantic query routing outperforms a baseline algorithm and thus provides a potentially effective way to connect user queries to qualified peer answerers.

Carmel et al. [6] studied the more general idea to personalize search results based off a user's social network. In their research, search results were re-ranked according to their relationships with a user's social network, as determined by multiple types of personalization: (1) familiarity-based networks determined by explicit connections, (2) similarity-based networks of people determined by social activity, and (3) overall networks that provide both relationship types. They conducted both an online and an offline study and found that all three personalizations provided better search results than non-personalized social search in both settings.

5.4.1 Statistical Analyses

Chi [7] states that users are motivated by a number of factors ranging from obligations to curiosity when seeking information from others during a search process. He believes that social search can facilitate the search process via statistical analyses of traces left behind by others. He examines trends—such as interest in collaborative, collocated search and social bookmarking—to argue that search processes should no longer be considered solitary activities. He classifies two categories of social search systems:

1. *Social answering systems* , which utilize people with certain expertise or opinions to answer a domain-specific question with success dependent upon recommendation algorithms to return the most relevant past answers, thus allowing for a better constructed knowledge base
2. *Social feedback systems*, which utilize implicitly or explicitly obtained social attention data to rank search results or information items

Chi [7] believes that both systems deserve more sophisticated statistical and analytical structure-based analytics (e.g., expertise-finding algorithms and data-mining algorithms) to improve social search and experience. He discusses the Mr Taggy system, which uses statistical machine learning to construct a Web browsing guide using social tagging data.

Goel et al. [17] define the "algorithmic small world hypothesis," which states that not only are pairs of individuals in a large social network connected by small paths but also that ordinary individuals can find these paths. "Paths," in this case, refer to the number of steps needed to connect to an information network; they measure the efficiency of information and other transport over a social network. In order to gather a more complete picture of small world chains, these authors used data from two small world experiments to model heterogeneity in chain attrition rates as a function of individual attributes. They then introduced a supposedly unbiased way to establish chain lengths.

With their findings, Goel et al. [17] provide mixed support for the algorithmic hypothesis. Some chains could be completed in six or seven steps, while others involved much longer mean estimates, and thus suggest that, for some parts of the population, the world is not "small." Their study concludes that search distances in social networks are fundamentally different from topological distances.

Adamic and Adar [1] present an earlier look at one specific attribute of small world experiments. Specifically, they examine how participants are able to find short paths in a social network using only local information about their immediate contacts. They simulate experiences on two separate networks: email contacts and a student social networking site. On the email network, they found that small world attributes, such as relative physical or hierarchical positions, could be used to locate a contact. On the student social networking site, they found that incomplete data and ambiguous hierarchical structures rendered those search strategies less effective. Their study broke new ground by applying social network theories to small world experiment theories, and determining which types of networks (in this case, email networks) best worked with small world experiments. Results impacted software development practices by demonstrating that different data collection techniques impact resulting social networks. According to Adamic and Adar [1], when data is incomplete or from a nonhierarchical structure, tools that support social search should provide a broader view of local user communities or directly assist users via global analysis of network data.

5.4.2 Social Annotations and Bookmarking

Muralidharan et al. [29] take a unique approach to social search by examining how to present social annotations—or annotations associated with a Web resource that can be modified or removed without modifying the resource itself—of search results. Before their research, practice dictated that faces and names drew attention, and the same presentation format was used independently of social connection strength and search query topic. Using mixed-method eye-tracking and interview experiments, the authors found that, depending on the search topic, only certain social contacts are useful sources of information. Additionally, faces lose their power to draw attention when they are rendered small as part of a social search result annotation. And finally, due to each search result page's respective visual parsing behaviors, social annotations go largely unnoticed by viewers. With these findings in mind, social annotations can improve their design and content to become more noticeable and useful.

Similarly, Heymann et al. [21] question whether social bookmarking can improve overall Web search. With social bookmarking, users can store and share links to Web pages using social bookmarking sites. To see whether these sites' data can be used to augment search systems, Heymann et al. [21] gathered a large dataset from a social bookmarking site that represented about forty million bookmarks from Delicious.[3] They characterized posts based on how many bookmarks existed (about 115 million, at the time), how fast the site was growing, and the URLs' activity (found to be very active). They also found that certain tags used by bookmarkers tended to gravitate toward particular domains, and vice versa. Tags occurred frequently throughout user-annotated pages, page text, back link page text, and forward link page text. Their findings suggest that social bookmarking can provide unique search data, though at the time it lacked the size and distribution of tags necessary to make a significant impact.

[3] https://delicious.com.

Social search is discussed extensively in information seeking literature as an evolving and increasingly important aspect of information retrieval processes. Whether it be implicit, explicit, synchronous, asynchronous, or characterized by other factors, it is clear that its practices and resulting data can and will influence information science and the design of online search systems.

5.5 Co-browsing or Collaborative Navigation

Co-browsing or social navigation is a process that allows a set of participants to navigate, browse, and share information with a possible intermediate interface. Root [31] introduced the idea of social browsing to support distributed cooperative work with unplanned and informal social interaction. He described a "social interface," which provided direct, low-cost access to other people through the use of multimedia communications channels. The design of his conceptual system, called Cruiser, incorporated three basic concepts: social browsing, a virtual workspace, and interaction protocols. He believed that by integrating all of our digital media into a richly interconnected workspace, we could significantly extend and enrich the available context of our workgroup activities.

Root's idea of facilitating informal and effortless interaction among a group of people was later explored by Donath and Robertson [9] and their conception of The Social Web, which allows a user to know that others are currently viewing the same Webpage and gives them the opportunity to communicate with those people. These researchers believe that users accessing the same page are likely to be in search of the same type of information and share similar interests. Providing them with the ability to communicate with each other can facilitate information searches and help foster community.

Cabri et al. [5] presented a system for synchronous cooperative browsing that permitted users within a workgroup to share information and cooperate toward a common goal. This was done using a proxy without changing the browsers on user ends. Gerosa et al. [16] presented a similar idea of proxy-based co-browsing with the application of e-learning. They called this symmetric synchronous collaborative navigation, a form of social navigation where users virtually share a Web browser. They presented a symmetric, proxy-based architecture implemented without the need for a special browser or other software. Again, the motivation behind such lightweight interfaces was to allow the users to emerge into a collaborative environment with as little effort as possible. Esenther [10] emphasized having a lightweight real-time collaborative Web browsing service and providing an instant co-browsing facility. That system was targeted toward casual (nontechnical) users and allowed remote participants to easily synchronize pointing, scrolling, and browsing of uploaded content in their Web browsers.

Another example of a collaborative browsing application is AntWorld [26], a tool developed to make it easier for the members of a common-interest user group to collaborate in searching the Web. AntWorld harnesses the expertise of the members of a common interest group as displayed by their evaluation of documents encountered while searching. It stores users' judgments and uses this information to guide other users to pages they may find useful.

Sometimes people want to co-browse and share more than Web pages; they may also want to examine other objects such as bookmarks. Keller et al. [23] presented WebTagger, a social bookmarking service similar to Delicious, which allows a group of users to tag and share Web pages. WebTagger enables users to supply feedback on the utility of the resources that they bookmarked relative to their information needs and provides dynamically updated ranking of resources based on incremental user feedback.

Several other systems used their own interfaces instead of relying on a Web browser. For instance, GroupWeb [20] is a browser that allows group members to visually share and navigate World Wide Web pages in real time. Its groupware features include document and view slaving for synchronizing information sharing, telepointers for enacting gestures, and "what you see is what I see" views to handle display differences. GroupWeb also incorporated a groupware text editor that lets groups create and attach annotations to pages. Similarly, GroupScape [19] was a multiuser HTML browser to support synchronous groupware applications and browsing of HTML documents on the Web.

Yet another architecture to support multiuser browsing is CoVitesse [24], a groupware interface that enables collaborative navigation on the Web based on a collaborative task model. This system saw users collaboratively navigating in an information space made of results from a query submitted to a search engine. In contrast to the above systems, which are primarily designed for remotely located participants, CoSearch [2] provides multi-device support for collaborative browsing among co-located participants.

Some applications allow their users to play different roles during social or collaborative information browsing. For instance, Pickens et al. [30] proposed the roles of Prospector and Miner in a collaborative video search environment, the former being responsible for seeking out various areas where relevant information could be found, and the latter being responsible for digging deeper in a given sub-domain with high potential or useful information. A collaborative navigation system proposed by Gerosa et al. [16] had a provision where each user could take the lead and guide others in visiting Websites. However, Aneiros and Estivill-Castro [3] advocated against controlled co-browsing where one user guides the browsing process for the others (what they referred to as the master/slave model) and proposed a model with unconstrained collaborative Web browsing. They argued that such unconstrained collaborative navigation is essential to allow natural information flow among multiple users.

5.6 Summary

We have all accepted that search is an effective and common information seeking strategy, but we often don't acknowledge that search can involve multiple people. And perhaps if it wasn't for the Web 2.0 and social media revolutions that we have seen in the early part of the twenty-first century, we may not be talking about that possibility at all. But the world has changed; specifically the World Wide Web has changed. We are drenched in social media streams. It's not uncommon for us to learn new information (whether we were looking for it or not) through these channels, as we saw in Chap. 3. And so when we are looking for information, we can certainly take advantage of these social channels.

In this chapter, we saw how social search is characterized. For better or for worse, there is no one way to talk about it. But there are two main narratives: it's searching through socially constructed information or searching for information through social connections. Either way, the backbone of social search is either existing social media/networking services or a tool/platform specifically created to facilitate people sharing and searching information using social ties.

When it comes to providing social search functionalities, what we have learned so far is that specialized tools do not have as much success as those that are general-purpose social media/networking services. In other words, people are more comfortable using the familiar environments of Facebook, Twitter, and Instagram to seek and share information than learning a new tool that is specifically designed for letting people search with their friends. But we are still just scratching the surface, and more developments, modalities, and applications are going to make their way to our world (both physical and virtual) in an attempt to leverage our need for information and our desire to be connected.

Finally, while talking about the social aspect of information seeking, whether in this chapter or the one before, we couldn't escape the concept of collaboration. That shouldn't be surprising, and we have been setting the stage for a discussion of that topic since the first chapter. The next section of the book gives a proper treatment to the collaborative aspect of information seeking. We will start by reviewing it in the next chapter. Then, in the chapter that follows, we'll recognize that in many situations it's difficult to separate social and collaborative aspects of information seeking.

References

1. Adamic, L., Adar, E.: How to search a social network. Soc. Netw. **27**(3), 187–203 (2005)
2. Amershi, S., Morris, M.R.: CoSearch. In: Conference on Human Factors in Computing Systems Proceedings, pp. 1647–1656 (2008)
3. Aneiros, M., Estivill-Castro, V.: Foundations of unconstrained collaborative Web browsing with awareness. In: Proceedings IEEE/WIC International Conference on Web Intelligence (WI 2003), pp. 18–25. IEEE Computer Society, Washington (2003)

4. Borgatti, S.P., Cross, R.: A relational view of information seeking and learning in social networks. Manag. Sci. **49**(4), 432–445 (2003)
5. Cabri, G., Leonardi, L., Zambonelli, F.: A proxy-based framework to support synchronous cooperation on the Web. Softw. Pract. Exp. **29**(14), 1241–1263 (1999)
6. Carmel, D., Zwerdling, N., Guy, I., Ofek-Koifman, S., Har'el, N., Ronen, I., Uziel, E., Yogev, S., Chernov, S.: Personalized social search based on the user's social network. In: Proceedings of the 18th ACM Conference on Information and Knowledge Management - CIKM '09, p. 1227. ACM, New York, NY (2009)
7. Chi, E.H.: Information seeking can be social. Computer **42**(3), 42–46 (2009)
8. Condie, T., Kamvar, S.D., Garcia-Molina, H.: Adaptive peer-to-peer topologies. In: Proceedings of the Fourth International Conference on Peer-to-Peer Computing, 2004, pp. 53–62. IEEE, Zurich (2004)
9. Donath, J.S., Robertson, N.: The sociable web. In: Proceedings of the World Wide Web (WWW) Conference. CERN, Geneva (1994)
10. Esenther, A.W.: Instant co-browsing: lightweight real-time collaborative Web browsing. In: Proceedings of the World Wide Web (WWW) Conference, Honolulu, HI, pp. 107–114 (2002)
11. Evans, B.M., Chi, E.H.: Towards a model of understanding social search. In: Proceedings of the 2008 ACM Conference on Computer Supported Cooperative Work, pp. 485–494 (2008)
12. Evans, B.M., Chi, E.H.: An elaborated model of social search. Inf. Process. Manag. **46**(6), 656–678 (2009)
13. Evans, B.M., Chi, E.H.: An elaborated model of social search. Inf. Process. Manag. **46**(6), 656–678 (2010)
14. Evans, B.M., Kairam, S., Pirolli, P.: Do your friends make you smarter?: an analysis of social strategies in online information seeking. Inf. Process. Manag. **46**(6), 679–692 (2010)
15. Faye, D., Nachouki, G., Valduriez, P.: Semantic query routing in SenPeer, a P2P data management system. In: Proceedings of the First International Conference on Network-Based Information Systems, NBiS 2007 (2007)
16. Gerosa, L., Giordani, A., Ronchetti, M., Soller, A., Stevens, R.: Symmetric synchronous collaborative navigation. In: Proceedings of the IADIS International Conference on WWW/Internet, pp. 748–754 (2004)
17. Goel, S., Muhamad, R., Watts, D.: Social search in "small-world" experiments. In: WWW, pp. 701–710 (2009)
18. Golovchinsky, G., Qvarfordt, P., Pickens, J.: Collaborative information seeking. Computer **42**(3), 47–51 (2009)
19. Graham, T.C.N.: GroupScape: integrating synchronous groupware and the World Wide Web. In: Proceedings of INTERACT. Chapman and Hall, Sydney (1997)
20. Greenberg, S., Roseman, M.: GroupWeb: a WWW browser as real time groupware. In: Proceedings of the Conference on Human Factors in Computing Systems, pp. 271–272. ACM, Vancouver, BC (1996)
21. Heymann, P., Koutrika, G., Garcia-Molina, H.: Can social bookmarking improve web search? In: Proceedings of the International Conference on Web Search and Web Data Mining - WSDM '08, p. 195. ACM, New York, NY (2008)
22. Horowitz, D., Kamvar, S.D.: The anatomy of a large-scale social search engine. In: Proceedings of the 19th International Conference on World Wide Web, pp. 431–440 (2010)
23. Keller, R.M., Wolfe, S.R., Chen, J.R., Rabinowitz, J.L., Mathe, N.: A bookmarking service for organizing and sharing URLs. Comput. Netw. ISDN Syst. **29**(8–13), 1103–1114 (1997)
24. Laurillau, Y., Nigay, L.: Clover architecture for groupware. In: Proceedings of the ACM Conference on Computer Supported Cooperative Work, New Orleans, LA, pp. 236–245 (2002)
25. McDonnell, M., Shiri, A.: Social search: a taxonomy of, and a user-centred approach to, social web search. Program **45**, 6–28 (2011)
26. Menkov, V., Neu, D.J., Shi, Q.: AntWorld: a collaborative web search tool. In: Unger, H., Kropf, P.G., Babin, G., Plaice, J. (eds.) Third International Workshop on Distributed Communities on the Web, Quebec City, pp. 13–22. Springer, London (2000)

27. Morris, M.R.: A survey of collaborative Web search practices. In: Proceedings of ACM SIGCHI Conference on Human Factors in Computing Systems, Florence, pp. 1657–1660 (2008)
28. Morris, M.R., Teevan, J., Panovich, K.: What do people ask their social networks, and why? A survey study of status message Q & A behavior. In: CHI 10, pp. 1739–1748 (2010)
29. Muralidharan, A., Gyongyi, Z., Chi, E.: Social annotations in web search. In: Proceedings of the 2012 ACM Annual Conference on Human Factors in Computing Systems - CHI '12, pp. 1085–1094 (2012)
30. Pickens, J., Golovchinsky, G., Shah, C., Qvarfordt, P., Back, M.: Algorithmic mediation for collaborative exploratory search. In: Proceedings of the 31st Annual International ACM SIGIR Conference: Research & Development in Information Retrieval, pp. 315–322 (2008)
31. Root, R.W.: Design of a multi-media vehicle for social browsing. In: Proceedings of the Conference on Computer-Supported Cooperative Work (CSCW), pp. 25–38 (1988)
32. Twidale, M.B., Nichols, D.M., Paice, C.D.: Browsing is a collaborative process. Inf. Process. Manag. **33**(6), 761–783 (1997)
33. Watts, D.J., Dodds, P.S., Newman, M.E.J.: Identity and search in social networks. Science (New York, NY) **296**(5571), 1302–1305 (2002)

Part III
Collaborative Dimension of Information Seeking

This part adds another crucial dimension to one's information seeking process—collaboration. We first examine just the collaborative aspect of information seeking and then see what happens when we incorporate the social aspect as well.

Chapter 6
Collaborative Information Seeking

Abstract The notions that information seeking is not always an individual activity and that people working collaboratively for information-intensive tasks should be studied and supported are more prevalent now than ever before. Several new research questions, methodologies, and systems have emerged around these ideas that may even prove to be useful beyond the field of collaborative information seeking (CIS), as they are relevant to the broader areas of information seeking and behavior. This chapter provides an overview of several key research works from a variety of domains, including library and information science (LIS), computer-supported cooperative work (CSCW), human-computer interaction (HCI), and information retrieval (IR). It starts with explanations of collaboration and how CIS fits in different contexts, emphasizing the interactive, intentional, and mutually beneficial nature of CIS activities. CIS's relationships to similar and related fields such as collaborative information retrieval (CIR), collaborative information behavior (CIB), and collaborative filtering are also clarified. Finally, the chapter presents a synthesis of various frameworks and models that exist in the field today.

6.1 Introduction

While it is natural for us to collaboratively work on difficult or complex tasks [10], many situations involving search, retrieval, and synthesis of information are not typically conceived as communal processes. This apparent paradox can be seen in many daily scenarios. Imagine planning a vacation with your family (an example often used in the literature by Morris [49]; Morris and Horvitz [51]; Pickens and Golovchinsky [54]; and Golovchinsky et al. [29]). There are many parts of this complex project that revolve around looking for relevant information, comparing and synthesizing various pieces of information from multiple sources, making decisions, and finally using the synthesized solution(s). Typically, all interested parties (friends, family members) become involved in some or all of these processes. This is an example of people working together to accomplish an information seeking task. Other day-to-day life examples include coauthors working on a scholarly article, an engaged couple doing wedding planning, and a recruitment committee working on their new hiring project [61, 69]. Notice that these examples go beyond simply searching together; they include information seeking, sharing, synthesis, and

C. Shah, *Social Information Seeking*, The Information Retrieval Series 38,
DOI 10.1007/978-3-319-56756-3_6

decision-making. In addition, they all have a mutually beneficial end goal for all parties involved. Such CIS projects typically last several sessions and are motivated by participants' desire to contribute to and benefit from results. Not surprisingly, the whole process is highly interactive. To incorporate these characteristics, the focus in this chapter will be on collaborative processes that are intentional, interactive, and possibly mutually beneficial.

Before proceeding further, it is important to note that collaboration is not always useful or desired. A brief discussion on this is given in the proceeding "Limitations of Collaboration" subsection, with the remaining parts of the chapter focusing on the situations where collaboration is useful and/or required. Also, while collaboration itself has been studied widely in fields ranging from civil services (e.g., [30]) to CSCW (e.g., [59]), this chapter focuses on reviewing research that grapples with collaborative projects that largely involve information seeking, particularly in the Web environment. Having said that, there are two ways of looking at the connection between collaboration and information seeking.

6.1.1 Collaboration to Help Information Seeking

Collaboration is used to solve problems that are too difficult or complex for an individual, such as information seeking. Take, for example, searching for a house to buy. This project is quite complex in nature and typically involves multiple parties, including joint buyers, the real estate agent, and the mortgage consultant. Because they all have the same mutually beneficial goal (buying a house), this information seeking project is inherently collaborative, and thus an example of CIS.

6.1.2 Information Seeking to Help Collaboration

We can also look at the connection between collaboration and information seeking by acknowledging that a collaborative project often requires information seeking. Think about the family vacation example. The whole project is collaborative, and a part of it (planning) is focused on information seeking.

To summarize, one could participate in CIS via an information seeking project or a collaborative project. It is often difficult to distinguish these two kinds of scenarios, and for the most part that will not affect the discussion in this chapter. However, it is important to point out these intertwined relationships among information retrieval/seeking and collaboration for conceptual understanding. Figure 6.1 is a simplistic view of these connections, showing CIS in the context of information seeking, information retrieval, and collaboration.

Given this *dual* nature of CIS, the material presented here will approach the topic from two different sides: collaboration and information seeking. The next section will provide a brief summary of various views on collaboration, and the following

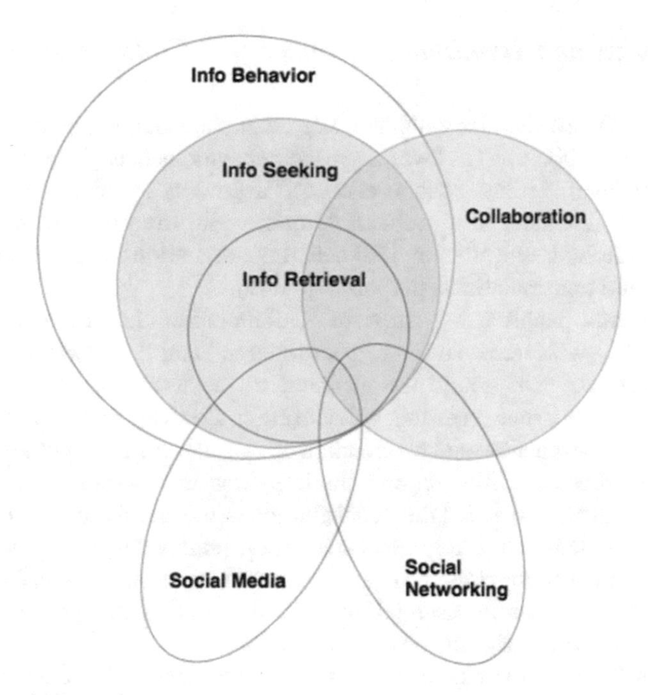

Fig. 6.1 A schematic view of collaborative information seeking in the context of related concepts

section will detail CIS in the context of information seeking/retrieval, as well as several other related concepts such as co-search and co-browsing. Then we will dive into some of the frameworks and models that are used in CIS studies. Some of these will come from the CSCW field.

Note that much of the material is taken from a previously published book by the same author and the same publisher [64], as well as the author's review article in the Journal of Association for Information Science and Technology (JASIST) [65].

6.2 Defining and Situating Collaboration

The discussion in this section is divided in three parts: explanation of how collaboration and related terms are viewed and presented, disclosure of the limitations of collaboration, and details on how collaboration can be studied in the context of information-intensive tasks.

6.2.1 Terms and Terminology Concerning Collaboration

Collaboration is not singularly defined. For example, London [46] interpreted the meaning of "collaboration" as "working together synergistically" (p. 8). Gray [30], on the other hand, defined collaboration as "a process of joint decision-making among key stakeholders of a problem domain about the future of that domain" (p. 11). Still, Roberts and Bradley [58] called collaboration "an interactive process having a shared transmutational purpose" (p. 209).

We often find people using the term "collaboration" in various contexts and interchangeably with terms such as "coordination" and "cooperation." It is very important that we first ground the meaning of the term "collaboration" before addressing various issues regarding collaboration. Denning and Yaholkovsky [11] suggested that coordination and cooperation are weaker forms of working together, though all of these activities require sharing some information with each other. Taylor-Powell et al. [74] added their contribution to this discussion, as they realized that effective collaboration requires each group member to make an individual contribution to the overarching process. Using communication, contribution, coordination, and cooperation as essential steps to collaboration, they showed how a true collaboration requires a tighter form of integration.

Based on these two works, a model of collaboration, called the C5 Model, is synthesized and presented in Fig. 6.2. This was originally presented in Shah [61] and then rectified in his later studies, [64] and [65]. It was most recently used by Shah and Leeder [66] to study collaborative work among graduate students. This model has five sets: communication (information exchange), contribution, coordination, cooperation, and collaboration. Using the idea of a set, the C5 Model demonstrates how various activities support each other. For instance, coordination is a subset of collaboration, which indicates that, for a meaningful collaboration, we need to have some way of coordinating people and events. Collaboration is a superset of cooperation, which means in order to have a true collaboration, we need more than mere cooperative behavior. The model applies to various situations where people work together or even simply interact and also identifies the nature of involved parties' joint configuration. For instance, we can classify scheduling a meeting as a coordinating task instead of collaborative one. In addition, the model allows us to recognize various components of a collaborative process. Let us take the same vacation-planning example mentioned earlier. While planning a trip, Claudia usually handles booking the flights and hotels, whereas her husband Charles starts researching their excursions, including food, attractions, and entertainment. They have particular interests and skills for both areas, and each one accepts the other person's authority in their specialty (cooperation). They both have the same goal, which is accomplished by coordinated efforts that help them each work independently and solve some subproblems (contribution). Often, they consult each other before finalizing a decision (communication). More applications and implications of this model can be found in Shah [61] and Shah and Leeder [66].

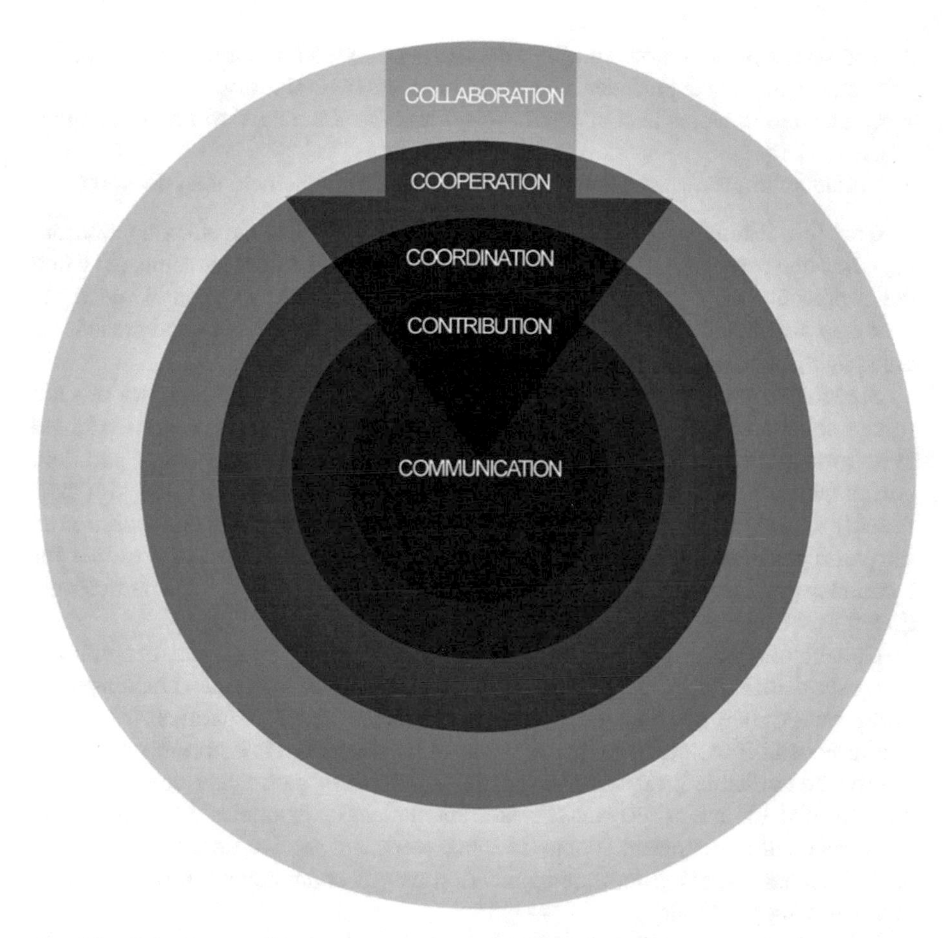

Fig. 6.2 C5 Model—a set-based organization of collaboration and related concepts. An inner set is essential to or supports the outer set

6.2.2 Limitations of Collaboration

It seems like collaboration is a great way to get things done, but is that always the case? Earlier, we noted that in many situations, collaboration is a natural choice, especially for solving difficult problems [11]. However, one must also understand the costs and benefits associated with a collaborative process in order to evaluate the usefulness and the effectiveness of that undertaking. London [46] identified the following limitations of a collaborative process:

1. Collaboration is a notoriously time-consuming process and is not suitable for problems that require quick and decisive action.
2. Power inequalities among the parties can derail the process.

3. The norms of consensus and joint decision-making sometimes require that the common good take precedence over the interests of a minority.
4. Collaboration works best in small groups and often breaks down in groups that are too large.
5. Collaboration is meaningless without the power to implement final decisions.

Gray [30] listed five circumstances under which it is best to avoid collaboration: (1) when one party has unchallenged power to influence the final outcome, (2) when the conflict is rooted in deep-seated ideological differences, (3) when the power is unevenly distributed, (4) when constitutional issues are involved or legal precedents are sought, and (5) when a legitimate convener cannot be found.

Sometimes we see collaboration forced on a group of people. Examples of such forced collaborations include the merger of two companies or instructor-enforced class groups. In such situations, the process may begin with acts of cooperation, during which the participants are merely following a set of rules to work with their fellow group members. Later, such cooperative events may result in collaboration as the participants take action (intentions) to drive the process of working together for a common goal. However, collaboration may still be unsuccessful if the participants do not trust each other or if power and benefits are unbalanced [30, 46].

Collaboration can also have limited advantages if the costs and benefits are unevenly distributed among the participants. As one of the eight challenges of groupware system development, Grudin [31] talked about disparities in benefits and responsibilities among the participants. He claimed that it is almost impossible to have an equitable groupware system in which every participant does the same amount of work and/or receives the same benefits. His examples show that some participants of a groupware system do more work and receive fewer rewards. Due to such inequality, the groupware application may become increasingly less useful and may even phase out.

While the kind of collaboration that is considered here (intentional and mutually beneficial) is slightly different than Grudin's notion of groupware, and the discussed CIS systems are considerably different than the groupware systems Grudin talked about, several of the issues he raised and the recommendations he made are relevant. For instance, for the abovementioned challenge, Grudin recommends that a system developer ensure that the process benefits all participants. This recommendation stemmed from the realization that many groupware systems were failing due to uneven cost-benefit ratios among their users (e.g., managers benefiting more than average workers while contributing less to the coordinated efforts). At the same time, Grudin identified the challenge this poses developers because the very authority figures who gain more benefits with less effort are the decision-makers. Pleasing the upper management personnel is equally important as (or more important than) pleasing other participants who have to do additional work.

This disparity of benefits also stems from the highly asymmetric roles that can be involved in such collaborations. Ensuring diversity among participants could be very useful for a successful collaboration [73], but as Aneiros and Estivill-Castro [2] argued, roles dictated by positions (manager vs. knowledge workers) could

Table 6.1 Various group activities and examples to demonstrate how aspects of collaboration play a role in information-intensive tasks

Activity	Definition	Examples
Communication	Exchanging information between two agents	Email, chat
Contribution	Offering of an individual agent to others	Online support groups, social Q&A
Coordination	Connecting different agents in a harmonious action	Conference call, net meeting
Cooperation	Agents following some rules of interaction	Wikipedia, Second Life
Collaboration	Working together synergistically to achieve a common goal	Brainstorming, coauthorship

create several constraints to CIS processes. They advised against such a master/slave model of collaboration and proposed a method of unconstrained co-browsing with asymmetric roles.

6.2.3 Collaboration in the Context of Information-Intensive Tasks

To understand the model of collaboration presented earlier (Fig. 6.2) in the context of information seeking, these five sets are listed in Table 6.1 with examples.

Sending an email or conversing on an IM client are forms of communication that could be parts of a collaborative project (see that communication is a subset of collaboration in Fig. 6.2). In fact, email is one of the most commonly employed methods of communication in collaborative work [50]. While communication tools can generally be used to share contributions between agents, there are specialized tools and places for doing so. Among these, online support groups and social Q&A sites, such as Yahoo! Answers, are very popular. The askers and answerers (contributors) on these sites, however, are not truly collaborating; one agent (user) is merely helping the other with their information need. To make this type of assistance more effective and explicit, people use conference calls or net meetings, which require coordinating the agents (people as well as systems). Once again, such a coordinated event could be one component of a collaborative project. If we combine coordinated contribution with a set of rules that the participating agents need to follow, we have examples of cooperation. On Wikipedia,[1] the participants not only contribute in a coordinated fashion but also follow rules when participating and

[1] https://www.wikipedia.org.

contributing. When users disagree, there are guidelines that suggest how to make such an interaction work. Beyond cooperative activities, true collaboration involves a group of agents working toward a common goal with explicit interactions. This can occur, for example, when coauthoring an article. The authors involved in this project not only contribute and coordinate with each other, but they also follow some set of rules that guide the aggregation of contributions and their mutual interactions. The authors also interact with each other to create this common product, which may be greater than the summation of their individual contributions.

We can draw on the terms "coordination" and "cooperation" to see how they fit around this understanding of collaboration. Austin and Baldwin [3] noted that while there are obvious similarities between cooperation and collaboration, the former involves preestablished interests, while the latter involves collectively defined goals. Malone [47] defined coordination as "the additional information processing performed when multiple, connected actors pursue goals that a single actor pursuing the same goals would not perform" (p. 5). Though this definition echoes our ideas about collaboration, one can argue that it still fits in the model described in Fig. 6.2 because it says nothing about creating solutions. For instance, organizing a meeting involves coordination among the attendees, but it is not a collaborative activity.

From the definitions and models described above, we can conclude that, in order to have a successful collaborative information seeking episode, we need to create a supportive environment where:

1. The participants of a team come with different backgrounds and expertise.
2. The participants have opportunities to explore information on their own without being influenced by the others, at least during a portion of the whole information seeking process.
3. The participants should be able to evaluate the discovered information without always consulting others in the group.
4. There has to be a way to aggregate individual contributions to arrive at the collective goal.

See Shah [65] for more information on how these four points were derived. They are missing one important aspect: the type of task involved in a collaborative project. There may not be a real reason to collaborate for simple fact-finding information tasks. As Morris and Horvitz [51] hypothesized, tasks that are exploratory in nature are likely to benefit from collaboration.

6.3 Collaborative Information Seeking in Context

It is often difficult for researchers and practitioners in this field to agree on a definition for CIS. Even if they do come to a common understanding of this term, there is still the question of how it relates to many other seemingly similar terms. The literature is filled with concepts such as collaborative search [71], collaborative information retrieval [5, 19, 38], social searching [13, 17], concurrent search [4], collaborative exploratory search [54, 55], co-browsing [16, 27, 33], collaborative navigation [43, 44], collaborative information behavior [39, 57], collaborative information synthesis [6], and collaborative information seeking [24, 36, 69]. Many definitions and conceptual understandings exist in previous research. Foster [24] defined CIS as "the study of the systems and practices that enable individuals to collaborate during the seeking, searching, and retrieval of information" (p. 330). Shah [61] referred to CIS as a process of information seeking "that is defined explicitly among the participants, interactive, and mutually beneficial" (p. 1). Table 6.2 summarizes several of these related works, along with the primary context of the collaborative activity each studied and the roles that both systems and users played.

Using this table and the earlier discussion on how CIS relates to concepts such as information seeking, information retrieval, and collaboration (Fig. 6.1), one can identify the following key aspects of CIS (see [63] for details on how these aspects were derived):

1. *Common goal and/or mutual benefits.* This is covered in the definition of the kind of collaboration that we're considering here. Often, it is the common goal and/or the possibility of mutual benefits that brings people together for collaboration. For the most part, this is not a function of a system. While systems can provide support for people with common goals who want to collaborate and reap the benefits of that collaboration, they do not typically spur a collaborative undertaking. On the other hand, a few systems are able to connect their visitors to the same Websites to foster collaboration. Donath [12] provides an example. These systems operate based on the assumption that people browsing the same Websites may have the same information needs.
2. *Complex task.* Morris and Horvitz [51] showed that simple tasks, such as fact-finding, do not significantly benefit from collaboration. Denning and Yaholkovsky [11] also recognized the larger benefit of collaborating while solving "messy" or "wicked" problems. While listing the conditions under which it is not useful to collaborate, London [46] argued that if a task is simple enough, it does not warrant collaboration. This may imply that the task should be exploratory in nature and may span several sessions.
3. *High benefits to overhead ratio.* Often, a simple divide and conquer strategy could make collaboration successful. However, such a process may have its overhead. London [46] noted that collaboration is only useful if such an overhead is appropriate for the given situation. Fidel et al. [21] showed that collaboration induces an additional cognitive load, what they referred to as the collaboration load. The collaboration in question has to meet or exceed expected benefits for it to be viable with the cognitive load that it brings.
4. *Insufficient knowledge or skills.* A common reason to collaborate is the insufficient knowledge or skills an individual possesses for solving a complex problem. In such cases, the participants can collaborate so that they can achieve something bigger or better than their individual potential. In other words, the whole can be bigger than the sum of its parts.

Table 6.2 Summary of CIS-related works, their focus, and contexts, as well as system and user roles

Research works	Information-related operations	Context	System role	User role
Collaborative search [71]	Search and retrieve	Filtering search results within a group/organization	Actively manipulating results	Recipients of filtered results
Collaborative information retrieval [5, 20, 38]	Search and retrieve	Search and retrieval of information with often colocated group	Support mechanism	Actively sharing and discussing results
Social searching [13, 17]	Search and retrieve	Social interactions among people while searching online	Support mechanism	Actively searching, sharing, and discussing results
Collaborative exploratory search [54, 55]	Search and retrieve	Recall-oriented tasks performed by a pair of users with the help of specialized search systems	Actively manipulating results and their rankings	Assuming different roles to optimize collaboration
Co-browsing [16, 27, 33]	Browse	Serendipitously creating connections among like-minded people based on their information tasks in Web environment	Monitoring and supporting user activities	Casual browsing turned to more intentional collaboration while looking through Websites
Collaborative navigation [43, 44]	Browse and locate	Serendipitously creating connections among like-minded people based on their information tasks in Web environment	Monitoring and supporting user activities	Casual browsing turned to more intentional collaboration while navigating through Websites
Collaborative information behavior [39, 57]	Seek, share, and use	Collaboration among healthcare professionals during diagnosis, patient care, and treatment	Support mechanism	Actively seeking, sharing, and analyzing information
Collaborative information synthesis [6]	Collect and consolidate	Collaborative behaviors of scientists in medical and public health	Support mechanism	Actively seeking and communicating information
Collaborative information seeking [23, 65]	Seek, retrieve, and use	Information seekers in online environments doing complex tasks	Both a support mechanism and an active component based on the task at hand	Active participants doing seeking, retrieving, sharing, and using information

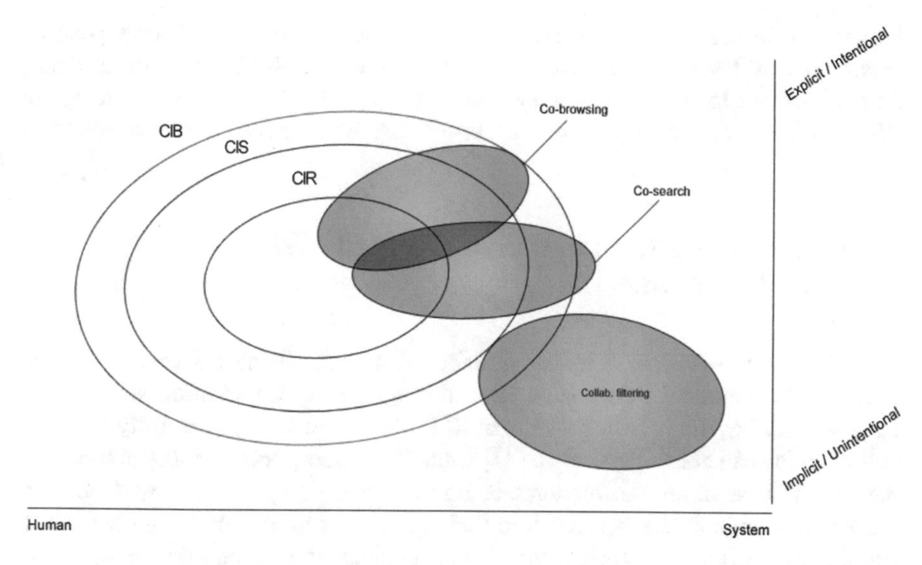

Fig. 6.3 Depiction of collaborative information seeking (CIS) and related topics, such as collaborative information retrieval (CIR) and collaborative information behavior (CIB), using the dimensions of human-system and explicit-implicit collaboration

Based on these points and related works, CIS can be defined as an information seeking process that takes place among a small group of participants (potentially with different sets of skills and/or roles) who are working on a collaborative project (possibly a complex task) that is intentional, interactive, and mutually beneficial. Note that such a collaborative project could itself be an information seeking endeavor (e.g., siblings looking for diabetes-friendly recipes for their mother), or it could include information seeking as only one of its components (e.g., coauthors searching for and sharing relevant literature as a part of writing an article). Here, "information seeking" could mean more than searching and retrieving; browsing, sharing, evaluating, and synthesizing information may also be involved.

Now, we'll attempt to classify various related works into categories that include labels such as collaborative IR (CIR), co-browsing, and social search. We'll also explore the relevant topic of collaborative filtering. Figure 6.3 is a depiction of various concepts around CIS.

As seen, these concepts are placed on dimensions of human-system and explicit-implicit collaboration. While the figure is not drawn to scale by any measures and researchers have not reached a firm agreement as to how different fields connect and overlap, it provides a schematic view of how various domains related to CIS can be seen in context. For instance, co-browsing and co-searching span across CIR, CIS, and CIB depending on the task at hand. Examples include CoVitesse system [44] for co-browsing that allows search and retrieval in addition to serendipitous browsing and CoSearch system [1] for co-searching that could also facilitate group sense-making (later implemented as CoSense system [53]). There is also a slight overlap between co-browsing and co-search since often these systems (and corresponding research) could support and study both searching and browsing. For instance, SearchTogether [51], a co-search system, could also let its participants engage in Web browsing activities to find novel information that may be relevant to their task.

6.3.1 Collaborative Information Retrieval (CIR) and Co-search

The discussion will now focus on collaborative setup scenarios where the goal is to satisfy a mutual information need through group information seeking. As discussed earlier, if/when the problem of IR is difficult to solve, a carefully executed collaboration can help. Smyth et al. [71] argued that incorporating collaboration into the search phase of an information seeking process is one possible way to connect users to information that is difficult to find. They showed how collaborative search could act as a front end for existing search engines and re-rank results based on the learned preferences of a community of users. They attempted to demonstrate this concept by implementing the I-Spy system [25]. I-Spy captures the queries and related results for a given workgroup and uses that information to provide users with filtered content that is, presumably, more relevant. Thus, I-Spy acts more as a collaborative filtering process than a synchronous collaborative searching tool.

While I-Spy attempts to extend content-based filtering techniques by incorporating communities, several collaborative IR systems have been developed by extending a traditional IR model to incorporate multiple users. However, such an extension is often ineffective or nontrivial. For instance, Hyldegård [37], who studied information seeking and retrieval in a group-based education setting, found that although people in a collaborative group to some extent demonstrated similar cognitive experiences as the individuals in Kuhlthau's information search process (ISP) model [41], these experiences did not only result from information seeking activities but also from work-task activities and intragroup interactions. Her further work also indicated that group-based problem solving is a dynamic process that shifts between a group perspective and an individual perspective [38]. Such a finding necessitates a thorough investigation into CIS that moves beyond an extension of a traditional IR system for multiple users. As Olson et al. [52] suggested, "The development of schemes to support group work, whether behavioral methods or new technologies like groupware, should be based on detailed knowledge about how groups work, what they do well, and what they have trouble with" (p. 347).

Unlike applications for co-browsing, which typically focus on Web browsing, works on CIR often focus on specialized domains for searching. For instance, Twidale and Nichols [77] presented the Ariadne system, which allowed a user to collaborate with an information expert remotely and synchronously over a library catalogue. The idea behind Ariadne was to allow the patron (naive user) to collaborate with a reference librarian (search expert) for an information need in a library situation. The authors identified the importance of supporting the social aspects involved in information searching and showed how their system can address them. However, Ariadne did not have support for asynchronous collaboration.

Morris and Horvitz [51] presented the SearchTogether system that allowed a group of remote users to collaborate synchronously or asynchronously. Awareness, division of labor, and persistent collaboration provided this system's foundation. In terms of awareness, they posited that it might enable lightweight collaboration, which would reduce overhead involved in explicitly asking group members to provide related information. Awareness was provided using per-user query histories, page-specific metadata, and annotations. Division of labor was implemented using integrated IM as well as a recommendation mechanism, by which a participant can recommend a page to another participant. SearchTogether also provided "Split Search" and "Multi-Engine Search" options for automatic division of labor. Finally, persistence was implemented by not only storing all session states but also automatically creating a shared artifact that summarizes a collaborative search's findings.

MUSE [40] supports synchronous, remote collaboration between two people searching a medical database. MUSE lets its users perform standard single-user searches, with a provision of chat and the ability to share metadata that pertains to current database results with their partners. S3 system [51] is not quite a CIS system, but its relevance lies in the fact that a set of its users can asynchronously share retrieved results.

A stream of research came out of the CIR group at the University of Washington. They studied situations where members of a work team are collaboratively seeking, searching, and using information and showed how such a process can be realized in a multi-team setting. This started with Fidel et al.'s work [19], where the authors defined CIR "as any activity that collectively resolves an information problem taken by members of a work-team regardless of the nature of the actual retrieval of information" (p. 604). They employed a cognitive work analysis framework to guide a field study examining information seekers' social, organizational, cognitive, and individual characteristics and then focused their findings on collaborative situations [19]. From their studies involving two design teams working in collaboration, Bruce et al. [8] found that (1) the nature of the task and the structure and the culture of the organization in which tasks are performed are important factors that determine CIR behavior, and (2) not all information behavior takes place collaboratively, even in teams that carry out CIR. In their further work in this realm, Poltrock et al. [56] found that (1) any information retrieval activity (identifying information needs, formulating queries, retrieving information, evaluating it, and applying it to address the need) may be performed by an individual on behalf of the team, by an ad hoc group, or by the team working together in a meeting, and (2) technologies intended to support teamwork could be more effective by recognizing and supporting collaboration in the activities that comprise information retrieval and their coordination. This suggests that a successful CIR/CIS system should not try to lock the users down in a certain type of imposed framework; it should rather let the participants choose their own way of collaborating and provide enough support for carrying out those various methods.

The efforts of connecting multiple users for information seeking (retrieval or browsing) continue to produce systems either by reinventing the wheel of traditional IR or by extending existing IR systems to accommodate more than one user. In practice, none of these systems have been widely adopted. Why? Several reasons contribute to the narrow visibility of collaborative systems, including the cognitive load involved in using these systems, the learning curve to start using these environments, and the sparsity of integration of information seeking into other parts of a collaborative process. Further, explanations to why such groupware systems fail and what can be done to address their problems can be found in [31].

6.4 Frameworks and Models for CIS

In this section, we will explore different ways in which researchers have studied CIS and its various aspects. This will start with the traditional way of classifying collaborative activities along space and time dimensions, move on to control-communication-awareness framework, and then to the nature of mediation in CIS. Finally, a synthesis of these frameworks and models using an extended set of dimensions for defining and studying collaborative activities will be presented.

6.4.1 Space and Time Aspects of CIS

The classic way to organize collaborative activities is based on two factors: location and time [59]. Recently, Hansen and Järvelin [34] and Golovchinsky et al. [28] also classified approaches to collaborative IR using these two attributes. Figure 6.4, inspired by Twidale and Nichols' [75] depiction, shows various activities, methods, and environments on these two dimensions.

As we can see from this figure, the majority of collaborative activities in conventional libraries are colocated and synchronous (e.g., face-to-face meetings, reference interviews), whereas collaborative activities relating to digital libraries are more often remote and synchronous (e.g., digital referencing, virtual meetings). Social information filtering, or collaborative filtering—a process benefiting from other users' actions—is asynchronous and mostly remote. Email also serves as a tool for doing asynchronous collaboration among users who are not colocated. Chat, or IM, enables synchronous and remote collaboration. For a detailed literature synthesis on how remotely located scientific collaborations are conducted and studied using laboratory without walls, or collaboratives, see an excellent review by Finholt [22].

The placement of a CIS environment on this figure has implications for its implementation, functionalities, and evaluation. For instance, Adobe Connect facilitates

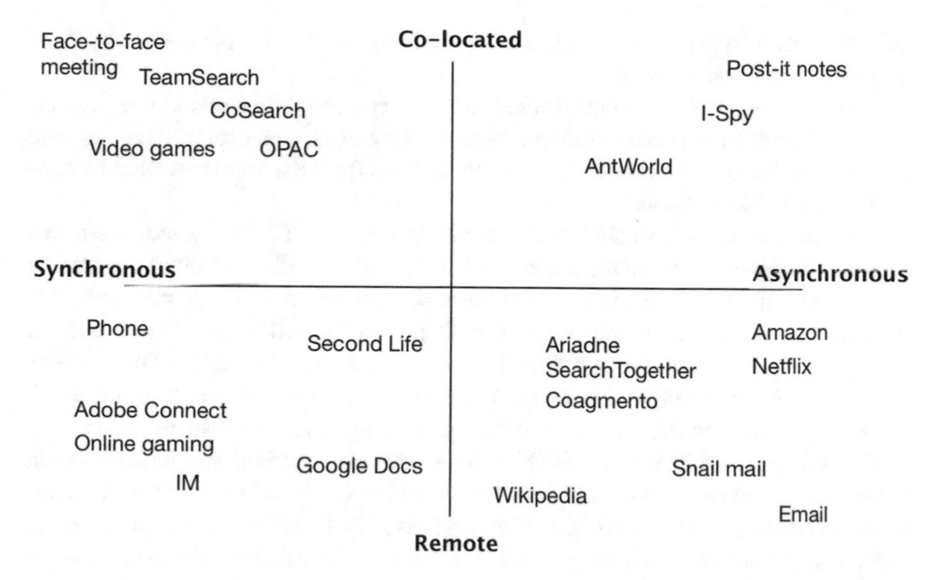

Fig. 6.4 Various collaborative activities, tools, and methods organized on space-time dimensions

online meetings where the participants can share and discuss information. Such an environment will fall under synchronous remote collaboration in Fig. 6.4. Thus, this environment needs to have (1) a way to connect remote participants, (2) a shared space for exchanging information, and (3) a communication channel to provide real-time message passing among the participants.

6.4.2 *Control, Communication, and Awareness in a CIS Environment*

Three components specific to group work or collaboration that are highly predominant in the CIS or CSCW literature are control, communication, and awareness.

6.4.2.1 Control

Rodden [59] identified the value of control in CSCW systems and listed a number of projects with their corresponding schemes for implementing control. For instance, the COSMOS project [78] represented system control with a formal structure. It used roles to represent people or automatons and rules to represent the flow and processes. Roles included a supervisor, processor, or analyst. Rules defined conditions that must be satisfied in order to start or finish a process. Due to structures seen in projects like COSMOS, Rodden classified these control systems as procedural-based systems.

Most of these systems were studied in office environments, where the subjects interacted with one another through personal conversations, group meetings, and phone calls. Several recommendations and findings from these studies were primarily based on observations.

To express control in a collaborative environment, early CSCW systems used various mechanisms to spread messages, which were often called structured definition language (SDL) messages. In the most basic sense, these were email messages that were sent back and forth among a collaborative project's participants. However, such a project requires more support than a simple messaging exchange. SDL provides this support by imposing a structure to these messages and incorporating additional fields of information that can be used to appropriately filter and distribute them.

For instance, Malone et al. [48] proposed the InformationLens framework, in which the messages carried additional information (some of which was automatically generated). This could later filter and classify these messages, thus suiting individuals' needs within their group. Later, Malone extended the above framework to ObjectLens [42], in which the participants could create objects in addition to messages to purvey information. Each of these objects would be imbued with a similar structure that could guide further control and distribution processes. ObjectLens also let people create links among the objects they formed. Malone pointed out that this was similar to hypertexts on the World Wide Web.

6.4.2.2 Communication

This is one of the most critical components of any collaboration. In fact, Rodden [59] identified message or communication systems as the class of systems in CSCW that is most mature and most widely used.

In order to craft CIS systems that allow their participants to engage in an intentional and interactive collaboration, there must be a way for the participants to communicate. In fact, collaboration could begin when a group of users is allowed to communicate with each other. For instance, Donath and Robertson [13] presented a system that allowed a user to connect with others who were viewing the same Web page and then communicate with those people to initiate a possible collaboration or at least a co-browsing experience. Providing communication capabilities even in an environment that was not originally designed for carrying out collaboration is an interesting way to encourage collaboration.

Using four multidisciplinary design situations in the United States and Europe, Sonnenwald [72] came up with 13 communication roles. The author showed how these roles can support collaboration, other aspects of an information seeking process such as knowledge exploration and integration, and task and project completion. Filtering and providing information, as well as negotiating differences across organizational, task, discipline, and personal boundaries, facilitated all of these processes and activities.

6.4.2.3 Awareness

Awareness is one of the most important issues that is identified and addressed in the literature. One of the often-asked questions about awareness is "awareness of what?" Schmidt [60] argued that we should talk about awareness not as a separate entity but as someone's consciousness of some particular occurrence. In other words, the term "awareness" is only meaningful if it refers to a person's awareness of something. Heath et al. [35] suggested that awareness is not simply a "state of mind" or a "cognitive ability" but rather a feature of practical action that is systematically accomplished within the course of everyday activities.

The literature uses several related terms and definitions to discuss awareness in collaborative projects. For instance, Dourish and Bellotti [14] defined awareness as "an understanding of the activities of others, which provides a context for your own activity" (p. 107). Dourish and Bly [15] suggested the following definition for awareness: "Awareness involves knowing who is 'around', what activities are occurring, who is talking with whom; it provides a view of one another in the daily work environments. Awareness may lead to informal interactions, spontaneous connections, and the development of shared cultures – all important aspects of maintaining working relationships which are denied to groups distributed across multiple sites" (p. 541).

Early works detailed a set of theories and models for understanding and providing awareness. Gaver [26] argued that focused collaboration in which people work closely toward a mutual goal is characterized by an intense sharing of awareness. He further claimed that less awareness is needed for division of labor, and that more casual awareness can lead to serendipitous communication, which can turn into collaboration. Bly et al. [7] also identified the importance of such general awareness by saying, "When groups are geographically distributed, it is particularly important not to neglect the need for informal interactions, spontaneous conversations, and even general awareness of people and events at other sites" (p. 29).

There are several ways of defining and implementing awareness. Various research projects have used their own taxonomy and interpretation of awareness for creating frameworks and systems. For instance, Gutwin and Greenberg [32] classified awareness into two types—situational and workspace—and suggested that situational awareness underlies the idea of workspace awareness in groupware systems. Unlike other definitions that focused on awareness of the workspace itself, their work accounted for personal reactions within the workspace. Simone and Bandini [70] identified two kinds of awareness: by-product awareness that is generated in the course of the activities required to accomplish a group's collaborative tasks and add-on awareness that stems from an additional activity. Add-on awareness can cost collaborators something within their tasks and is discretionary because it depends on their assessment of the contingent situation. Chalmers [9], likewise, divided awareness into two kinds: awareness of people and awareness of information artifacts. He suggested implementing an activity-centered awareness tool that would focus on presenting people's ongoing appearances and activities.

Shah and Marchionini [67] extensively used four kinds of awareness as presented by Liechti and Sumi [45] for their work with CIS. They are listed below:

1. *Group awareness*. This type of awareness includes providing information to each group member about the status and activities of the other collaborators at a given time.
2. *Workspace awareness*. This refers to a common shared workspace where group members can bring and discuss their findings and create a common product.
3. *Contextual awareness*. This type of awareness applies to the application domain rather than its users. Here, the objective is to identify what content is useful for the group and what the goals are for the current project.
4. *Peripheral awareness*. This relates to the type of information that results from an individual's and the group's collective histories and should be kept separate from what a participant is currently viewing or doing.

6.4.3 Materializing Control, Communication, and Awareness

Several systems supporting collaboration have identified the issues of control, communication, and awareness as critical to their design. For instance, Farooq et al. [18] presented a collaborative design for CiteSeer,[2] a search engine and digital library of research literature in the computer and information science disciplines. Based on a survey and follow-up interviews with CiteSeer users, the authors presented four novel implications for designing the CiteSeer collaboratory: (1) visualize query-based social networks to identify scholarly communities of interest, (2) provide online collaborative tool support for upstream stages of scientific collaboration, (3) support activity awareness for staying cognizant of online scientific activities, and (4) use notification systems to convey scientific activity awareness.

Depending on the domain and type of application, different CIS systems have different ways of providing awareness to the collaborators. Take, for example, Ariadne [76], developed to support the collaborative learning of database browsing skills. To facilitate complex collaborative browsing processes, Ariadne presents a visualization of the search process. This visualization consists of thumbnails of screens that look like playing cards, which represent command-output pairs. Any such card can be expanded to reveal its details. The support for awareness, in this case, is driven by the specific domain (library) and application (catalogue search).

SearchTogether [51], on the other hand, was based on information seeking (application) on the Web (domain). It instantiates awareness in several ways, one of which is per-user query histories. This is done by showing each group member's screen name and their photo and queries in the "Query Awareness" region. The access to the query histories is immediate and interactive, as clicking on a query

[2]citeseerx.ist.psu.edu.

brings back the results from when it was executed. Because query awareness allows group members to both share their search strings and learn from each other's formulation techniques, the authors identified it as a very important feature in collaborative searching. Another component of SearchTogether that facilitates awareness is the display of page-specific metadata. This region includes several pieces of information about the displayed page, including group members who viewed the given page, and their comments and ratings. The authors claim that such visitation information can help a participant either avoid another group member's previously visited pages, thereby minimizing wasted duplication, or perhaps choose to visit pages that appear to be promising leads as indicated by the presence of comments and/or ratings.

6.4.4 Nature and Level of Mediation

Yet another way to study CIS (or generally, collaborative) systems is by looking at how collaboration is mediated. Pickens et al. [55] saw two extremes: system or algorithmically mediated and user or interface mediated.

6.4.4.1 System/Algorithmically Mediated Collaboration

Here, the system (more specifically, the behind-the-scenes part of the system) acts as an active component for collaboration and helps the collaborators get the most out of their shared projects by doing any of the following:

- Combining various inputs from the users (e.g., queries, annotations) to produce better versions of them
- Joining multiple streams of results—produced by different people doing the same action (e.g., search)—into a better set of results
- Redistributing the results, keeping in mind every participant's abilities, roles, and responsibilities
- Optimizing workload for each individual involved in collaboration

Pickens et al. [55] showed how algorithmic mediation could be provided in a time-bound, recall-oriented task to allow the collaborators to find results that they would have individually missed. Their algorithm was based on catering to different (predefined) roles played by the collaborators. Later, Shah et al. [69] showed how a system-mediated collaboration that considers collaborators' asymmetric roles could enhance both relevance and novelty in retrieval.

Often, system-mediated CIS systems come close to being collaborative filtering tools but are set apart by the notion of intention. Because those working with system-mediated collaboration are explicitly involved in the process, it appears that they have the intention to collaborate. Collaborative filtering, on the other hand, may not have the explicit consent or intentionality of those involved or affected.

6.4.4.2 User/Interface-Mediated Collaboration

This method of collaboration implies that either the participants fully control the collaborative processes and/or such control is being exercised through the system's user interface. In other words, the collaboration in question is very transparent to the involved parties, and the control rests with the users. To keep control with the users, the system serves as a passive element that helps with aspects such as communication and awareness.

For example, the Ariadne system [75] allows the collaborators (a reference librarian and an information seeker) to work through their information seeking process using the system's co-browsing interface, which does nothing more than respond to user actions. Recent systems such as SearchTogether [51] and Coagmento [62][3] could also be seen as interface-mediated CIS tools where the users maintain control, though such systems often employ a few system-mediatory components. For instance, SearchTogether has a split search feature, whereby a team could ask the system to intelligently split the search results among the collaborators. The authors, however, found this feature to be underused [51].

6.5 Summary

In different fields and contexts, researchers have recognized the need to study and support people working in collaboration. In the area of information seeking/behavior, the focus has been on extending single-user environments to accommodate multiple participants in information-intensive situations. However, most of these approaches have been application driven, and we still need a set of models, specialized tools, and best practices that help us effectively support CIS. This chapter identifies these gaps and offers a research agenda in its conclusion. We discussed a set of key works from various fields to put collaboration and CIS in perspective. Early works primarily focused on support for collaboration in information-intensive domains within office environments or library settings. More recent projects have targeted online information seeking situations.

CIS stands at a very interesting intersection. It is both a long-standing domain within CSCW and a relatively young field that has been shaped by several veteran domains such as IR, CSCW/groupware, and HCI. Another way to think about CIS-centric research is that while we have seen a tremendous amount of interest and outcomes in the recent years as evident by the publications, systems, and events around CIS, many ideas have come from previous research in well-established forums of SIGIR, CSCW, and CHI. Having said that, it is worth noting that while modern CIS's interdisciplinary nature retains the traces of these domains, it is also

[3]http://coagmento.org.

constantly evolving and creating its own identity by carving out a unique space of research problems.

There are several issues that emerge from different aspects of the CIS field. For instance, a researcher who wishes to pursue the HCI components of CIS may study issues such as interface design for CIS systems, how to reduce participants' collaborative load, and how to foster appropriate amounts and kinds of awareness.

The advent of the Web 2.0 and the fact that an increasing number of people have access to online information sources have steered new CIS developments toward building tools that leverage on these provisions. However, it is time we start paying more attention to some of the fundamental issues in CIS. They include understanding user requirements and behavior in CIS environments, identifying motivations and best practices for people doing collaboration, and sketching effective design guidelines for CIS systems. Above all, there is a dire need to devise new models, theories, and evaluation matrices for CIS. These issues are at the core of the CIS domain (see [63] for more discussion on this), and studying them could help us get closer to better understanding people's behavior in CIS environments and better designing of CIS systems.

Finally, we need to acknowledge that "collaboration" and "social" are not just some two independent dimensions but rather quite intertwined in most cases and should be studied together. The next chapter takes us in that direction.

References

1. Amershi, S., Morris, M.R.: CoSearch. In: Proceedings of the Twenty-Sixth Annual CHI Conference on Human Factors in Computing Systems - CHI '08, p. 1647. ACM, New York, NY (2008)
2. Aneiros, M., Estivill-Castro, V.: Usability of real-time unconstrained WWW-co-browsing for educational settings. In: The 2005 IEEE/WIC/ACM International Conference on Web Intelligence (WI'05), pp. 105–111. IEEE, Washington (2005)
3. Austin, R.G., Baldwin, A.E.: Faculty collaboration: enhancing the quality of scholarship and teaching. ASHE-ERIC Higher Education Report No. 7, 1991. Technical report, Association for the Study of Higher Education, ERIC Clearinghouse on Higher Education, George Washington University, Washington DC, School of Education and Human Development, Washington, DC (1991)
4. Baecker, R.M.: Readings in Human-Computer Interaction: Towards the Year 2000. Morgan Kaufmann, San Francisco (1995)
5. Blackwell, A.F., Stringer, M., Toye, E.F., Rode, J.A.: Tangible interface for collaborative information retrieval. In: Extended Abstracts of the 2004 Conference on Human Factors and Computing Systems - CHI '04, p. 1473. ACM, New York, NY (2004)
6. Blake, C., Pratt, W.: Collaborative information synthesis I: a model of information behaviors of scientists in medicine and public health. J. Am. Soc. Inf. Sci. Technol. **57**(13), 1740–1749 (2006)
7. Bly, S.A., Harrison, S.R., Irwin, S.: Media spaces: bringing people together in a video, audio, and computing environment. Commun. ACM **36**(1), 28–46 (1993)
8. Bruce, H., Fidel, R., Pejtersen, A.M., Dumais, S., Grudin, J., Poltrock, S.: A comparison of the collaborative information retrieval behaviour of two design teams. N. Rev. Inf. Behav. Res. **4**(1), 139–153 (2003)

9. Chalmers, M.: Awareness, representation and interpretation. Comput. Supported Coop. Work: J. Collab. Comput. **11**(3/4), 389–409 (2002)
10. Denning, P.J.: Mastering the mess. Commun. ACM **50**(4), 21 (2007)
11. Denning, P.J., Yaholkovsky, P.: Getting to 'we'. Commun. ACM **51**(4), 19 (2008)
12. Donath, J.S.: Casual collaboration. In: Proceedings of the International Conference on Multimedia Computing and Systems, Boston, MA, pp. 490–495 (1994)
13. Donath, J.S., Robertson, N.: The sociable web. In: Proceedings of the World Wide Web (WWW) Conference. CERN, Geneva (1994)
14. Dourish, P., Bellotti, V.: Awareness and coordination in shared workspaces. In: Proceedings of the Conference on Computer-Supported Cooperative Work, pp. 107–114. ACM, Toronto, ON (1992)
15. Dourish, P., Bly, S.: Portholes. In: Conference on Human Factors in Computing Systems Proceedings, pp. 541–547 (1992)
16. Esenther, A.W.: Instant co-browsing: lightweight real-time collaborative Web browsing. In: Proceedings of the World Wide Web (WWW) Conference, Honolulu, HI, pp. 107–114 (2002)
17. Evans, B.M., Chi, E.H.: An elaborated model of social search. Inf. Process. Manag. **46**(6), 656–678 (2009)
18. Farooq, U., Ganoe, C.H., Carroll, J.M., Giles, C.L.: Designing for e-science: requirements gathering for collaboration in CiteSeer. Int. J. Hum. Comput. Stud. **67**(4), 297–312 (2009)
19. Fidel, R., Bruce, H.: Collaborative information retrieval. In: Proceedings of the ASIST Annual Meeting, p. 604 (1999)
20. Fidel, R., Bruce, H., Pejtersen, A.M., Dumais, S.: Collaborative information retrieval (CIR). N. Rev. Inf. Behav. Res. **1**, 235–247 (2000)
21. Fidel, R., Pejtersen, A.M., Cleal, B., Bruce, H.: A multidimensional approach to the study of human-information interaction: a case study of collaborative information retrieval. J. Am. Soc. Inf. Sci. Technol. **55**(11), 939–953 (2004)
22. Finholt, T.A.: Collaboratories. Annu. Rev. Inf. Sci. Technol. **36**(1), 73–107 (2005)
23. Foster, J.: Collaborative information seeking and retrieval. Annu. Rev. Inf. Sci. Technol. **40**, 329–356 (2006)
24. Foster, J.: Collaborative information seeking and retrieval. Annu. Rev. Inf. Sci. Technol. **40**(1), 329–356 (2007)
25. Freyne, J., Smyth, B., Coyle, M., Balfe, E., Briggs, P.: Further experiments on collaborative ranking in community-based Web search. Artif. Intell. Rev. **21**, 229–252 (2004)
26. Gaver, W.W.: Technology affordances. In: Proceedings of the SIGCHI Conference: Human Factors in Computing Systems, pp. 79–84 (1991)
27. Gerosa, L., Giordani, A., Ronchetti, M., Soller, A., Stevens, R.: Symmetric synchronous collaborative navigation. In: Proceedings of the IADIS International Conference on WWW/Internet, pp. 748–754 (2004)
28. Golovchinsky, G., Adcock, J., Pickens, J., Qvarfordt, P., Back, M.: Cerchiamo: a collaborative exploratory search tool. In: Proceedings of Computer Supported Cooperative Work (CSCW). ACM, New York, NY (2008)
29. Golovchinsky, G., Pickens, J., Back, M.: A taxonomy of collaboration in online information seeking (2009). Preprint, arXiv:0908.0704
30. Gray, B.: Collaborating: Finding Common Ground for Multiparty Problems. Jossey-Bass, San Francisco (1989)
31. Grudin, J.: Groupware and social dynamics: eight challenges for developers. Commun. ACM **37**(1), 92–105 (1994)
32. Gutwin, C., Greenberg, S.: A descriptive framework of workspace awareness for real-time groupware. Comput. Supported Coop. Work: J. Collab. Comput. **11**(3/4), 411–446 (2002)
33. Han, R., Perret, V., Naghshineh, M.: WebSplitter: a unified XML framework for multi-device collaborative Web browsing. In: Proceedings of the 2000 ACM Conference on Computer Supported Cooperative Work, pp. 221–230 (2000)
34. Hansen, P., Järvelin, K.: Collaborative information retrieval in an information-intensive domain. Inf. Process. Manag. **41**(5), 1101–1119 (2005)

35. Heath, C., Svensson, M.S., Hindmarsh, J., Luff, P., vom Lehn, D.: Configuring awareness. Comput. Supported Coop. Work **11**(3–4), 317–347 (2002)
36. Hertzum, M.: Collaborative information seeking: the combined activity of information seeking and collaborative grounding. Inf. Process. Manag. **44**(2), 957–962 (2008)
37. Hyldegård, J.: Using diaries in group based information behavior research: a methodological study. In: Proceedings of the 1st International Conference on Information Interaction in Context, vol. 176, pp. 153–161 (2006)
38. Hyldegård, J.: Beyond the search process: exploring group members' information behavior in context. Inf. Process. Manag. **45**(1), 142–158 (2009)
39. Karunakaran, A., Reddy, M.C., Spence, P.R.: Toward a model of collaborative information behavior in organizations. J. Am. Soc. Inf. Sci. Technol. **64**(12), 2437–2451 (2013)
40. Krishnappa, R.:. Multi-user search engine: supporting collaborative information seeking and retrieval. Master's thesis, University of Missouri-Rolla (2005)
41. Kuhlthau, C.C.: Towards collaboration between information seeking and information retrieval. Inf. Res. Int. Electron. J. **10**(2), 225 (2005)
42. Lai, K., Malone, T.W., Yu, K.: Object lens: a 'spreadsheet' for cooperative work. ACM Trans. Off. Inf. Syst. **6**(4), 332–353 (1988)
43. Laurillau, Y.: Synchronous collaborative navigation on the WWW. In: CHI '99 Extended Abstracts on Human Factors in Computing Systems - CHI '99, p. 308. ACM, New York, NY (1999)
44. Laurillau, Y., Nigay, L.: Clover architecture for groupware. In: Proceedings of the ACM Conference on Computer Supported Cooperative Work, New Orleans, LA, pp. 236–245 (2002)
45. Liechti, O., Sumi, Y.: Editorial: awareness and the WWW. Int. J. Hum. Comput. Stud. **56**(1), 1–5 (2002)
46. London, S.: Collaboration and community. http://scottlondon.com/reports/ppcc.html (1995)
47. Malone, T.W.: What is coordination theory? Technical Report SSM WP # 2051–88. Massachusetts Institute of Technology, Cambridge, MA (1988)
48. Malone, T.W., Grant, K.R., Turbak, F.A., Brobst, S.A., Cohen, M.D.: Intelligent information-sharing systems. Commun. ACM **30**(5), 390–402 (1987)
49. Morris, M.R.: Interfaces for collaborative exploratory Web search: motivations and directions for multi-user design. In: Proceedings of ACM SIGCHI Conference on Human Factors in Computing Systems 2007 Workshop on Exploratory Search and HCI: Designing and Evaluating Interfaces to Support Exploratory Search Interaction, pp. 9–12 (2007)
50. Morris, M.R.: A survey of collaborative Web search practices. In: Proceedings of ACM SIGCHI Conference on Human Factors in Computing Systems, Florence, pp. 1657–1660 (2008)
51. Morris, M.R., Horvitz, E.: SearchTogether: an interface for collaborative Web search. In: Proceedings of the 2007 ACM Symposium on User Interface Software and Technology (UIST 2007), pp. 3–12. ACM, New York, NY (2007)
52. Olson, G.M., Olson, J.S., Carter, M.R., Sorrosten, M.: Small group design meetings: an analysis of collaboration. Hum. Comput. Interact. **7**(4), 347–374 (1992)
53. Paul, S.A., Morris, M.R.: CoSense. In: Proceedings of the 27th International Conference on Human Factors in Computing Systems - CHI 09, p. 1771. ACM, New York, NY (2009)
54. Pickens, J., Golovchinsky, G.: Collaborative exploratory search. In: Proceedings of Workshop on Human-Computer Interaction and Information Retrieval, Cambridge, MA, pp. 21–22 (2007)
55. Pickens, J., Golovchinsky, G., Shah, C., Qvarfordt, P., Back, M.: Algorithmic mediation for collaborative exploratory search. In: Proceedings of the 31st Annual International ACM SIGIR Conference: Research & Development in Information Retrieval, pp. 315–322 (2008)
56. Poltrock, S., Fidel, R., Bruce, H., Grudin, J., Dumais, S., Pejtersen, A.M.: Information seeking and sharing in design teams. In: Pendergast, M., Schmidt, K., Simone, C., Tremaine, M. (eds.) Proceedings of the International ACM SIGGROUP Conference on Supporting Group Work, Sanibel Island, FL, pp. 239–247 (2003)
57. Reddy, M.C., Jansen, B.J.: A model for understanding collaborative information behavior in context: a study of two healthcare teams. Inf. Process. Manag. **44**(1), 256–273 (2008)

58. Roberts, R.T., Bradley, N.C.: Stakeholder collaboration and innovation: a study of public policy initiation at the state level. J. Appl. Behav. Sci. **27**(2), 209–238 (1991)
59. Rodden, T.: A survey of CSCW systems. Interact. Comput. **3**(3), 319–353 (1991)
60. Schmidt, K.: The problem with 'awareness'. Comput. Supported Coop. Work: J. Collab. Comput. **11**(3/4), 285–298 (2002)
61. Shah, C.: Understanding system implementation and user behavior in a collaborative information seeking environment. In: Proceedings of the 31st Annual International ACM SIGIR Conference: Research & Development in Information Retrieval, p. 896 (2008)
62. Shah, C.: Coagmento: a collaborative information seeking, synthesis and sense-Making framework (an integrated demo). In: Proceedings of Computer Supported Cooperative Work (CSCW), Savannah, GA (2010)
63. Shah, C.: Brief overview of computer-mediated communication (CMC). In: Collaborative Information Seeking. The Information Retrieval Series, vol. 34, pp. 173–178. Springer, Berlin/Heidelberg (2012)
64. Shah, C.: Collaborative Information Seeking: The Art and Science of Making the Whole Greater than the Sum of All. Information Retrieval Series. Springer, Berlin/Heidelberg (2012)
65. Shah, C.: Collaborative information seeking. J. Assoc. Inf. Sci. Technol. **65**(2), 215–236 (2014)
66. Shah, C., Leeder, C.: Exploring collaborative work among graduate students through the C5 model of collaboration: a diary study. J. Inf. Sci. **42**(5), 609–629 (2015)
67. Shah, C., Marchionini, G.: Awareness in collaborative information seeking. J. Am. Soc. Inf. Sci. Technol. **61**(10), 1970–1986 (2010)
68. Shah, C., Pomerantz, J.: Evaluating and predicting answer quality in community QA. In: Proceedings of the 33rd International ACM SIGIR Conference on Research and Development in Information Retrieval - SIGIR '10, p. 411. ACM, New York, NY (2010)
69. Shah, C., Pickens, J., Golovchinsky, G.: Role-based results redistribution for collaborative information retrieval. Inf. Process. Manag. **46**(6), 773–781 (2010)
70. Simone, C., Bandini, S.: Integrating awareness in cooperative applications through the reaction-diffusion metaphor. Comput. Supported Coop. Work: J. Collab. Comput. **11**(3/4), 495–530 (2002)
71. Smyth, B., Balfe, E., Briggs, P., Coyle, M., Freyne, J.: Collaborative Web search. In: Proceedings of the International Joint Conference on Artificial Intelligence (IJCAI), pp. 1417–1419. Morgan Kaufmann, Acapulco (2003)
72. Sonnenwald, D.H.: Communication roles that support collaboration during the design process. Des. Stud. **17**(3), 277–301 (1996)
73. Surowiecki, J.: The Wisdom of Crowds: Why the Many Are Smarter than the Few and How Collective Wisdom Shapes Business, Economies, Societies, and Nations, 1st edn. Doubleday, New York (2004)
74. Taylor-Powell, J., Rossing, E., Geran, B.: Evaluating Collaboratives: Reaching the Potential. University of Wisconsin-Extension, Madison, WI (1998)
75. Twidale, M.B., Nichols, D.M.: Collaborative browsing and visualization of the search process. ASLIB Proc. **48**, 177–182 (1996)
76. Twidale, M.B., Nichols, D.M., Mariani, J.A., Rodden, T., Sawyer, P.: Supporting the active learning of collaborative database browsing techniques. Res. Learn. Technol. **3**(1), 75–79 (1995)
77. Twidale, M.B., Nichols, D.M., Paice, C.D.: Browsing is a collaborative process. Inf. Process. Manag. **33**(6), 761–783 (1997)
78. Wilbur, S.B., Young, R.E.: The COSMOS project: a multi-disciplinary approach to design of computer supported group working. In: Speth, R. (ed.) EUTECO 88: Research into Networks and Distributed Applications, Vienna, pp. 20–22 (1988)

Chapter 7
Social and Collaborative Information Seeking

Abstract The social and collaborative aspects of information seeking described in the previous chapters are often hard to separate. This chapter presents the notion of social and collaborative information seeking (SCIS) that attempts to study both of those aspects at the same time. There are two main reasons to bring the areas of social information seeking (SIS) and collaborative information seeking (CIS) together: it is often difficult to separate a project's social and collaborative dimensions, and their combination could greatly improve our ability to support human information behavior. This chapter will first present a brief synthesis of SIS and CIS work. Next, it will consider SCIS as a new field that integrates and extends SIS and CIS. The chapter will explore the many benefits of this approach and finally present a research agenda that outlines the opportunities and challenges unique to SCIS.

7.1 Introduction

The need to use social and collaborative ties to search, retrieve, and use information pervades multiple dimensions of our everyday lives. Consider this scenario from a day in Carol's life. Carol is part of a corporate team that must gather business intelligence. When she returns home exhausted from work, she and her husband Mark spend their evening planning a relaxing vacation. Before she goes to bed, Carol spends time online trying to find information and support regarding treatment options for her aging parents' diabetes diagnoses. As her activities demonstrate, the importance of information access and processing is becoming only more critical to our daily activities.

Scholars in the fields of information and computer science have recently been investigating both individuals' engagement in social and collaborative information seeking and processing and information systems' ability to support these needs. Though this research is in its early stages, it has resulted in new tools for information seeking and new models for studying SIS and CIS. Future research, however, must address a slew of challenges that include creating suitable data collection and analysis methods, constructing new evaluation frameworks, and developing integrated systems that incorporate people's social and collaborative behaviors.

C. Shah, *Social Information Seeking*, The Information Retrieval Series 38,
DOI 10.1007/978-3-319-56756-3_7

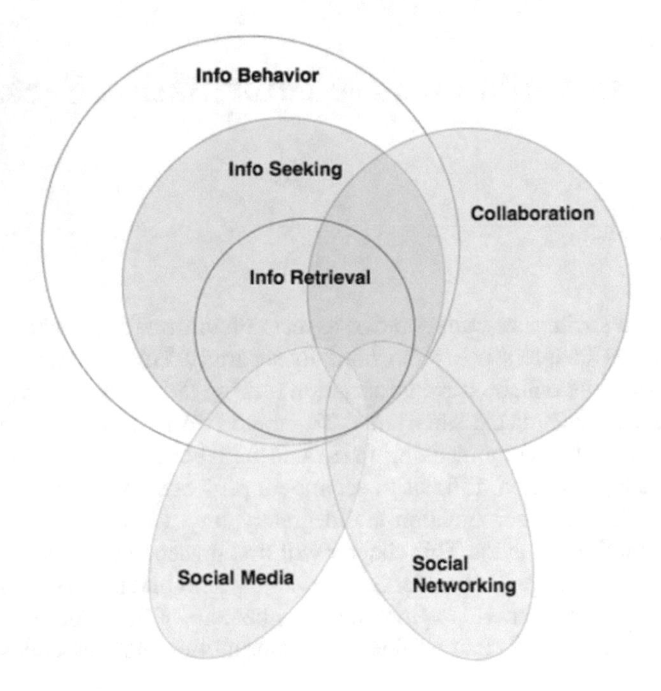

Fig. 7.1 A schematic view of social and collaborative information seeking (SCIS) as a union of SIS and CIS

Before we can confront these challenges, we need to establish a clear path for future research directions. It would be immensely productive to combine some of the past efforts in both SIS and CIS in order to create a unified domain. We'll call that domain social and collaborative information seeking (SCIS). Conceptually, SCIS sits at the union of SIS and CIS as shown in Fig. 7.1.

You may be wondering why SCIS is so important. After all, can combining two already-popular research fields really have an impact on SIS? The answer is "yes." SCIS allows people to address problems that are too difficult or even impossible for one person to solve because it allows people with different skills, knowledge, and backgrounds to share information and work together to solve problems [53]. And to support these collaborations, SCIS technologies and tools can efficiently and effectively assist information seeking activities across a range of situations. With SCIS studies, we can gain insight into collaborative workers' needs and behaviors and then respond to those needs with supportive tools that impact a variety of situations and contexts.

If the scenario that begins this chapter doesn't excite you, consider this: SCIS can impact situations in which tools are needed to support human activities and responses during difficult events. Imagine better plans, systems, and responses during emergencies, disasters, and logistical situations. SCIS need not solely focus on the mundane or the leisurely; tools and systems may act as a part of a larger system of responsive relief. For example, instruments may support intrinsic and implicit collaborations through establishing formal or informal "contracts" between parties without the need to preprocess the procedures of an established network of collaborators [3]. That's potential that needs to be realized, don't you think?

7.2 Background

Despite the predominant focus on individual information seeking, several scholars have argued that information seeking is a social activity [55]. And although the systems for accessing/retrieving information are designed with individual information seekers in mind, users are increasingly turning to others for information seeking assistance [22, 30, 31].

Both SIS and CIS trace this phenomenon. But despite their commonalities, SIS has largely focused on situations in which people seek information through or from other people, whereas CIS focuses on seeking information in conjunction with other people. Thus, CIS participants tend to set mutual goals, while those in SIS may have different goals depending on their roles (e.g., information seeker vs. provider). SIS examples include engaging in question-answering on Yahoo! Answers or reaching out to a social network for restaurant suggestions. In these scenarios, one person typically consults the "crowd" to receive answers or advice that will satisfy their information need. Two types of SIS emerge in the literature: situations where people seek information from known sources (social networks, e.g., Facebook) or situations where people seek information from unknown sources (crowd/community, e.g., Yahoo! Answers). CIS, on the other hand, encompasses situations where participants work together to seek information. A group of students may need to collect information for a term project, or a team of advertisers may need to analyze market data. Although collaborators' specific roles and skills may differ, CIS cases are typically driven by shared goals.

We do find a few cases in which scholars have connected the dots between social and collaborative dimensions to form one concrete concept. For instance, Evans and Chi [11] used social search as "an umbrella term used to describe search acts that make use of social interactions with others. These interactions may be explicit or implicit, co-located or remote, synchronous or asynchronous." (p. 657). "Search" refers to a specific method of information seeking, while "social" is one quality of that method, though here they are morphed into a more generalized form of information seeking that could incorporate both social and collaborative components. Shah [41] builds on this concept to argue that CIS could (and should) encapsulate areas such as social media/networking. Again, we see that a concept with a specific focus (e.g., CIS) can connect to a larger idea.

This chapter actually strives to subsume both SIS and CIS into a larger model of SCIS, which captures the common components of both concepts: they involve groups of people in the process of finding, identifying, and making sense of information.

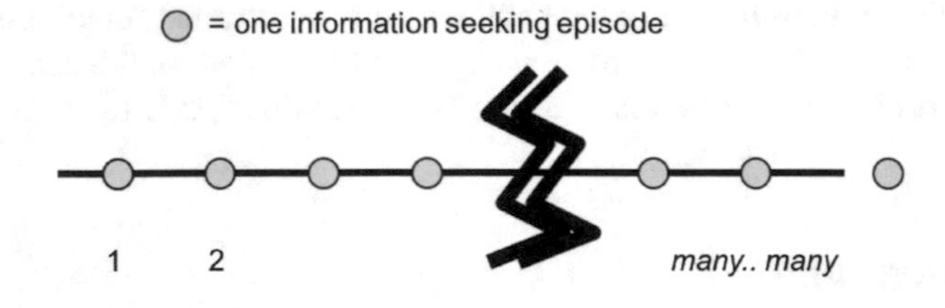

Fig. 7.2 Individual information seeking over multiple episodes

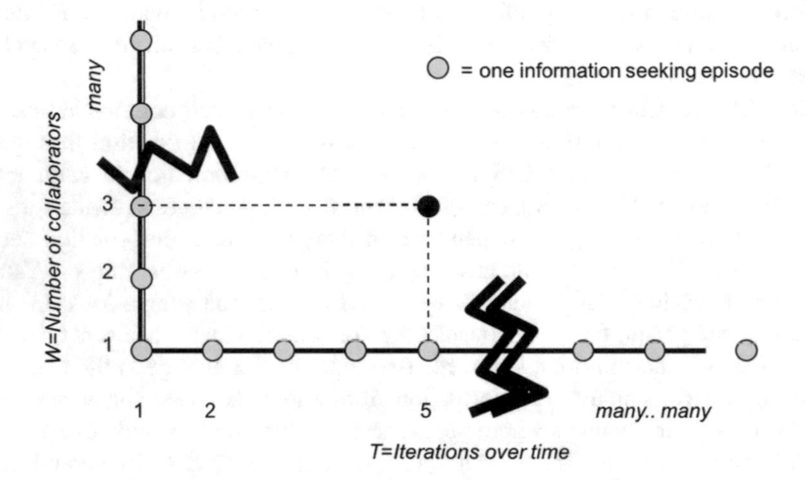

Fig. 7.3 Collaborative information seeking (CIS)

Figures 7.2, 7.3, 7.4, and 7.5 illustrate a gradual buildup of SCIS behavior. As shown, the SCIS research includes both individual-based information seeking activities (either single episodes or several episodes over time) and group-based activities as special cases of the overall SCIS model.

Figure 7.2 depicts the dominant model of information seeking in which a single individual looks for specific information over time. Over the past few decades, several scholars have explored this persistent or iterated information need, moving to the right along the *T* axis as shown here.

Things start to get interesting with Figs. 7.3 and 7.4. Here, we demonstrate how SCIS can extend the space of information seeking into two innovative additional dimensions. Figure 7.3 depicts the collaborative dimension. The black dot represents a team of three who search on five different occasions. Figure 7.4 adds the crucial third "dimension" that represents the social nature and degree of affiliation among the searchers. It is shown as orthogonal to the other axes to indicate that it will vary independently of the other two characteristics of the search. Unlike the first two axes, the social axis represents possible relations among people and is not necessarily expressible on a ratio scale, or even an ordinal scale.

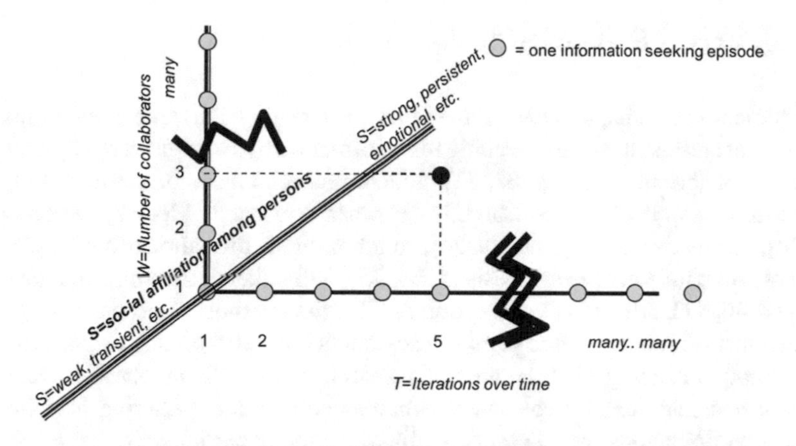

Fig. 7.4 Adding the social dimension to CIS

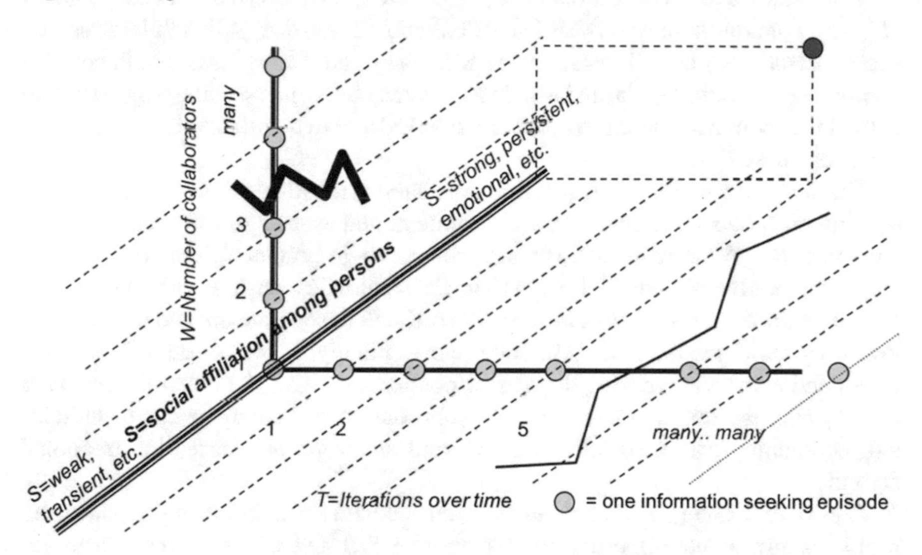

Fig. 7.5 Incorporating social and collaborative dimensions in information seeking activities

The three-axis conception space shown in Fig. 7.5 situates the various components of SCIS. For example, the red dot represents an information seeking activity involving three collaborators who share a strong, persistent emotional social relationship and engage in five episodes of information seeking. Note that collaboration can also be quite independent of social relations. In fact, much of the work in CIS has focused on characterizing collaborative activities along dimensions such as time (synchronous vs. asynchronous) and space (remote vs. colocated) [54], depth of collaboration [19], kind of mediation [37], and intentionality of the collaborators [18].

7.3 Current State of SCIS Research

The previous few chapters have shown that we already have quite a few terms and works that address seeking/searching for information by multiple people. Examples include collaborative search [32, 51], collaborative information retrieval [13, 24], concurrent search [2, 4], collaborative exploratory search [36, 37], co-browsing [9, 20], collaborative navigation [9, 26], collaborative information behavior [25, 38], collaborative information synthesis [5, 34, 35], and collaborative information seeking [14, 40, 41]. All address some form of CIS, though most focus on small groups of information seekers (often pairs). Researchers have also distinguished CIS from collaborative filtering [39], an area of research in IR. CIS involves participants' explicit and intentional involvement, whereas collaborative filtering may involve passive participations and/or scant coordination among participants.

Some studies focus on various forms of online Q&A, referred to as social Q&A [17, 45], community-based Q&A [1], or collaborative Q&A [49]. While these and social search [10] are all examples of SIS, they could also have a collaborative component as shown by Gazan [16]. So as you may have guessed, the opportunity to extend CIS with a social dimension, or extend SIS with a collaborative dimension, has been missed!

The literature implies that social and collaborative dimensions of information seeking must be studied and supported as integrated aspects of information search and retrieval. We can distinguish between three important drives. First, social and collaborative behaviors share certain characteristics, such as communication, coordination, and cooperation. Second, it's difficult to separate the two in situations involving multi-session and multimodal work. Finally, if we situate CIS and SIS on a continuum with varying degrees of connection strength among the involved participants, we could create seamless solutions to ultimately integrate individual, community-based, socially oriented, and small group-focused informational activities.

And if that potential doesn't excite you, consider the following unaddressed problems and unmet opportunities apparent in SIS and CIS research. There are several works in CIS that investigate the effects of roles (e.g., [52]), and there are works in SIS that look at information seeking through peers (e.g., [15]) or experts [49], but we do not know if/when and how people can/should switch from or assume roles with their collaborators and the outside world. Another example: CIS works have focused on awareness and its influence on search behaviors (e.g., [8, 44]), and SIS works have focused on privacy (e.g., [12]). Perhaps these are two sides of the same coin and should/could be studied together to provide better support for people working together. Bringing these research activities under a larger umbrella of SCIS and creating a framework that supports them could not only lead to solutions to these problems but could also even lead to better insights into respective CIS and SIS processes.

7.4 Research and Development Trajectory for SCIS

Even with the advancements that have been made in SCIS, CIS, SIS, and related areas, we still have our work cut out for us regarding remaining questions and unmet challenges. In this section, you'll find an overview of important questions and challenges in SCIS. The resulting research agenda is grounded in ideas, discussions, and challenges identified in a series of SCIS-focused workshops organized by a number of scholars (present author included!) in recent years (e.g., [46–48, 50]).

Over the last 10–15 years, collaborative aspects of life in general—or, more specifically, situations where people handle, exchange, and make decisions about or based off information—have radically changed. Innovative tools, systems, and apps support emerging types of collaboration and traditional collaborative situations and behaviors. Some of these technologies are specially geared toward supporting collaborative work, but others can be reasonably applied to enable and support group efforts [6]. Thus, to study collaboration and design systems in different situations, we need to determine new angles from which we can approach SCIS and examine traditional models from the perspective of new technologies. These situations may be known or unknown, meaning we have to remain open-minded when developing and utilizing frameworks, tools, and methods that can study these phenomena.

7.4.1 *Methodological Issues and Challenges*

Preparing to study information seeking carried out by two or more people certainly diverges from studying how one person engages in searching behaviors. SCIS inherently adds many additional factors and challenges to the research process. Consider the wide array of factors that can affect SCIS-related activities: multiple people and personalities, knowledge sharing, coordination, different roles and motivations, etc. Goals and outcome measures do not only vary based on the task scenario; an individual's role may also be a factor. In prior work, a variety of different methods have been utilized to study CIS. Even though both ethnographic and empirical research exist, fewer works present in-depth and thorough discussions of how to study CIS on a general level. Shah wrote one such work [42] to propose a new framework for studying CIS problems and evaluating CIS systems. The study presented a structure of evaluation that could measure both the system side and the user side in a CIS environment.

Another general CIS framework hails from Hyldegård et al. [23]. Their work identifies three distinct, predominantly qualitative longitudinal methods: multi-dimensional exploration, task-structured observation, and condensed observation. When conducting multidimensional exploration, researchers would use several general-purpose methods at different stages in concert. This, for example, could apply to an assignment process in order to explore behavior over time. On the other hand, a researcher conducting task-structured observation would need to observe a set of selected work tasks. This method is based on task-based process structuring, and could be used in any domain that uses work task as the unit of observation and involves a set of supporting data-collecting methods. Finally, a researcher utilizing condensed observation would observe a regularly recurring event—a series of meetings, for example—that constitutes a CIS activity and includes an account of the period since the previous instance of the event [23]. So if a group of students met once a week to work on a final project, and reviewed their previous meetings' occurrences before beginning their new session, they could provide a sample for condensed observation.

Other methods are constructed around different types of data collection. Researchers may wish to gather qualitative data, quantitative data, or use mixed methods. We need to foster discussions of data collection for studies of SCIS. What types of data collection and data analysis methods are best suited for specific types of SCIS scholarship? Given the diverse theoretical goals and research questions within the field, this is a pressing issue.

Most of the existing research in SCIS has been accomplished by observing SCIS phenomena in a variety of different domains [33] using a variety of different methods. Though we do have a small sample of empirical and experimental studies, it is worth considering a more systematic, focused approach to SCIS research. As a research community, we should start to discuss and create SCIS test collections, categories of tasks, scenarios, and evaluation/measurement frameworks that can be collectively shared and used to inspire future work. Currently, experimental platforms open to the general research public can be found at NIST TREC, the European CLEF platform, NTCIR in Japan, and FIRE in India. Establishing SCIS-focused tracks at these worldwide research events could both focus SCIS research and send it in new directions. SCIS could, for example, be part of a NIST TREC track or part of the CLEF environment. It could even encourage researchers to explore algorithmic approaches and tasks that have more user-oriented and interactive approaches. But to actualize these potentials, we need to build resources and locate dedicated partners. So if you're interested, we could use you!

7.4.2 Studying SCIS in Specific Domains

Several specific domains were identified as promising areas for future research at a recently held SCIS workshop [50]. Education, health, cross-language information retrieval, and e-discovery all hold possibilities. Each field hosts important challenges that SCIS could help overcome. In fact, prominent scholars believe that we should focus the next generation of SCIS research around several specific domains. Theory and practice suggest that SCIS research benefits from having specific, "real-world" problems to address, while the individual domains it tackles benefit from the tools and knowledge that such studies develop. Consider the following outline of directions for SCIS research in each of these areas.

7.4.2.1 SCIS Support for Education

We can develop SCIS support for educational platforms in a variety of ways. For example, SCIS research could explore ways to support known, established educational tasks such as: (a) helping teachers and students with their need to communicate and coordinate as part of the learning process; (b) supporting teachers in their individual and collaborative tasks with other teachers (e.g., administrative and educational processes); (c) supporting students in their learning process through tools that help with sharing information and data, cowriting assignments, and peer-reviewing procedures [21]; and (d) supporting educational analytics to help teachers, students, and administrators with their use of educational and learning components.

But can SCIS really encourage, foster, and measure learning? Believe it or not, yes. If we integrate learning dimensions into information seeking processes, we can extend the usage of information access systems into different learning contexts [27–29, 43]. We must also acknowledge that information access systems do not only apply to collaboratively "searching and browsing" for information. On the contrary, research could investigate collaborative seeking as one wheel of a larger vehicle for learning in both academic and professional contexts.

By nature of their job descriptions, information workers must be able to effectively work with others on search tasks. SCIS can sometimes support learning through an intentional flow of information from a knowledge holder to a knowledge seeker. Within social Q&A sites, for example, information flow is intentional and prescribed through the mechanisms of posting and responding to questions. Outside of these platforms, individuals may want to work in a close group to mutually help each other discover and learn new information. Future research could help identify how collaborative search systems and tools can support users in these group-learning settings.

But what if people indirectly work together? SCIS has us covered. Another exciting opportunity involves support of indirect collaborative learning. Consider this: in many situations, people learn from observing others. So if a user does not know how to begin a search in a new domain, they could benefit from exposure to search trails utilized by previous information seekers for similar topics [7].

7.4.2.2 SCIS Support for Health Information Seeking

When supporting a patient with a medical condition, multiple people assume multiple roles to seek health-related information. These roles may be played by the patient, their family, caregivers, and health-care providers, all of whom work in an ongoing CIS process. At the recent SCIS workshop, a breakout group proposed that "exemplary cases" were needed to help generalize and characterize these kinds of tasks [50]. Defining tasks, roles, relevance cues, and evaluation criteria are all challenges to be addressed in this area.

Across many of the outlined application areas, the need for mediated collaboration [18, 52] is an important future area for SCIS research. After all, systems can help mediate information seeking processes that involve humans with varying skill sets, languages, roles, and goals. Health information seeking exemplifies the salience of this task. As we said, these scenarios tend to involve many different bodies with many different roles, skills, and backgrounds. Already tense by nature, the uncertainty that can ensue from these interactions can be unproductive and, depending on context, frightening. Imagine what could happen if a system efficiently and effectively helped all parties engage in meaningful CIS!

7.4.2.3 SCIS Support for Cross-Language Information Retrieval

Cross-language information retrieval (CLIR) is an important area of IR that could greatly benefit from SCIS. CLIR has gained traction in a variety of contexts that either currently involve SCIS or could profit from its incorporation. Consider this: machine translation (MT) can be applied to many CLIR situations, but it currently has its limits. These boundaries could be broken by human translators/interpreters that could help users design meaningful queries, explain the nuances and dimensions of retrieved results, and provide translations to help tune and refine MT systems. Perhaps the inclusion of features to help users chat with document curators—who may very well use a different language than the searcher—could be useful. Even a simple option to help users improve their queries could have significant results.

7.4.2.4 SCIS Support for E-Discovery

E-discovery is a legal process employed to request relevant evidence/documents in a legal proceeding. Its current practices involve keyword searching and manual document review, but SCIS holds great potential for its future. The domain provides several interesting challenges for SCIS, especially in the area of algorithmic mediation. At the recent SCIS workshop, a breakout group addressed these issues by outlining a Collaborative Technology Assisted Review (CTAR) system in which human annotators provide training data to an automatic classification system that then supports human assessors in reviewing future documents (see [50] for more details).

7.4.2.5 SCIS Support for Other Domains

The above examples are not the only areas that could benefit from systems that include and support socio-collaborative connections. It may seem silly, but try placing the word "collaborative" in front of an existing area to explore this opportunity. What about collaborative analytics? We could explore new possibilities of doing analytics processes with a group of workers (e.g., analysts) who strive to address the needs of an organization (perhaps a government agency) in analyzing streams of data and producing insights for decision-making [56].

We can even find SCIS embedded in other social media or professional and commercial collaborative platforms for co-work and team/group project work, especially within business processes. Take e-governance, where SCIS may be explored to create more open discussion and communication among local and national governmental authorities. It follows that SCIS platforms could serve to enhance and empower individual or group-wide democratic values and processes. These systems may become community builders that shift the ways in which citizens collaborate, debate, and communicate at various social and political levels.

Let's think back to the idea that a great deal of previous information seeking scholarship examines tasks completed by individuals. Why couldn't we expand SCIS research to apply social and/or collaborative dimensions to improve these tasks' efficiency and effectiveness? That's certainly worth exploring. SCIS research could even expand into new domains, contexts, and situations that may include various everyday situations, manufacturing contexts, and consumer contexts. The possibilities are endless.

7.4.2.6 Cross-Disciplinary Research

SCIS is inherently cross-disciplinary. It draws from aspects of information science, HCI and interaction design, information retrieval, social networks, collaboration, and other areas. Given its vast expanse, its future success depends on the involvement of both system-focused and user-focused researchers, and there are benefits to bringing the two together. Integrated research could improve machine-learning classifiers and features, develop new methods for algorithmic mediation, and improve systems to support collaboration among participants with diverse skills and backgrounds (and among humans and algorithmic components). For SCIS to support complex multi-agent systems, it is important to involve researchers with algorithmic, computer science, and engineering backgrounds.

7.5 Summary

Neither SIS nor CIS are static fields; they constantly evolve as new technologies and tools bring new challenges and opportunities. Changes in societal conditions also beget new ways of interaction and communication. If we think about SIS and CIS as part of an integrated model of SCIS rather than two concrete concepts, we can improve circumstances for technology scholars, practitioners, designers, and end users. The integrated model of SCIS introduced here includes explicit social and collaborative dimensions to help situate specific information seeking situations. If we want to help designers to better support groups of information seekers (and we do!), we must consider these combined dimensions. Collaborators will be able to find, identify, and make sense of information in more efficient and effective ways.

In this chapter, we identified a number of domains in which applied, cross-disciplinary SCIS research may hold significant practical importance, including education and learning, health information seeking, cross-language information retrieval, e-discovery, e-governance and community involvement, and other work/group settings that involve collaboration and coordination. But to reach maximum impact, we have also identified a strong need to develop methods, practices, and cross-disciplinary approaches to collaboratively address practical problems in these domains. To address these needs, researchers, practitioners, and developers working in SCIS-related areas must, funny enough, work collaboratively; structure and organization are needed to effectively share resources (e.g., tools, systems, study design templates), data sets, methods, and findings. In this chapter, we presented an integrated view of SCIS and a research agenda to provide a foundation for impactful, cross-disciplinary work. In the future, let's hope we improve tools, processes, and systems to support users in a variety of important information seeking situations.

References

1. Agichtein, E., Castillo, C., Donato, D., Gionis, A., Mishne, G.: Finding high-quality content in social media. In: Proceedings of the International Conference on Web Search and Web Data Mining - WSDM'08, pp. 183–194. ACM Press, New York (2008)
2. Amershi, S., Morris, M.R.: CoSearch. In: Proceedings of the Twenty-Sixth Annual CHI Conference on Human Factors in Computing Systems - CHI'08, pp. 1647. ACM Press, New York (2008)
3. Bjurling, B., Hansen, P.: Contracts for information sharing in collaborative networks. In: ISCRAM 2010 - 7th International Conference on Information Systems for Crisis Response and Management: Defining Crisis Management 3.0, Proceedings, Seattle, WA (2010)
4. Blackwell, A.F., Stringer, M., Toye, E.F., Rode, J.A.: Tangible interface for collaborative information retrieval. In: Extended Abstracts of the 2004 Conference on Human Factors and Computing Systems - CHI'04, p. 1473. ACM Press, New York (2004)
5. Blake, C., Pratt, W.: Collaborative information synthesis I: a model of information behaviors of scientists in medicine and public health. J. Am. Soc. Inf. Sci. **57**(13), 1740–1749 (2006)
6. Capra, R., Marchionini, G., Velasco-Martin, J., Muller, K.: Tools-at-hand and learning in multi-session, collaborative search. In: Proceedings of the 28th International Conference on Human Factors in Computing Systems - CHI'10, pp. 951. ACM Press, New York (2010)
7. Capra, R., Arguello, J., Crescenzi, A., Vardell, E.: Differences in the use of search assistance for tasks of varying complexity. In: Proceedings of the 38th International ACM SIGIR Conference on Research and Development in Information Retrieval - SIGIR'15, pp. 23–32. ACM Press, New York (2015)
8. Chen, A.T., Capra, R., Wu, W.-C.: An investigation of the effects of awareness and task orientation on collaborative search. Proc. Am. Soc. Inf. Sci. Technol. **51**(1), 1–10 (2014)
9. Esenther, A.W.: Instant co-browsing: lightweight real-time collaborative Web browsing. In: Proceedings of the World Wide Web (WWW) Conference, Honolulu, HI, pp. 107–114 (2002)
10. Evans, B.M., Chi, Ed.H.: An elaborated model of social search. Inf. Process. Manag. **46**(6), 656–678 (2009)
11. Evans, B.M., Chi, Ed.H.: An elaborated model of social search. Inf. Process. Manag. **46**(6), 656–678 (2010)
12. Evans, B.M., Kairam, S., Pirolli, P.: Do your friends make you smarter?: an analysis of social strategies in online information seeking. Inf. Process. Manag. **46**(6), 679–692 (2010)

13. Fidel, R., Bruce, H., Pejtersen, A.M., Dumais, S.: Collaborative information retrieval (CIR). New Rev. Inf. Behav. Res. **1**, 235–247 (2000)
14. Foster, J.: Collaborative information seeking and retrieval. Annu. Rev. Inf. Sci. Technol. **40**(1), 329–356 (2007)
15. Gazan, R.: Seekers, sloths and social reference: homework questions submitted to a question-answering community. New Rev. Hypermedia Multimedia **13**(2), 239–248 (2007)
16. Gazan, R.: Microcollaborations in a social Q&A community. Inf. Process. Manag. **46**(6), 693–702 (2010)
17. Gazan, R.: Advances in information science social Q & A. J. Am. Soc. Inf. Sci. Technol. **62**(12), 2301–2312 (2011)
18. Golovchinsky, G., Pickens, J., & Back, M. (2009). A taxonomy of collaboration in online information seeking. Preprint, arXiv:0908.0704
19. Golovchinsky, G., Qvarfordt, P., Pickens, J.: Collaborative information seeking. IEEE Comput. **42**, 47–51 (2009)
20. Han, R., Perret, V., Naghshineh, M.: WebSplitter: a unified XML framework for multi-device collaborative Web browsing. In: Proceedings of the 2000 ACM Conference on Computer Supported Cooperative Work, pp. 221–230 (2000)
21. Hansen, P., Hansson, H.: Optimizing student and supervisor interaction during the SciPro thesis process: concepts and design. In: Li, F.W.B., et al. (eds.) Advances in Web-Based Learning: ICWL 2015, pp. 245–250. Springer, Cham (2015)
22. Hansen, P., Järvelin, K.: Collaborative information retrieval in an information-intensive domain. Inf. Process. Manag. **41**(5), 1101–1119 (2005)
23. Hyldegård, J., Hertzum, M., Hansen, P.: Studying collaborative information seeking: experiences with three methods. In: Hansen, P., Shah, C., Klas, C.P. (eds.) Collaborative Information Seeking, pp. 17–35. Springer, Cham (2015)
24. Karamuftuoglu, M.: Collaborative information retrieval: toward a social informatics view of IR interaction. J. Am. Soc. Inf. Sci. **49**(12), 1070–1080 (1998)
25. Karunakaran, A., Reddy, M.C., Spence, P.R.: Toward a model of collaborative information behavior in organizations. J. Am. Soc. Inf. Sci. Technol. **64**(12), 2437–2451 (2013)
26. Laurillau, Y., Nigay, L.: Clover architecture for groupware. In: Proceedings of the ACM Conference on Computer Supported Cooperative Work, New Orleans, LA, pp. 236–245 (2002)
27. Leeder, C., Shah, C.: Collaborative information seeking in student group projects. Aslib J. Inf. Manage. **68**(5), 526–544 (2016)
28. Leeder, C., Shah, C.: Measuring the effect of virtual librarian intervention on student online search. J. Acad. Librariansh. **42**(1), 2–7 (2016)
29. Leeder, C., Shah, C.: Practicing critical evaluation of online sources improves student search behavior. J. Acad. Librariansh. **42**(4), 459–468 (2016)
30. Morris, M.R.: A survey of collaborative Web search practices. In: Proceedings of the Twenty-Sixth Annual CHI Conference on Human Factors in Computing Systems - CHI'08, p. 1657. ACM Press, New York (2008)
31. Morris, M.R.: Collaborative search revisited. In: Proceedings of the 2013 Conference on Computer Supported Cooperative Work - CSCW'13, p. 1181. ACM Press, New York (2013)
32. Morris, M.R., Horvitz, E.: SearchTogether: an interface for collaborative Web search. In: Proceedings of the 2007 ACM Symposium on User Interface Software and Technology (UIST 2007), pp. 3–12. ACM Press, New York (2007)
33. Newman, K., Knight, S., Hansen, P., Elbeshausen, S.: Situating CIS: the importance of context in collaborative information seeking. In: Hansen, P., Shah, C., Klas, C.P. (eds.) Collaborative Information Seeking, pp. 37–54. Springer, Cham (2015)
34. Olson, G.M., Olson, J.S., Carter, M.R., Sorrosten, M.: Small group design meetings: an analysis of collaboration. Hum. Comput. Interact. **7**(4), 347–374 (1992)
35. Olson, J.S., Olson, G.M., Storrøsten, M., Carter, M.: Groupwork close up: a comparison of the group design process with and without a simple group editor. ACM Trans. Inf. Syst. **11**(4), 321–348 (1993)

36. Pickens, J., Golovchinsky, G.: Collaborative exploratory search. In: Proceedings of Workshop on Human-Computer Interaction and Information Retrieval, Cambridge, MA, pp. 21–22 (2007)
37. Pickens, J., Golovchinsky, G., Shah, C., Qvarfordt, P., Back, M.: Algorithmic mediation for collaborative exploratory search. In: Proceedings of the 31st Annual International ACM SIGIR Conference: Research & Development in Information Retrieval, pp. 315–322 (2008)
38. Reddy, M.C., Jansen, B.J.: A model for understanding collaborative information behavior in context: A study of two healthcare teams. Inf. Process. Manag. **44**(1), 256–273 (2008)
39. Shah, C.: Toward collaborative information seeking (CIS). In: Proceedings of JCDL 2008 Workshop on Collaborative Exploratory Search, Pittsburgh, PA (2009)
40. Shah, C.: Collaborative Information Seeking: The Art and Science of Making the Whole Greater than the Sum of All. Information Retrieval Series. Springer, Berlin (2012)
41. Shah, C.: Collaborative information seeking. J. Assoc. Inf. Sci. Technol. **65**(2), 215–236 (2014)
42. Shah, C.: Evaluating collaborative information seeking: synthesis, suggestions, and structure. J. Inf. Sci. **40**(4), 460–475 (2014)
43. Shah, C., Leeder, C.: Exploring collaborative work among graduate students through the C5 model of collaboration: a diary study. J. Inf. Sci. **42**(5), 609–629 (2015)
44. Shah, C., Marchionini, G.: Awareness in collaborative information seeking. J. Am. Soc. Inf. Sci. Technol. **61**(10), 1970–1986 (2010)
45. Shah, C., Oh, S., Oh, J.S.: Research agenda for social Q&A. Libr. Inf. Sci. Res. **31**(4), 205–209 (2009)
46. Shah, C., Reddy, M., Twidale, M.: In: First Workshop on Collaborative Information Seeking (2010)
47. Shah, C., Hansen, P., Capra, R.: In: Second Workshop on Collaborative Information Seeking (2011)
48. Shah, C., Hansen, P., Capra, R.: In: Third Workshop on Collaborative Information Seeking (2013)
49. Shah, C., Kitzie, V., Choi, E.: Modalities, motivations, and materials - investigating traditional and social online Q&A services. J. Inf. Sci. **40**(5), 669–687 (2014)
50. Shah, C., Capra, R., Hansen, P.: Workshop on social and collaborative information seeking (SCIS). SIGIR Forum **49**(2), 117–122 (2015)
51. Smyth, B., Balfe, E., Briggs, P., Coyle, M., Freyne, J.: Collaborative Web search. In: Proceedings of the International Joint Conference on Artificial Intelligence (IJCAI), Acapulco, pp. 1417–1419. Morgan Kaufmann, San Francisco (2003)
52. Soulier, L., Shah, C., Tamine, L.: User-driven system-mediated collaborative information retrieval. In: Proceedings of the 37th International ACM SIGIR Conference on Research & Development in Information Retrieval - SIGIR'14, pp. 485–494. ACM Press, New York (2014)
53. Talja, S., Hansen, P.: Information Sharing. Springer, Dordrecht (2006)
54. Twidale, M.B., Nichols, D.M.: Collaborative browsing and visualization of the search process. Aslib Proc. **48**, 177–182 (1996)
55. Twidale, M.B., Nichols, D.M., Paice, C.D.: Browsing is a collaborative process. Inf. Process. Manag. **33**(6), 761–783 (1997)
56. Widen, G., Hansen, P.: Managing collaborative information sharing: bridging research on information culture and collaborative information behaviour. Inf. Res. Int. Electron. J. **17**(4), paper 538 (2012)

Part IV
Current State and Future Directions

This part provides a synthesis of several of the concepts and works covered thus far in this book. This is done by consolidating methods, systems, and evaluation techniques relating to social and collaborative information seeking. Finally, we conclude this book by listing challenges and opportunities for further work in this domain.

Chapter 8
SIS in Research and Practice

Abstract This chapter provides an overview of how SIS research studies are done; how different SIS systems, services, and users are evaluated; and how all of the above are implemented. First, we present a brief description of common research methods for SIS studies. These methods include observations, interviews, content analysis, and mixed methods. Next, we recognize the challenge of evaluating SIS. We'll explain some of the popular methods for evaluation in this field, which include usability testing, system-based training-testing, quantitative evaluations, and qualitative evaluations. Finally, various products and services that implement and/or facilitate SIS are introduced. They include different forms of communication tools and methods, peer-driven services, expert-driven services, and social live streaming services (SLSSs).

8.1 Introduction

The previous two parts of this book covered a lot of ground regarding SIS and a number of related areas. As we often saw, these areas are not easy to separate. It follows that now we will bring many of them together to discuss SIS as a larger area that covers all forms of social and collaborative aspects of information seeking/searching/browsing processes. We'll focus on how SIS studies are conducted, how evaluations of users and systems are performed, and where we can see SIS-related ideas in real-life applications.

Unsurprisingly, several of these ideas are already discussed in the previous chapters of this book, but they are sprinkled throughout the text. In this chapter, we will try to consolidate them as we discuss research and practice ideas for SIS, CIS, SCIS, social search, etc. We once again look at the familiar figure that organizes all of these concepts in Fig. 8.1, which reminds us where SIS lies.

C. Shah, *Social Information Seeking*, The Information Retrieval Series 38,
DOI 10.1007/978-3-319-56756-3_8

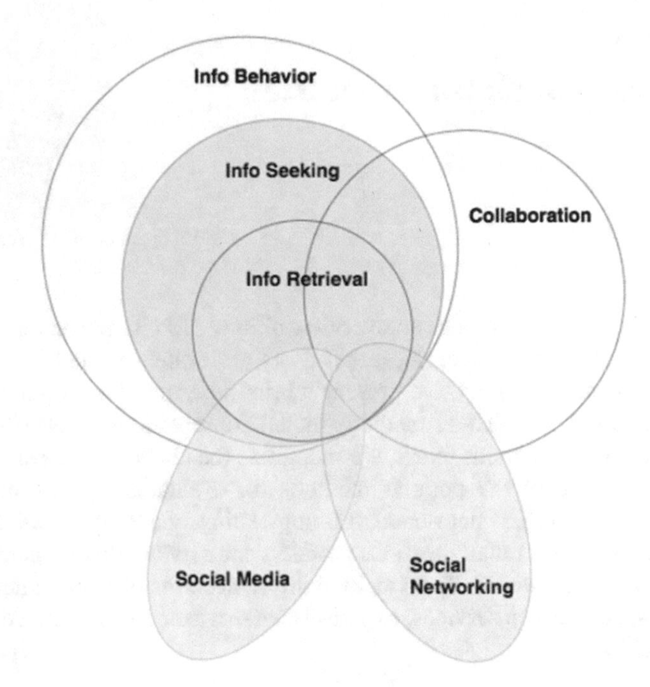

Fig. 8.1 A schematic view of social information seeking (SIS)

8.2 Studying SIS

Scholars who study SIS and related areas such as social Q&A, social information retrieval, collaborative search, co-browse, and co-search use a variety of methods to conduct their research. These methods can be classified into a few main categories that are not all that different from what one may find in studies that fall at the intersection of social and computational sciences. The subsections below provide brief descriptions with examples and should be seen as starting points for these explorations involving SIS studies.

8.2.1 Direct Observation

Who are these people engaged in SIS? What are they doing? Several studies in the areas of SIS and related topics involve looking at people in their natural environments. Sometimes this also includes giving those people tasks to complete.

Many researchers present subjects with specific information seeking tasks and then observe the said subjects' behavior as they carry out their work. These tasks typically take place within a specific online platform, such as Amazon's Mechanical Turk. Evans et al. [13], for example, studied the cognitive benefits of online social interactions by assigning exploratory search tasks to their subjects and then using talk-aloud protocol and video capture to formulate their results. Because these researchers directly observed users' interactions with a variety of platforms, such as SNSs and private online communication channels, they were able to draw conclusions about the effectiveness of these platforms' functions. Based on their findings, they suggest that online social tools could be better integrated with each other and existing search facilities. Observational methods often allow scholars to make inferences about both user behavior and system design.

8.2.2 Interviews

While observations can tell researchers about *who*, *what*, and *when*, they often don't shed enough light on *why*. And that's where actually talking to participants in question could be very useful.

Scholars may present their subjects with exploratory search tasks and then conduct in-depth interviews to draw conclusions about SIS behaviors. Participants in O'Brien et al.'s [23] study, for instance, used an online news Website to select three items of interest, which they then rated during post-search interviews where they also articulated their motivations for choosing each item. From data collected during these interviews, the researchers concluded that while personal interests and curiosity play important roles in SIS, a wide range of situational factors and goals also come into play. Interviews often allow researchers to discover nuances and motivational factors that strict observation can miss.

In other research, theorists have used interviews to determine how and why information seekers favor certain tools, such as search engines, over others, such as academic databases. Bøyum and Aabø [9], for example, interviewed PhD students to discover their information seeking practices. Using a phenomenological approach, they gathered data on these students' preferred tools, methods for keeping up-to-date, and contexts in which they used formal or social information seeking practices. The authors believe that their study and other related studies can help libraries and other institutions improve their services and acquire relevant resources for their users. Tian [44] used a similar interview approach to determine how students in Hong Kong used SNSs in SIS.

As an alternative or supplement to in-person interviews, scholars may present their research participants with questionnaires that inquire about social searching practices and/or follow the completion of an assigned information seeking task. These can be surveys or diary logs kept by participants and are discussed further amidst mixed methods. Researchers have also used Skype[1] and other video calling services as a way to collect face-to-face interview data without geographic restraint [7, 11].

---

[1] https://www.skype.com.

8.2.3 Content Analysis

When it comes to SIS-related work, there is no shortage of content, as an increasing number of people are generating, sharing, and reproducing more and more information every day. One can also slice and dice these productions in many ways to conduct all kinds of interesting analyses. Therefore, it is not surprising that there are plenty of studies in this area that involve analyzing content. These materials involve questions, answers, comments, documents, segments, and almost everything in-between that can be digitally created and shared. A few scholars analyze such information manually, but most do it using automated techniques. And when it comes to automating content analysis, it's almost imperative that researchers complete some form of feature extraction and selection.

Take an example of work by Liu et al. [18]. The authors proposed the Asker Satisfaction Prediction (ASP) framework that included textual and semantic features of questions and answers, history of answer satisfaction by category, and askers' and answerers' past activity history. Agichtein et al. [2] used the ASP framework with 71 features and performed one of the first large-scale studies that combined content-based features and network-based features in order to identify quality answers as ranked by human coders within Yahoo! Answers. Their findings indicate that models trained on each set of features from the framework perform at a substandard level, but the combination of features leads to adequate classification performance, suggesting that each set of features provides independent information that makes a unique contribution to the model. Adamic et al. [1] similarly performed a large-scale content analysis of Yahoo! Answers with 8.4 million answers, 1.1 million questions, and 700,000 distinct users. They found that a user tends to provide more Best Answer ratings when their participation rate (e.g., asking, answering, evaluating) is lower.

Content analysis can be quantitative or qualitative, and often involves researchers' in-depth analysis of SIS services and user behaviors. Interactions—such as those between questioners and answerers within online Q&A services—are recorded, coded, classified, and studied in order to draw conclusions about SIS practices. Shah et al. [35] employed two types of content analysis during their study of traditional and social online Q&A services. First, they created a typology of Q&A services and classified questions from each type to compare and discuss results. Second, they focused on the relationship between platforms' non-textual features. The work revealed that six significant textual attributes contribute to the model with the highest percentage of accuracy: (1) interrogative words used at the beginning of a question; (2) the number of unique words in the question, which is an indicator that the information within the question is more specific; (3) the clarity score representing the complexity of the question; (4) presence of content that provides additional information in order to give the reader a better understanding of what the asker is looking for; (5) the number of question marks, which signifies how many questions the user asks; and (6) presence of taboo words, which indicates whether the question is socially appropriate. Feature extraction can certainly tell us a great deal about SIS practices and behaviors.

8.2.4 *Mixed Methods*

While SIS researchers do not often solely rely on quantitative methods, they do employ data collection as part of mixed-method strategies. Tashakkori and Teddlie [42, 43] believe that qualitative and quantitative approaches can complement each other, and the combination of both methods could allow for more comprehensive data analysis and a sharper understanding of findings.

Scholars can typically distribute online surveys with ease and use these tools to gather generalizable data concerning certain aspects of SIS, such as users' motivations for asking questions within the context of online Q&A. Choi and Shah [11] combined an Internet survey with a quantitative diary method. The initial survey provided preliminary findings and a way for the researchers to extract a smaller sample of in-depth participants. The diary method illustrated subjects' general searching behaviors and motivations for asking questions. According to Choi and Shah [11], data collection via diary entries can be particularly helpful, as it allows for the collection of real-time information about the moments in which online users engage in social Q&A. Their study followed the survey and diary methods with qualitative interviews, which provided depth and texture to an understanding of specific SIS situations and contexts.

Shah et al. [35] also employed a mixed-method approach that included quantitative measures. In addition to an in-depth, synthesized literature review and interviews, they utilized surveys to measure different facets of online Q&A exposure and use, as well as general information seeking behaviors on the Web. They also utilized content analysis to study non-textual features from Yahoo! Answers to determine relationships between these features, such as time taken to answer a question and answerer satisfaction. The researchers sorted questions and answers into specific categories to generate descriptive statistics over a 2-year period.

While methods such as survey distribution and diary collection are popular, they are typically combined with other methods and are rarely used alone.

8.3 Evaluating SIS

Evaluating SIS tools, techniques, and environments can be an enormous challenge because their complex designs involve a set of users, integrated systems, and a variety of interactions. One can evaluate an SIS system using typical measures of IR. But we know better. As discussed before, information seeking is not merely about retrieving information, and thus, evaluating an SIS system through its retrieval effectiveness may not be sufficient. While traditional IR evaluations can still be used to measure the retrieval performance of a collaborative filtering system, just as Smyth et al. [39] did, we need additional measures for SIS systems.

Baeza-Yates and Pino [4] presented some initial work that tried to develop a measure that can extend the evaluation of a single-user IR system for a socio-collaborative environment. While their work was based on retrieval performance,

Aneiros and Estivill-Castro [3] proposed evaluating the *goodness* of such a system via usability. In addition, Baeza-Yates and Pino [4] treated a group's performance as the summation of the performances of the individuals in said group. While this may work for simple information seeking and retrieval, we can imagine situations in which this is not true. For instance, if two people interacting can find twice as much information as either of them working independently, was that a good thing? How about the amount of time they spent cumulatively? The searchers may not be able to find twice as many results, but what if they achieved better understanding of the problem or the information because they worked together? Then there are other factors, such as engagement, social interactions, and social capital, which may be important depending on the application, but are usually not looked at in noninteractive or single-user IR evaluations.

Now, we'll review a number of evaluative methodologies that have been used for SIS and related areas (social search, social Q&A, CIS, SCIS). We'll follow that with a discussion about specific measures taken primarily from IR, HCI, and CSCW literatures that could help in evaluating SIS systems and approaches. These measures will be divided into two categories: system-based and user-based.

To commence the discussion of evaluation methods, we'll start with a broad overview of how researchers have approached this issue using different methodologies.

8.3.1 Evaluating Usability with User Studies

Most of the work reported in the literature that has attempted to evaluate the effectiveness of a collaborative system has looked at the usability of the social/collaborative interface. For instance, Morris and Horvitz [21] tested their SearchTogether system with a user study to evaluate how users implemented various tools offered in its interface and how those tools affected the act of collaboration. The authors used seven pairs of users and let each pair choose a mutually appealing topic. The evaluation was based on the log, observational, and questionnaire data. While the authors demonstrated their interface's effectiveness in letting people search together, they did not evaluate group-wide learning that stemmed from collaboration. Laurillau and Nigay [17] demonstrated how multiple users could navigate the Web in a collaborative environment with their CoVitesse system. They presented evaluations for the user interface as well as various network-related parameters. However, no clear understanding of the effects on the retrieval performance was reported. Aneiros and Estivill-Castro [3] presented their participants with a questionnaire to evaluate the usability of their Group Unified History (GUH) tool. Typical questions included: "[H]ow difficult was it to interpret the user identity symbols used in the tool?" and "[D]id you visit any websites found by your team/peers using the group history?"

Some of the application designers also let real users use their systems and evaluated the effectiveness of those systems based off users' feedback and/or success in solving real problems. For instance, Twidale et al. [46] invited volunteers to present a problem that they already knew they had to solve. Students from a wide range of academic backgrounds (including Psychology, Computing, Women's Studies, Chemistry, Religious Studies, and Environmental Science) used the authors' Ariadne system to conduct literature searches. The testing informed the iterative development of the system.

8.3.2 System-Based Training-Testing

Smyth et al. [38] tested their I-Spy system with a leave-one-out evaluation methodology. From 20 users, they left one user as a testing user and used the other 19 as training users. The relevancy results of the training users were extracted to populate I-Spy's hit matrix, and the results of each query were re-ranked using I-Spy's relevancy metric. Then, researchers counted the number of those results listed as relevant by the test user for various result-list sizes, and finally, they made the equivalent relevancy measurements by analyzing the results produced by the baseline untrained version of I-Spy.

Not surprisingly, this line of evaluation is more popular with system or algorithmically mediated connections among participants. For instance, Pickens et al. [25] used search query suggestions provided by individuals and showed how their algorithm could achieve an effective collaboration by way of simulation. Similarly, Shah et al. [34] used the notions of relevance and novelty to demonstrate how search processes that were virtually combined could lead to results that are both relevant and diverse. Soulier and her colleagues [40, 41] also used simulations as a technique to see how well a system could identify different roles among people working together, and how effectively it could leverage users' diverse skills in a search situation.

8.3.3 Qualitative Evaluation

Prekop [26] presented a qualitative way to evaluate people working together on search tasks. He measured information seeking patterns that described prototypical actions, interactions, and behaviors performed by participants in a socio-collaborative endeavor. The three patterns that the author described were information seeking by recommendation, direct questioning, and advertising information paths. Using a similar idea to study participants through an analysis of their behavior and patterns, Olson et al. [24] studied ten design meetings from four projects in two organizations. The meetings were videotaped, transcribed, and then analyzed using a coding scheme that classified participants' problem-solving methods and coordinating/managing activities. The authors also analyzed the structure of their design arguments. They claimed that the coding schemes developed might be useful for a wide range of problem-solving meetings other than design.

The concept of "social" is often understood to incorporate work-related connections beyond nonwork, social ties. Luo and Olson [19], in an effort to study communication in scientific collaborations, selected eight different collaboratories from around the world and interviewed 50 scientists. Their interviews included open-ended questions that were analyzed using qualitative methods. Results provided interesting insights into the communication aspect of scientific collaborations, including what support scientific collaboratives offer or lack when it comes to informal communication among scientists.

8.3.4 Task- or Application-Based Evaluation

Wilson and schraefel[2] [47] analyzed an evaluation framework for information seeking interfaces in terms of its applicability to collective search software. Extending Bates' tactics model [5] and Belkin's user model [6], they showed that the framework can be applied to both individual information seeking software and social/collaborative search interactions, but pointed out that additional considerations concerning individuals' group involvement must be maintained throughout the assessment. These efforts of evaluating various factors in SIS can be summarized as measuring (1) retrieval performance of the system, (2) effectiveness of the interface in facilitating collaboration, and (3) user satisfaction and involvement. There are also several new attempts that use previously atypical measures. These include awareness (e.g., [32]) and engagement (e.g., [23]).

8.4 SIS Products and Services

SIS occurs in a variety of settings and involves diverse products. The advent and expansion of Web-based platforms has exponentially increased individuals' ability to engage in SIS. According to Shah et al. [35], although many SIS tools exist, little scholarship can be found that defines or classifies their respective purposes. There is a plethora of services that cover one or several aspects of social connections, search/seeking/browsing, and producing or repurposing information. Figure 8.2 shows just some of them, organized on a collaboration grid.

Here, one axis is about the nature of information (text-based to multimedia), while the other axis indicates the nature of the social activity—from communicating to creating. Throughout this book we have seen many of these possibilities in the larger space of SIS. The following subsections provide a brief overview of some of these ideas.

[2]No, this is not a typo. This is how m.c. schraefel spells her name.

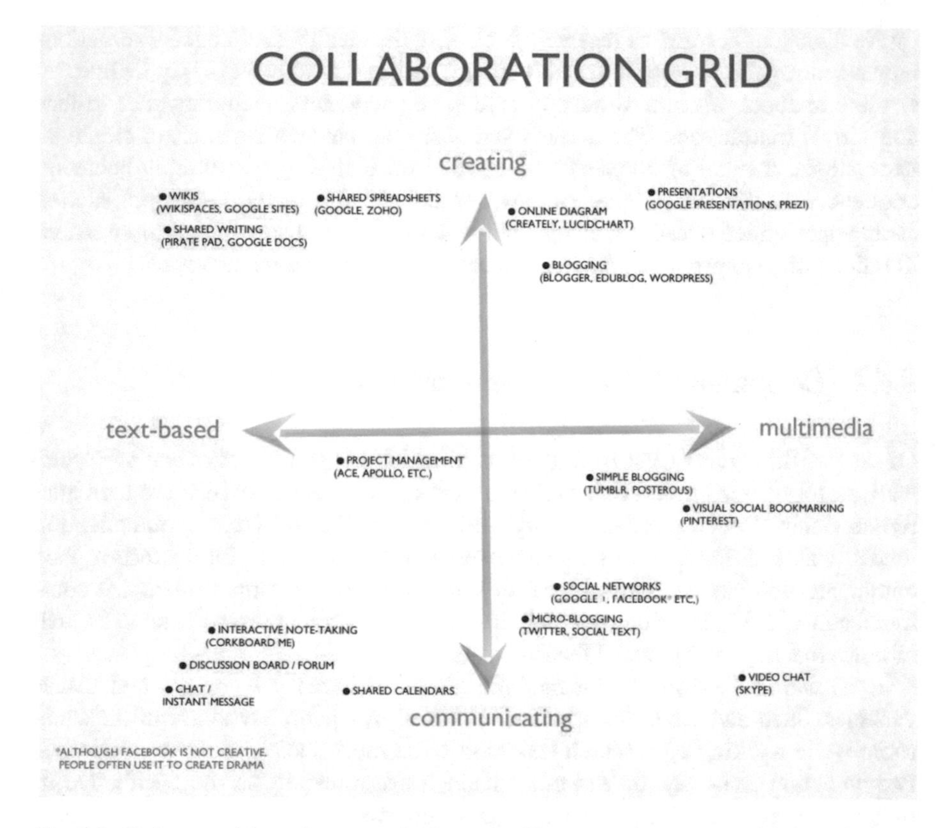

Fig. 8.2 Various social services organized on a grid representing nature of information and nature of group activity. Photo source: John Spencer. Collaboration grid. Retrieved from http://teachpaperless.blogspot.com/2012/03/collaboration-grid.html

8.4.1 Face-to-Face Communication

Due to the ubiquity and popularity of the Internet, many only consider online resources when discussing various SIS services and practices. Co-browsing, social searching, and other CIS techniques, however, existed long before technology's facilitation of socially based work. Face-to-face communications still comprise a large amount of SIS interactions and range from informal in-person meetings in which information is exchanged to formal traditional reference encounters between library patrons and staff.

Many scholars have tackled the reference interview in their research. Lynch [20] provided an early analysis of face-to-face reference encounters in traditional library settings. Her exploratory study sought to answer eight questions having to do with librarians' ability to parse actual information needs from patrons' initial questions. Using audio recording equipment, Lynch analyzed 309 interviews primarily using content analysis. Her work resulted in reference interview models and suggested future directions for further research, including the idea that reference transactions may not always be appropriate given certain questions. Ross et al. [27] quite literally wrote a textbook about a variety of reference encounters, including face-to-face and virtual transactions. The authors synthesized their own research to create an instructional manual of librarians' best practices, including questioning behavior, etiquette, and other information. Both works maintain that certain behaviors, such as asking open-ended questions, using a polite demeanor, and creating multiple search iterations when appropriate, make for successful library reference work.

8.4.2 Computer-Mediated Communication

Of course, these days most of our communication happens electronically. Specifically, a lot of our information exchange and coordination activities are mediated by computers. Social presence theory [36] suggests that different communication media enable different levels of social presence experience. While face-to-face communication has the highest level of social presence, computer-mediated communication (CMC) has a considerably lower level of social presence due to its lack of nonverbal cues and reduced feedback.

Even within CMC, different modalities offer different advantages and disadvantages. Shah and Gonzalez-Ibanez [31] found that people who are in the same room while working on a search task tend to be more social, but less productive. People sitting remotely, on the other hand, were found to be more effective in finding and producing informational objects, but were less social. The authors also found differences between communication channels (text, audio, video) preferred by remotely located participants. It turns out that while video offers more "richness" for communication, people preferred to either ignore their friends' video or just have text and/or audio channels while working on a search task. Media richness theory [12] provides insights into various media channels, such as their capability to provide feedback in terms of the number of channels they support (e.g., audio, visual).

A lot more can be said about CMC's role in SIS and, in general, our everyday lives, but we will stop here for now. A more detailed review of CMC, along with relevant theories, is presented in Appendix A.

8.4.3 Peer-Driven Services

Peer-driven services include SNSs such as Facebook, Twitter, and LinkedIn, as well as more specialized sites that pertain to certain domains or populations. We already saw three categories of such services in Chap. 4. They include social, community-based, and collaborative services, primarily in the form of question-answering (Q&A).

Research into social Q&A has greatly expanded since users' widespread adoption of social networking platforms. According to Shah et al. [33], these tools utilize the features of users' social networking sites to facilitate question-answering. Morris et al. [22] identify SNSs as uniquely characterized by trust and personalization. Often, but not always, those who engage in SIS via social Q&A are working with friends, acquaintances, or other personally related figures. Increasingly, organizations such as libraries are utilizing SNSs to connect with users and answer their reference questions. Many SNSs also offer unique "folksonomy" classification systems in which content is assigned user-generated tags. Tsur and Rappoport [45] delve into the creation and development of hashtags within microblogging platforms. Other scholars, such as Zimmer [48], examine how information seekers conduct research within the confines of social media platforms.

According to Shah et al. [33], community-based online platforms include three essential components: a mechanism for information seekers to submit questions in natural languages, answerers or responders who actively submit answers to questions, and a community built around this exchange. Frequent and/or well-regarded users often moderate these sites. Community-based sites may be vertical—meaning they pertain to a specific topic—or horizontal, meaning they cover a broad range of topics. Examples of these virtual SIS spaces include Yahoo! Answers, Answerbag, and Brainly. Liu et al. [18], Harper et al. [15], Kim and Oh [16], and many others have devoted significant scholarship to these Q&A sites.

Shah et al. [33] define collaborative spaces as those that facilitate the ability to edit and improve the phrasing of a question and/or answers over time by collaborating with other users. WikiAnswers serves as a popular collaborative space in which anyone can edit site-wide content. These communities are often regulated by their users and encourage co-creation. Popular platforms, such as those available through Google Drive,[3] also allow for collaboration. Unlike WikiAnswers, Google Drive and similar services are typically used among peers or associates to complete a common task. These tools uniquely expand the potential for global collaboration and remote collaborative working opportunities. Shah [30] provides a comprehensive overview of this and other types of CIS, while scholars such as Fidel and Bruce [14], Cho and Lee [10], Blake and Pratt [8], and many others have studied CIS across platforms, life circumstances, and professional disciplines.

8.4.4 Expert-Driven Services

Expert-driven Q&A services are similar to peer-driven services in that they consist of the same three essential components, with one major difference: paid or volunteer experts provide answers. Google Answers (now defunct), online chat support provided by various companies, and virtual reference services conducted by

[3]https://www.google.com/drive.

librarians all exemplify expert-based Q&A. Scholars have paid particular attention to virtual reference in libraries. These services include IM ("chat"), email, text, and telephone communications.

A number of researchers have focused on expert-based collaborative spaces. Sears [29] conducted a study at Auburn University that analyzed one semester's chat reference questions answered by various librarians. She examined traits such as types of questions, types of users, and whether questions were directly related to the specific library's resources. She found that askers' queries could be sorted into a few distinct categories: reference questions, policy and procedural questions, and directional questions. Because about two-thirds of inquiries were not at a research level, she postulated that askers turn to chat services to satisfy brief information needs. She also found that answering librarians often went outside their immediate library network to find information.

Smyth [37] analyzed virtual reference questions using Sears's typology. She found that, while it did classify askers' questions, it did not sufficiently address users' competency or stage in the research cycle. She contended that online Q&A facilitated by librarians can provide a wealth of potential research material, as it creates literal transcripts that can be analyzed as opposed to the fleeting moments in face-to-face encounters. In their textbook, Ross et al. [27] capitalize on this idea to instruct readers about the elements of successful and unsuccessful virtual collaborative encounters.

More details on these services are covered in Sect. 4.2.3 of this book.

8.4.5 Social Live Streaming Services

Rapidly evolving technology necessitates that SIS researchers stay abreast of emerging tools and services. Such tools include social live streaming services (SLSSs), such as Periscope[4] and recently popularized SNSs like Snapchat.[5] Many users have already popularized Facebook's live streaming service[6] (Fig. 8.3) in contexts ranging from personal and professional events (wedding, conference) to sports and video blogging.

Though studies on these tools are in their infancy, some scholars have already drawn attention to live streaming's potential for information seeking and sharing. Scheibe et al. [28], for example, studied YouNow[7] users' actions to analyze information production behavior (i.e., broadcasting) and information reception behavior (i.e., watching streams and commenting on them). Findings indicate that users enjoy chatting during live streams and rewarding performers with emoticons. Like many

[4]https://www.periscope.tv.

[5]https://www.snapchat.com.

[6]https://live.fb.com.

[7]https://www.younow.com.

Fig. 8.3 Facebook live streaming service. Photo source: Christine und Hagen Graf. facebook. Retrieved from https://flic.kr/p/998Jrn

SNSs, but unlike many Q&A platforms, SLSS broadcasters are not anonymous. The ability for any user to broadcast their life in real time has tremendous potential ranging from entertainment to law enforcement accountability.

8.5 Summary

We have come full circle with this chapter. Throughout this book, we have explored different topics that comprise SIS and related areas such as CIS, co-search, social search, and Q&A services. Here, we brought them all together to talk about how these subjects are studied, evaluated, and implemented.

Methods for studying SIS systems, services, users, and content are not very different from general research methods used in social and computational sciences. What makes SIS research interesting and challenging is its unique blend of people and information. That's because these socially engaged users define information, and vice versa. So what we have is a moving target that is tangled with another moving target! When we design or evaluate an SIS system, we can't simply evaluate just the content (information) or user behaviors; they both go together and affect each other in ways not easily covered by a single measure of assessment. What we saw in this chapter are some of the common methods for meeting this challenge, and a few categories of systems and services that implement SIS. As we develop a better understanding of these tools, and as more and more people become increasingly comfortable in SIS environments, we are going to see larger and more innovative solutions for leveraging people's social engagement attributes to enhance information access, exchange, and production.

References

1. Adamic, L.A., Zhang, J., Bakshy, E., Ackerman, M.S.: Knowledge sharing and yahoo answers: everyone knows something. In: Proceedings of the 17th International Conference on World Wide Web, vol. 4, pp. 665–674. ACM, New York (2008)
2. Agichtein, E., Castillo, C., Donato, D., Gionis, A., Mishne, G.: Finding high-quality content in social media. In: Proceedings of the International Conference on Web Search and Web Data Mining - WSDM'08, pp. 183–194. ACM Press, New York (2008)
3. Aneiros, M., Estivill-Castro, V.: Usability of real-time unconstrained WWW-co-browsing for educational settings. In: The 2005 IEEE/WIC/ACM International Conference on Web Intelligence (WI'05), pp. 105–111. IEEE, New York (2005)
4. Baeza-Yates, R., Pino, J.A.: First step to formally evaluate collaborative work. In: Hayne, S.C., Prinz W. (eds.) Proceedings of the International ACM SIGGROUP Conference on Supporting Group Work, Phoenix, AZ, pp. 56–60. ACM, New York (1997)
5. Bates, M.J.: Information search tactics. J. Am. Soc. Inf. Sci. **30**(4), 205–214 (1979)
6. Belkin, N.J., Marchetti, P.G., Cool, C.: BRAQUE: design of an interface to support user interaction in information retrieval. Inf. Process. Manag. **29**(3), 325–344 (1993)
7. Bertrand, C., Bourdeau, L.: Research interviews by Skype: a new data collection method. In: Proceedings of the 9th European Conference on Research Methods for Business and Managements Studies, pp. 70–79. IE Business School, Madrid (2010)
8. Blake, C., Pratt, W.: Collaborative information synthesis I: a model of information behaviors of scientists in medicine and public health. J. Am. Soc. Inf. Sci. Technol. **57**(13), 1740–1749 (2006)
9. Bøyum, I., Aabø, S.: The information practices of business PhD students. New Libr. World **116**(3/4), 187–200 (2015)
10. Cho, H., Lee, J.S.: Collaborative information seeking in intercultural computer-mediated communication groups: testing the influence of social context using social network analysis. Commun. Res. **35**(4), 548–573 (2008)
11. Choi, E., Shah, C.: User motivations for asking questions in online Q&A services. J. Assoc. Inf. Sci. Technol. **67**(5), 1182–1197 (2016)
12. Daft, R.L., Lengel, R.H.: Information richness: a new approach to managerial behavior and organization design. Technical Report (1983)
13. Evans, B.M., Kairam, S., Pirolli, P.: Do your friends make you smarter?: an analysis of social strategies in online information seeking. Inf. Process. Manag. **46**(6), 679–692 (2010)
14. Fidel, R., Bruce, H.: Collaborative information retrieval. In: Proceedings of the ASIST Annual Meeting, p. 604 (1999)

15. Harper, F.M., Raban, D., Rafaeli, S., Konstan, J.A.: Predictors of answer quality in online Q&A sites. In: Proceedings of ACM CHI 2008 Conference on Human Factors in Computing Systems, vol. 1, pp. 865–874 (2008)
16. Kim, S., Oh, S.: Users' relevance criteria for evaluating answers in a social Q&A site. J. Am. Soc. Inf. Sci. Technol. **60**(4), 716–727 (2009)
17. Laurillau, Y., Nigay, L.: Clover architecture for groupware. In: Proceedings of the ACM Conference on Computer Supported Cooperative Work, New Orleans, LA, pp. 236–245 (2002)
18. Liu, Y., Bian, J., Agichtein, E.: Predicting information seeker satisfaction in community question answering. In: Proceedings of the 31st Annual International ACM SIGIR Conference on Research and Development in Information Retrieval - SIGIR'08 (Section 2), p. 483 (2008)
19. Luo, A., Olson, J.S.: Informal communication in collaboratories. In: CHI'06 Extended Abstracts on Human Factors in Computing Systems - CHI EA'06, p. 1043. ACM Press, New York (2006)
20. Lynch, M.J.: Reference interviews in public libraries. Libr. Q. **48**(2), 119–142 (1978)
21. Morris, M.R., Horvitz, E.: SearchTogether: an interface for collaborative Web search. In: Proceedings of the 2007 ACM Symposium on User Interface Software and Technology (UIST 2007), pp. 3–12. ACM Press, New York (2007)
22. Morris, M.R., Teevan, J., Panovich, K.: A comparison of information seeking using search engines and social networks. In: ICWSM, pp. 23–26 (2010)
23. O'Brien, H., Freund, L., Westman, S.: What motivates the online news browser? News items selection in a social information seeking scenario. Inf. Res. Int. Electron. J. **19**(3), 95 (2014)
24. Olson, G.M., Olson, J.S., Carter, M.R., Sorrosten, M.: Small group design meetings: an analysis of collaboration. Hum. Comput. Interact. **7**(4), 347–374 (1992)
25. Pickens, J., Golovchinsky, G., Shah, C., Qvarfordt, P., Back, M.: Algorithmic mediation for collaborative exploratory search. In: Proceedings of the 31st Annual International ACM SIGIR Conference: Research & Development in Information Retrieval, pp. 315–322 (2008)
26. Prekop, P.: A qualitative study of collaborative information seeking. J. Doc. **58**(5), 533–547 (2002)
27. Ross, C.S., Nilsen, K., Radford, M.: Conducting the Reference Interview: A How-to-Do-It Manual for Librarians, 2nd edn. Neal-Schuman, New York (2009)
28. Scheibe, K., Fietkiewicz, K.J., Stock, W.G.: Information behavior on social live streaming services. J. Inf. Sci. Theory Pract. **4**(2), 6–20 (2016)
29. Sears, J.: Chat reference service: an analysis of one semester's data. Issues Sci. Technol. Librariansh. **32**, 92001 (2001). Retrieved from http://www.istl.org/01-fall/article2.html?a_aid=3598aabf
30. Shah, C.: Collaborative information seeking: a literature review. Adv. Librariansh. **32**, 3–33 (2010)
31. Shah, C., Gonzalez-Ibanez, R.: Evaluating the synergic effect of collaboration in information seeking. In: Proceedings of the Annual ACM Conference on Research and Development in Information Retrieval (SIGIR), Beijing, pp. 913–922 (2011)
32. Shah, C., Marchionini, G.: Awareness in collaborative information seeking. J. Am. Soc. Inf. Sci. Technol. **61**(10), 1970–1986 (2010)
33. Shah, C., Oh, J.S., Oh, S.: Research agenda for social Q&A. Libr. Inf. Sci. Res. **31**(4), 205–209 (2009)
34. Shah, C., Pickens, J., Golovchinsky, G.: Role-based results redistribution for collaborative information retrieval. Inf. Process. Manag. **46**(6), 773–781 (2010)
35. Shah, C., Kitzie, V., Choi, E.: Modalities, motivations, and materials - investigating traditional and social online Q&A services. J. Inf. Sci. **40**(5), 669–687 (2014)
36. Short, J., Williams, E., Christie, B.: The Social Psychology of Telecommunications, vol. 7. Wiley, New York (1976)
37. Smyth, J.: Virtual reference transcript analysis: a few models. Searcher **11**(3), 26 (2003)
38. Smyth, B., Balfe, E., Briggs, P., Coyle, M., Freyne, J.: Collaborative Web search. In: Proceedings of the International Joint Conference on Artificial Intelligence (IJCAI), Acapulco, pp. 1417–1419. Morgan Kaufmann, San Francisco (2003)

39. Smyth, B., Balfe, E., Boydell, O., Bradley, K., Briggs, P., Coyle, M., Freyne, J.: A live-user evaluation of collaborative Web search. In: Proceedings of the International Joint Conference on Artificial Intelligence (IJCAI), Edinburgh, pp. 1419–1424 (2005)
40. Soulier, L., Shah, C., Tamine, L.: User-driven system-mediated collaborative information retrieval. In: Proceedings of the 37th International ACM SIGIR Conference on Research & Development in Information Retrieval - SIGIR'14, pp. 485–494. ACM Press, New York (2014)
41. Soulier, L., Tamine, L., Bahsoun, W.: On domain expertise-based roles in collaborative information retrieval. Inf. Process. Manag. **50**(5), 752–774 (2014)
42. Tashakkori, A., Teddlie, C.: Mixed Methodology: Combining Qualitative and Quantitative Approaches, vol. 46. SAGE Publications, Thousand Oaks (1998)
43. Tashakkori, A., Teddlie, C.: The past and future of mixed methods research: from data triangulation to mixed model design. In: Tashakkori, A., Teddlie, C. (eds.) Handbook of Mixed Methods in Social and Behavioral Research, pp. 671–702. SAGE Publications, Thousand Oaks (2003)
44. Tian, X.: Network domains in social networking sites: expectations, meanings, and social capital. Inf. Commun. Soc. **19**(2), 188–202 (2016)
45. Tsur, O., Rappoport, A.: What's in a hashtag?: content based prediction of the spread of ideas in microblogging communities. In: Proceedings of the Fifth ACM International Conference on Web Search and Data Mining, pp. 643–652 (2012)
46. Twidale, M.B., Nichols, D.M., Mariani, J.A., Rodden, T., Sawyer, P.: Supporting the active learning of collaborative database browsing techniques. Res. Learn. Technol. **3**(1), 75–79 (1995)
47. Wilson, M.L., schraefel, m.c.: Evaluating collaborative search interfaces with information seeking theory. In: Workshop on Collaborative Information Retrieval, Pittsburgh, PA (2008)
48. Zimmer, M.: "But the data is already public": on the ethics of research in Facebook. Ethics Inf. Technol. **12**(4), 313–325 (2010)

Chapter 9
Conclusion

Abstract This chapter provides some important concluding remarks about social information seeking (SIS) and related topics. We'll start by revisiting the concept and manifestation of SIS. Next we'll discuss a framework that synthesizes several of the concepts described in this book to show how individual, crowd-based, social, and collaborative activities around information behavior are associated. Then another framework is presented that incorporates various social and information behavior activities on different dimensions. This framework shows that there are several competing ways in which SIS studies and applications can be conceptualized and evaluated. Finally, the chapter provides a synthesis of challenges and opportunities for researchers and developers working in SIS. This synthesis could serve as a starting point for students and scholars interested in studying and supporting human behaviors that incorporate socio-collaborative and information seeking aspects.

9.1 Introduction

Let's start by revisiting our favorite figure in this book—the one with several interconnected domains (Fig. 9.1). The concepts represented in this figure are the ones we have explored in this book, and after seeing each of them individually, it's time to look at the big picture again.

What we see in this picture is essentially a set of basic human behaviors: collaborative, social, and informational. As we put different behaviors in various combinations and contexts, we discover the themes covered in this book: information seeking, social media/networking, question-answering (Q&A), social search, collaborative information seeking (CIS), and of course, social information seeking (SIS). In Chaps. 2–7, we gave individual treatment to each of these themes, and in Chap. 8 we brought them together to discuss how they are studied, supported, and evaluated.

And now that we have covered all of that in different combinations, it's time to look at things with a more holistic perspective. What do all these topics mean? How do they all connect? Where do we go from here? And that's what the current chapter will try to answer. We start by putting together different ideas we discovered in this book into synthesized frameworks.

C. Shah, *Social Information Seeking*, The Information Retrieval Series 38,
DOI 10.1007/978-3-319-56756-3_9

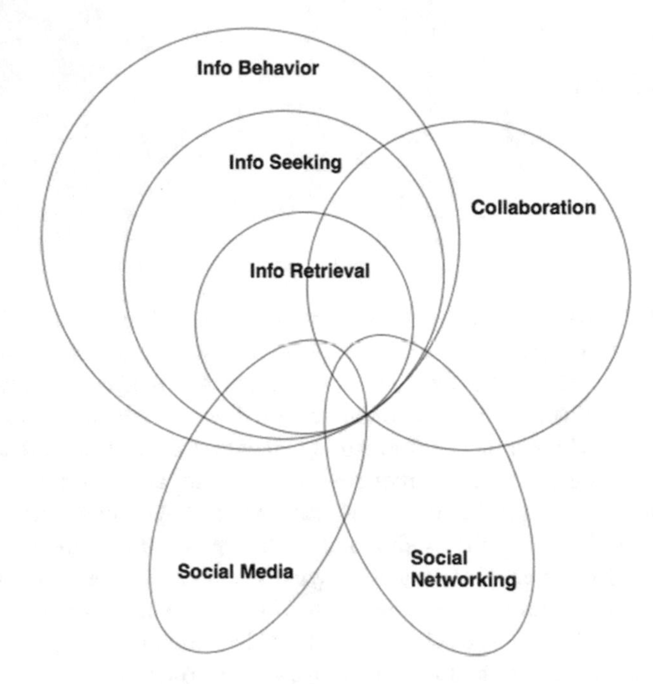

Fig. 9.1 A schematic view of larger concepts related to social information seeking (SIS)

9.2 Synthesis Frameworks with Social and Collaborative Dimensions

We begin by revisiting the C5 Model of collaboration [28]. As we saw in Chap. 6, there are five levels of people interacting with each other: communication, contribution, coordination, cooperation, and collaboration. Depending on the nature and the goal of interaction, a collective activity could fit into one or several of these levels. Chatting with a buddy to figure out when you could get together for a lunch fits both coordination and communication, whereas paying your taxes is an act of cooperation that includes communication (transferring your tax filing, getting confirmation in return), contribution (the tax you pay), and coordination (filing and contributing on a certain schedule and platform).

In Chap. 6, our objective was to use this model of collaboration to talk about CIS, but now we can expand that to think about all kinds of other activities that involve multiple people. Figure 9.2 provides a new framework that incorporates the C5 Model of collaboration with various social and informational activities and theories. Note that some of these theories are not covered in this book, but you can look at Appendix A for a brief overview.

This figure also incorporates the dimension of people participation (x-axis), which includes individual, crowd (where you are interacting with unknown people), social (where you are interacting with people you know), and collaboration ties. For

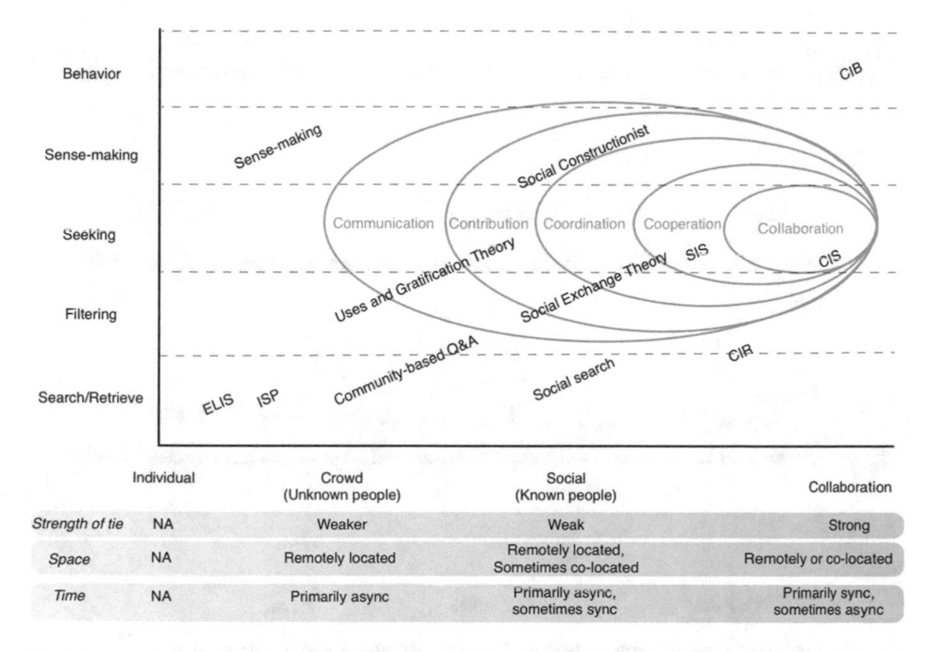

Fig. 9.2 A framework that depicts various related concepts using the C5 Model of collaboration [28], along with information seeking/behavior activities

each of these four options, the strength of the tie is considered to be a primary defining and differentiating factor. In addition, the classic “space” and “time” dimensions provide additional context to understand how these individual or group informational activities are carried out.

Having seen several frameworks for understanding SIS and CIS, it is easy to realize that the usefulness or validity of any of these depends on their context. Therefore, instead of trying to provide a comprehensive framework that fits all needs, we will enumerate various elements or dimensions of socio-collaborative systems here. One could, hopefully, pick and choose the elements needed to study or explain a given context for a socio-collaborative system from the list presented here (see the following subsections) and depicted in Figs. 9.3 and 9.4. Note that these figures and much of the description for these dimensions were presented previously by Shah [26].

9.2.1 Intent

This dimension describes the level of intention one has in a group process, or in other words, whether one explicitly defines their actions as social and/or collaborative. This dimension can be analyzed in the context of truly socio-collaborative systems, as well as those that merely serve as social or collaborative filtering systems.

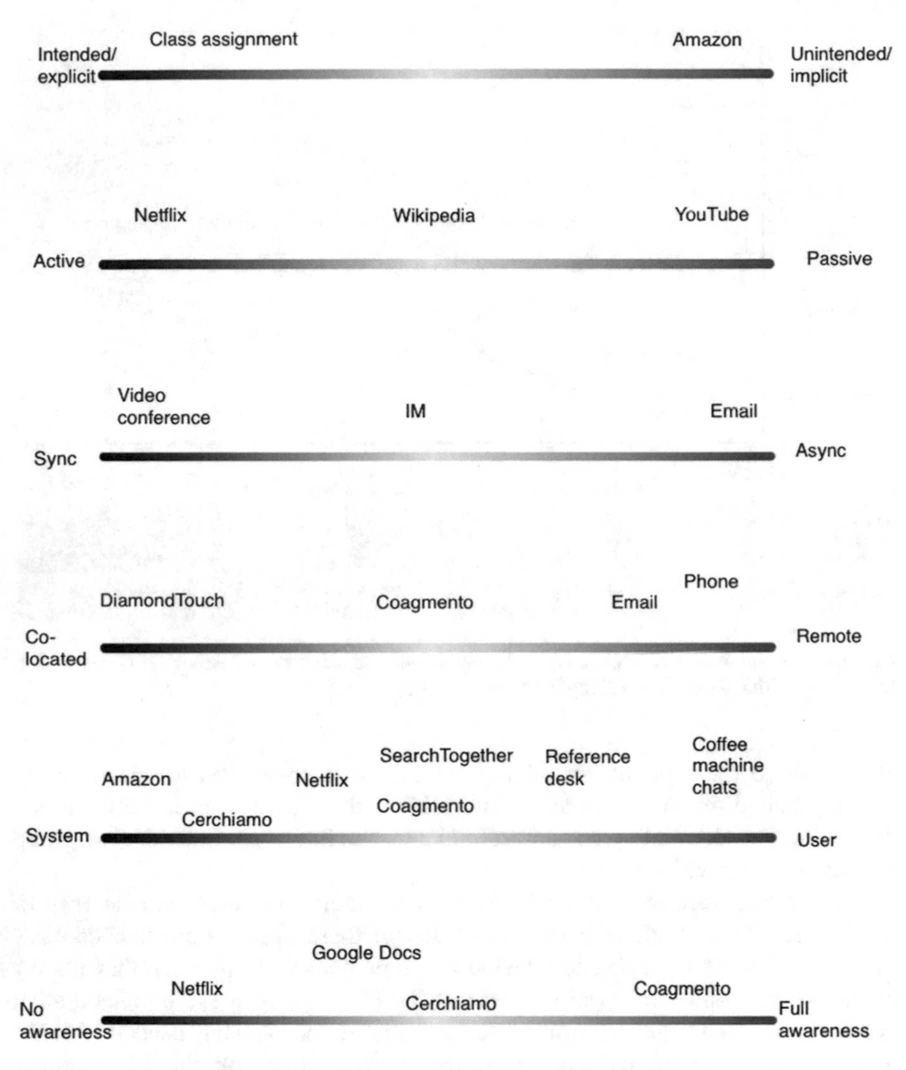

Fig. 9.3 A framework for socio-collaborative environments (part 1 of 2)

An intentional or explicitly defined group activity occurs when various aspects of the process are clearly stated and understood. For instance, a group of students working on a science project together knows (1) that they are collaborating and (2) who is responsible for specific tasks. A father who asks his sister to help him surprise his wife and kids with his family's cannoli recipe knows (1) that he is using his social connection and (2) what specifically he expects through this interaction. When such activities happen without explicit specifications, they can be considered

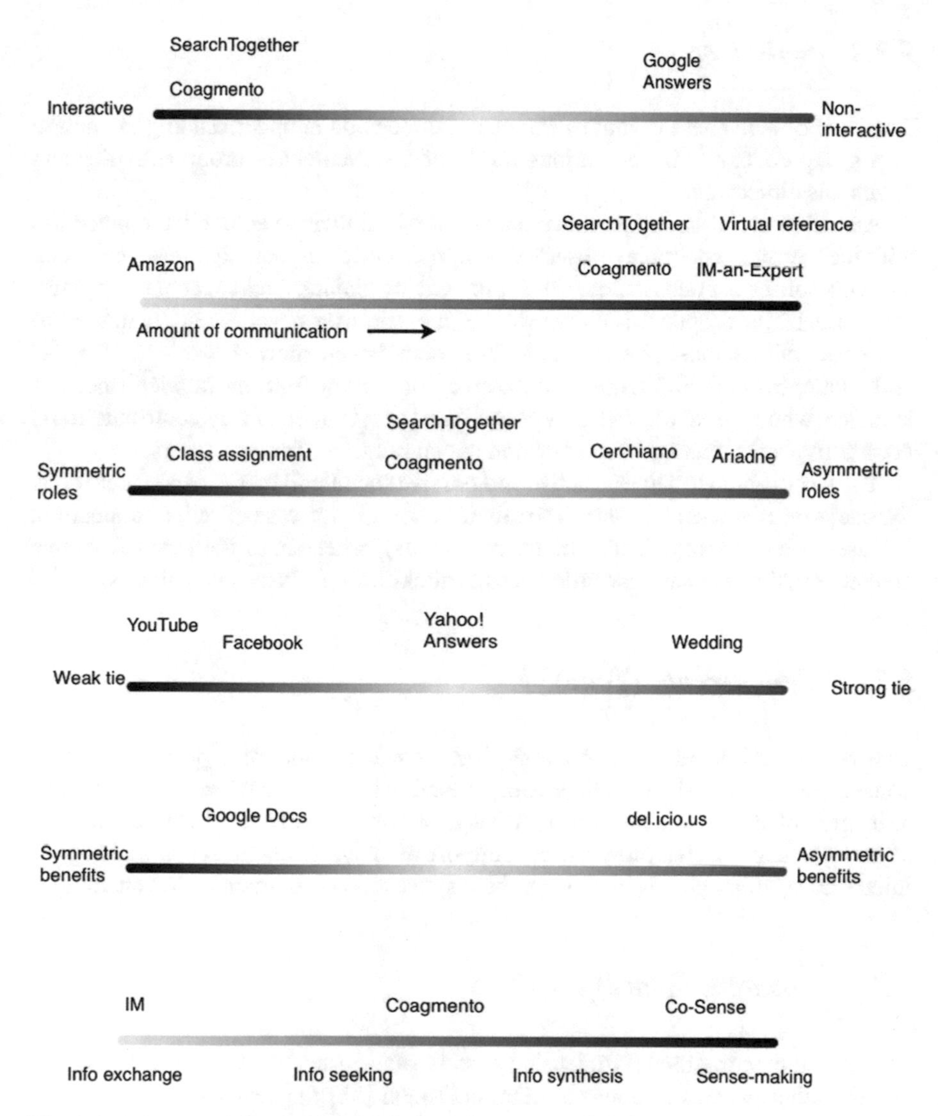

Fig. 9.4 A framework for socio-collaborative environments (part 2 of 2)

unintentional or implicitly defined. For instance, visitors to Amazon.com receive recommendations based on other people's searching and buying behavior without knowing those people. Early explorations of the potential benefits and problems with using implicit or unintentional actions in information interactions/filtering can be found in Nichols [22].

9.2.2 *Activeness*

The level of activeness is another important dimension in understanding the nature of a group endeavor. Users' various levels of involvement in group activities can frame this dimension.

An active social or collaborative connection is similar to an explicit connection with the key difference being a user's willingness and awareness. For instance, when a Netflix subscriber rates a movie, they are actively playing a part in connecting with other users. But despite this circumstance, the said user never explicitly agreed to work with others, most of whom they likely do not even know. A user's willingness and awareness also differentiates a passive connection from an implicit one. For instance, when a user watches a video on YouTube, they passively contribute to its popularity, thus affecting its ranking and social relevance for other users.

The key difference between active and passive social/collaborative connections is the user's willingness and control over their actions. In the case of active connection, the user agrees to participate (rating, comments), whereas, in the case of passive connection, the user has very little control (click-through, browsing patterns).

9.2.3 *Concurrency (Time)*

One of the traditional ways of classifying a socio-collaborative process is by its concurrency [11]. A videoconference or a meeting typically requires the participants to be present at the same time (synchronous), whereas email could help a team work asynchronously. A chat program can support both synchronous and asynchronous interactions, although it is intended to be a synchronous communication channel.

9.2.4 *Location (Space)*

This is another traditional dimension that is often used to place different socio-collaborative systems in context. DiamondTouch [31] requires the participants to be physically present around the system for a search session. SearchTogether [21] and Coagmento, on the other hand, facilitate searching and sharing among remotely located participants. See Shah and Gonzalez-Ibanez [29] for explorations on how the spatial aspect of collective work influences a socio-collaborative project's effectiveness.

9.2.5 *Role/Mediation of System and User*

Though a social and/or collaborative project can be entirely done by a group of people, it can also incorporate support from systems, such as computers and phones.

However, this dimension goes beyond that concept. In a socio-collaborative project, a system could mediate the interactions, in which case some underlying algorithm would drive the process. Alternatively, the people or the users of the system could do mediation themselves, making the system (if it is used) a passive component. Cerchiamo [10] is an example of the former, and Coagmento is an example of the latter.

9.2.6 *Level of Awareness*

Gaver [9] used awareness as a factor to identify different situations for people interacting and working together. He claimed that less awareness is needed for division of labor, and that more casual awareness can lead to serendipitous communication, which can beget stronger connections. An individual's or group's level of awareness, therefore, is an important dimension to consider.

The amount and the type of awareness present in a group environment depend on several factors, including cost/benefit analysis, available technology, and privacy. On one hand, services such as Netflix and Amazon connect multiple users without making them aware of one another. On Google Docs, one has workspace awareness, whereby group members can collaboratively work on their collective artifact without knowing who contributed what specifically. Cerchiamo provides a system-driven collaboration, where the users have limited and filtered access to their collaborators' actions and results. Coagmento, on the other extreme, provides a very transparent interface, in which a user can be aware of the task at hand, the shared workspace, and the group's history and products.

9.2.7 *Level of Interaction*

Again, to differentiate systems with very little or no user interaction from those that are highly interactive, we need a dimension that considers this factor to define the relative interactiveness of a given platform. Systems such as SearchTogether and Coagmento are designed to support interactive connections. Google Answers, on the other hand, was a noninteractive service, where the information seeker could pose their questions to experts and receive answers without going back and forth.

9.2.8 *Amount of Communication*

Similar to the level of interaction, socio-collaborative systems also vary in terms of the amount of communication that takes place among the participants. In fact, dimensions such as intention and communication could help us even determine if a given system is truly a socio-collaborative system. For instance, on Amazon, the users do not necessarily directly talk to accomplish a common goal. Systems such as Coagmento, on the other hand, provide explicit support for communication since the participants are expected to directly interact while working on their collective project. So where do we put Amazon? Well, if we look back to Fig. 9.2, we realize that there is something other than "social" and "collaborative," and that's "crowd," wherein people interact with strangers in a community.

9.2.9 User Roles

While an effective socio-collaborative connection must be democratic and inclusive—that is, it must be free from hierarchies of any kind and it must include all parties who have a stake in the problem [19]—different scenarios inevitably unfold among various groups of people, and we should consider their roles in such group activity.

Division of labor and combining diverse sets of skills are two of the most appealing aspects of socio-collaborative projects. Invariably, the former assumes symmetric roles, and the latter assumes asymmetric roles of the participants. For example, a group project for a class typically involves students who all have roughly the same background and skills. Ariadne [34], on the other hand, was designed to connect a patron to a reference librarian—each with a different background.

9.2.10 Strength of the Connection

As reflected in the literature review on social networking, tie strength differentiates a social group from a collaborative group. Often, one group can become the other as ties develop. A collaborative endeavor, for instance, could involve more or less of the social element.

Facebook is an SNS where connected users may not have strong ties or common goals. Coauthoring a research article, on the other hand, involves multiple parties who are more strongly bound together.

9.2.11 Balance of Benefits

This dimension stems from user roles as well as the strength of the connection. While typical collaboration is mutually beneficial for its participants, there can be a gradation of these benefits. Coauthoring a research article benefits all the involved authors, whereas one's collection of useful bookmarks on Delicious may benefit the author and the subscribers in different ways.

9.2.12 Usage of Information

This final dimension allows us to see how information flows in the system. Often, social and/or collaborative informational activities focus on information exchange. For example, many online help services use chat messengers. This dimension could also include information seeking, information synthesis, and sense-making. A socio-collaborative system could support one or several of these elements.

It is important to note that these twelve dimensions are not mutually exclusive. They have an interaction effect; i.e., fixing or altering one dimension changes the rest appropriately. For instance, if we fix the "Location" dimension to colocated as opposed to remote, our options for the "Concurrency" dimension are reduced to synchronous, as the participants engaged in the group activity are likely to be meeting with each other at the same place and time. If, on the other hand, the participants could not meet face-to-face (remotely located), they may use synchronous (e.g., chat) or asynchronous (e.g., email) communication. Several of the dimensions exhibit an apparent correlation. For instance, there is a high level of match between "Communication" and "System-user" dimensions.

9.3 Opportunities and Challenges in SIS

Now that we have looked at where things stand—both on theoretical and practical grounds—it's time to think about where we can go from here. There are many issues that still need to be addressed, and with that comes a unique set of opportunities and challenges. The following two subsections will take a detailed look at many of these theoretical and experimental issues in SIS, CIS, and related fields.

9.3.1 Theoretical Issues

For better or worse, a lot of work in SIS has happened organically. In other words, for the most part scholars recognized a need to fill some gap in our knowledge of human information seeking behaviors in social settings and then proceeded to address those gaps with ideas, methods, and tools. But now that we have been doing this for a while and know that it's not just a passing fad, it's time to rethink the foundational ideas for this quickly emerging field.

Currently there is a lack of comparable SIS theories and models similar to those developed by Belkin [3], Marchionini [20], and Wilson [36] to study individual information seeking behavior. Development of sustainable SIS models will depend on addressing some of the fundamental issues in the field, including user motivations and methods for establishing social ties, individual and group benefits, user roles, SIS system design challenges, and a number of aspects concerning the user and the system in an SIS environment.

Similarly, information synthesis and sense-making processes have been addressed in the context of individual information seeking but need to be identified and understood when people work with or through other people. We have models for information search process (ISP), such as the one by Kuhlthau [17, 18], and a mapping of this model onto SIS/CIS [14, 15, 27]. Similar extensions need to be explored that look beyond ISP toward other processes in a social/collaborative context.

If we take a step back and consider the larger idea of social and collaborative behaviors, a few researchers, such as Reddy and Jansen [24], have examined these topics in specific fields like health care. There is even a preliminary model on collaborative information behavior (CIB) by Karunakaran et al. [16] within the health-care sector. Such efforts need to be extended to encompass more situations and domains.

Of course, one needs to start somewhere more specific, and that's where some of the models and frameworks presented in this book, and specifically in this chapter, could come in handy. Take, for example, the C5 Model of collaboration [28] that was revisited earlier in this chapter to show how various social and collaborative activities associated with information seeking could be explained and studied.

Figure 9.5 provides a couple of such examples. If we look at the "communication" dimension of a socio-collaborative activity, we can think about issues such as understanding topics and intentions in that exchange, identifying which messages concern topic/work and which provide socio-emotional support, and extracting strategies expressed through people's interactions. Similarly, studying the "contribution" dimension may involve looking at issues of how people resolve conflict, what techniques and methods are used to achieve synergy (making 1+1>2), and how various ties are socially balanced.

These few examples only scratch the surface of SIS research potential. There are many other lenses through which one could look at these issues and even more methods to study them. Rather than enumerate all those possibilities, here we will provide a list of specific issues and questions on the theoretical front of SIS that we need to address next.

1. We have a fairly good understanding of why people want to socialize and why they may want to collaborate. However, people do not often take advantage of situations in which being connected in some way (social and collaborative) could work to their mutual benefit. Often, even if a social/collaborative tie could be useful, people do not see the value in working together. We need to identify such situations and learn to promote socio-collaborative connections. Similarly, the literature points us to a list of tools and methods used to forge connections. However, the relative merits of these tools and methods are not very clear. As we saw in this book, people often seek information with or through others using tools that were not specifically designed for such tasks. One could argue that we need specialized tools to support SIS, but we do not know what such tools may look like and how we could promote them to people without burdening them.

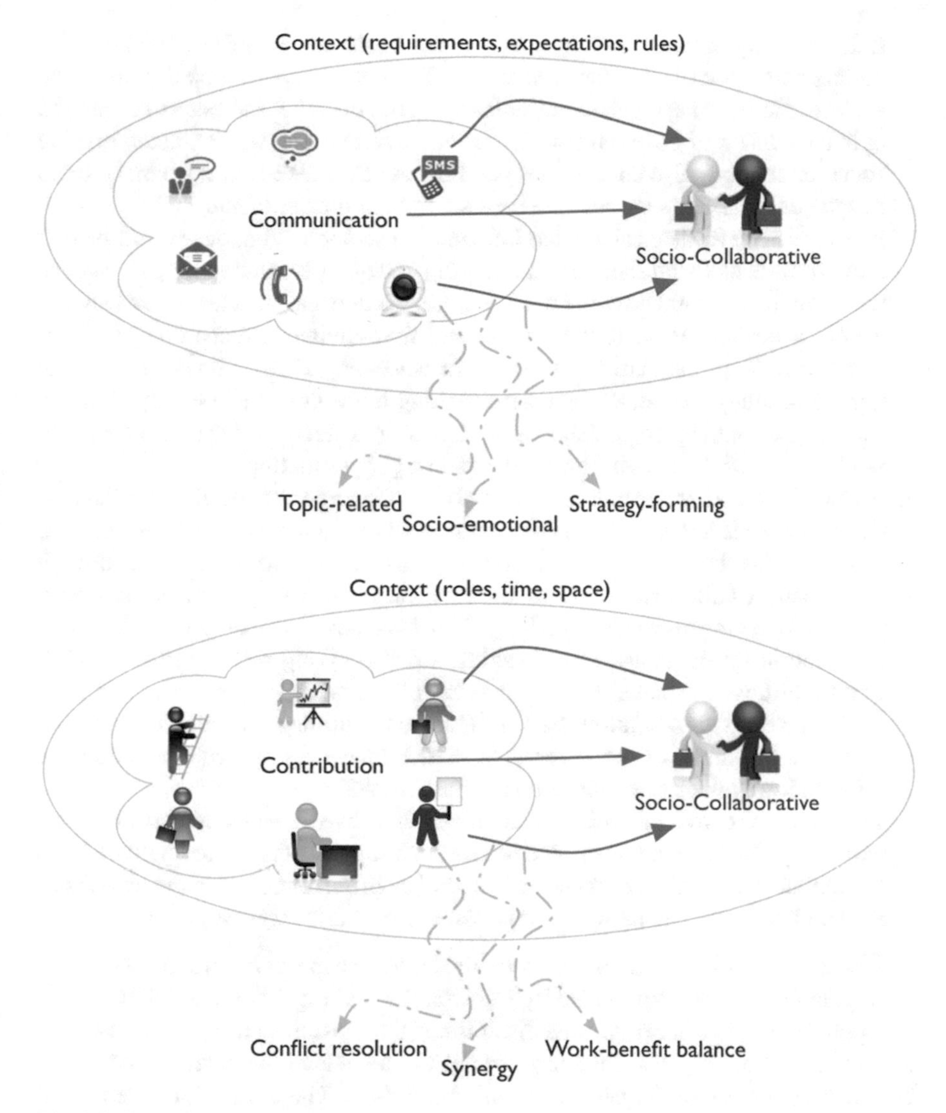

Fig. 9.5 Examples of how elements of the C5 Model could be used to address missing knowledge in different contexts

2. We have seen a number of undertakings that seek to understand how people work with socio-collaborative systems such as SearchTogether [21] and Coagmento [25], as well as how they behave in online communities and social networking sites [5, 6]. As of yet, there is no connecting link between these two environments. In other words, we do not know how we can leverage people's engagement in SNSs to promote collaborations or support various social activities with collaborative systems.

3. It is currently unclear how to measure the costs and benefits of having and maintaining social and collaborative ties. There are ways to look at things like social anxiety [35] and collaborative load [8], but these "costs" need to be looked at in the context of potential benefits. Because in real life, we don't stop making social or collaborative connections just because they take effort; we make them in spite of those costs because we have something greater to gain.
4. It is necessary to determine what information seeking situations would benefit most from establishing and/or maintaining social/collaborative ties, as well as what situations would be better off. We acknowledge that such ties are not always useful or desired; it would be helpful and time-saving to focus on only those situations where they are intentional and beneficial. Further investigations are needed to study the situations where making these ties is potentially harmful. This understanding could help us complete a better cost-benefit analysis of working in social and collaborative tasks in a given situation.
5. As identified earlier, we must determine how to incorporate social and collaborative dimensions into individual information seeking, synthesis, and sense-making models. This book focused on people working toward goals met through social and/or collaborative information seeking, and so much of our attention was focused on information seeking. But it is possible that certain forms of information synthesis and sense-making are also taking place during SIS/CIS. For simplification's sake, here such possibilities were ignored, but they need further investigation in future studies. This book outlined several traditional and emerging SIS and CIS frameworks. Similar frameworks for socio-collaborative information synthesis and sense-making are needed.
6. The ability to convert a social tie into a collaborative tie and vice versa is worth exploring. The literature presented in this book suggests that there might be ways to facilitate collaborative processes in social environments. Given the ubiquitous nature of online social networks, this issue merits further investigation.

While SIS is still trying to take a more defined shape as a field and lacks the strong theoretical foundation held by information seeking and related fields, there are opportunities to learn from other disciplines' theories and concepts. For instance, we could look at cognitive load theory [32] to understand the extent to which an individual plans to participate in an SIS interaction. There are also several rich theories that we could borrow from computer-mediated communication (CMC) to develop a communication-focused theoretical framework for SIS. For instance, the media richness theory [7] considers media outlets and content according to their ability to provide feedback in terms of the number of channels they support (e.g., audio, visual). This can be useful in understanding the effectiveness or appropriateness of using a particular communication channel during a socio-collaborative project set within a given time-space situation (see, e.g., [12]).

9.3.2 *Experimental and Practical Issues*

Since SIS has emerged as an interdisciplinary field, it is no surprise that it has borrowed methods and experimental frameworks from IR, HCI, and CSCW, among others. Some of the most common methods for conducting experiments have been laboratory studies, interviews, surveys, observations, and to some extent field studies and simulations. There are opportunities to explore other ways to collect and analyze data that are more tailored to SIS research needs. Following are some of the pressing issues concerning experimental and practical aspects of SIS and/or CIS research.

1. Several of the research studies reported in the literature are targeted toward specific populations—college students, professionals in social sciences, and knowledge workers. Investigations are needed to study other specialized populations, such as families with health issues or intelligence analysts working in teams. These future studies could employ different research methods, including cognitive walk-throughs and empirical observations.
2. The laboratory studies employed by many researchers can be extended to field studies, allowing the participants to work without some of the limitations of a controlled laboratory setting. The participants in a field study could work with the system as they please, creating their own projects of interest and initiating connections with their colleagues and friends as they see fit. If we run a field study over a long period of time (at least a few weeks), we could study long-term adoption effects, appropriation factors, and system-based feature's specializations.
3. Similarly, while content analysis-based methods are quite prominent with studies borderlining social media, those are often not sufficient to answer the "why" question. Such studies should be complemented using methods that could provide richer data (albeit at the expense of scale) such as surveys and interviews. In essence, there is a dire need for mixed-method approaches.
4. It would be prudent to determine what type of visualization methods can be useful for SIS and CIS interfaces. Systems such as Mr Taggy [4], SearchTogether [21], and Coagmento [25] provide a very basic interface for viewing personal and shared information. During participatory design sessions that Shah et al. [30] conducted, however, the issue of having new kinds of dynamic and interactive interfaces appeared highly important. This issue deserves more advance treatment with interface designs and experimentation.
5. Given a specific domain, we should determine what additional tools are required to enhance existing methods of people working with and through others. Such domains may include office environments, educational settings, or even domestic projects. We know that extending an individual information seeking process to SIS/CIS requires two things: (1) we need to create a support system that connects the participants and makes it easy for them to communicate; and (2)

we need to provide appropriate and adequate awareness.[1] Such requirements and specifications may vary from domain to domain.

6. By considering a pair/team/community, as opposed to an individual, as the unit of analysis, we can extend analyses done for many of the socio-collaborative experiments. Though fostering groups of all sizes and studying their respective dynamics can be a very complex procedure, it can provide us with very insightful details into how people connect with one another and what type of support they need to make those connections more effective and engaging.
7. A few researchers offer suggestions for evaluating an SIS/CIS system as well as users' performance while working with such a system (e.g., [2]). However, there is still a debate to determine what factors we should measure and how. These likely depend on the application's domain. For instance, for a time-bound recall-oriented task such as the one reported in Pickens et al. [23], we can use relevance and efficiency as measures. But, such metrics may not be appropriate for an education setting, where learning is probably a more important factor to measure. We need a taxonomy of evaluation metrics for different SIS/CIS situations.
8. Once again, SIS can benefit from other related fields for further work concerning such system design, development, and deployment issues. For instance, Grudin's [13] guidelines for groupware system developers are still both valid and relevant to those building and evaluating SIS systems.

In the end, we need to think about the future of SIS in two ways: it can help us address information seeking problems using social connections—something that is not easy or even possible through conventional methods of information seeking as we saw in this book—and it can provide us with opportunities that haven't existed thus far. Most of the discussions in this section focused on the former, but it's important to keep the latter case in mind as well.

For example, students are increasingly using online crowdsourcing and social networking services to look for help, opinions, and ideas. A 2011–2012 analysis of 28 million course papers submitted to Turnitin [33] revealed that social networking and other user-generated content sites were cited in 23% of the papers written by students in higher education institutions. The same report also lists online Q&A sites such as Yahoo! Answers and WikiAnswers as second only to Wikipedia among sources used by students (p.6). It's impossible to forbid students from doing this, and so instead of trying to stop them (as some teachers do) from using such online resources, we may want to help them make the most out of such methods. In fact, we should even encourage this behavior. The Association of College and Research Libraries (ACRL) Information Literacy Standards Task Force [1] recommends that the next iteration of the standards must acknowledge the role of students as content creators and curators and acknowledge the value of information in diverse formats.

[1]Note that awareness is not all that important for crowd-based and community-based services. It's more important to know the online status of a friend you are chatting with than a stranger on a Q&A service.

Acknowledging and understanding people's SIS and CIS behaviors in education settings could help us leverage students' socio-collaborative ties for the betterment of their information seeking, synthesis, and sense-making activities, leading to better learning experiences and outcomes.

Of course, this is easier said than done. But that's where we should go—looking to unravel more opportunities and possibilities at places and in domains where we haven't traditionally thought about incorporating, extending, and leveraging social and collaborative aspects of human behavior.

References

1. ACRL: Association of College and Research Libraries: Information Literacy Competency Standards Task Force Recommendations (2014)
2. Baeza-Yates, R., Pino, J.A.: First step to formally evaluate collaborative work. In: Hayne, S.C., Prinz W. (eds.) Proceedings of the International ACM SIGGROUP Conference on Supporting Group Work, Phoenix, AZ, pp. 56–60. ACM, New York (1997)
3. Belkin, N.: Anomalous states of knowledge as a basis for information retrieval. Can. J. Inf. Sci. **5**, 133–143 (1980)
4. Chi, Ed.H.: Information seeking can be social. Computer **42**(3), 42–46 (2009)
5. Choi, E., Shah, C.: Asking for more than an answer: What do askers expect in online Q&A services? J. Inf. Sci. **42**(2), 0165551516645530 (2016)
6. Choi, E., Shah, C.: User motivations for asking questions in online Q&A services. J. Assoc. Inf. Sci. Technol. **67**(5), 1182–1197 (2016)
7. Daft, R.L., Lengel, R.H.: Information richness - a new approach to managerial behavior and organization design. Res. Organ. Behav. **6**, 191–233 (1984)
8. Fidel, R., Mark Pejtersen, A., Cleal, B., Bruce, H.: A multidimensional approach to the study of human-information interaction: a case study of collaborative information retrieval. J. Am. Soc. Inf. Sci. Technol. **55**(11), 939–953 (2004)
9. Gaver, W.W.: Technology affordances. In: Proceedings of the SIGCHI Conference: Human Factors in Computing Systems, pp. 79–84 (1991)
10. Golovchinsky, G., Adcock, J., Pickens, J., Qvarfordt, P., Back, M.: Cerchiamo: a collaborative exploratory search tool. In: Proceedings of Computer Supported Cooperative Work (CSCW). ACM Press, New York (2008)
11. Golovchinsky, G., Pickens, J., Back, M.: A taxonomy of collaboration in online information seeking (2009). Preprint, arXiv:0908.0704
12. González-Ibáñez, R., Haseki, M., Shah, C.: Time and space in collaborative information seeking: the clash of effectiveness and uniqueness. In: Annual Meeting of the American Society for Information Science & Technology (ASIST), Baltimore, MD (2012)
13. Grudin, J.: Groupware and social dynamics: eight challenges for developers. Commun. ACM **37**(1), 92–105 (1994)
14. Hyldegård, J.: Collaborative information behaviour: exploring Kuhlthau's information search process model in a group-based educational setting. Inf. Process. Manag. **42**(1), 276–298 (2006)
15. Hyldegård, J.: Beyond the search process: exploring group members' information behavior in context. Inf. Process. Manag. **45**(1), 142–158 (2009)
16. Karunakaran, A., Reddy, M.C., Spence, P.R.: Toward a model of collaborative information behavior in organizations. J. Am. Soc. Inf. Sci. Technol. **64**(12), 2437–2451 (2013)
17. Kuhlthau, C.C.: Seeking Meaning: A Process Approach to Library and Information Services. Ablex Publishing, Norwood (1994)

18. Kuhlthau, C.C.: Towards collaboration between information seeking and information retrieval. Inf. Res. Int. Electron. J. **10**(2), 225 (2005)
19. London, S.: Collaboration and Community. http://scottlondon.com/reports/ppcc.html (1995)
20. Marchionini, G.: Information-seeking strategies of novices using a full-text electronic encyclopedia. J. Am. Soc. Inf. Sci. **40**(1), 54–66 (1989)
21. Morris, M.R., Horvitz, E.: SearchTogether: an interface for collaborative Web search. In: Proceedings of the 2007 ACM Symposium on User interface software and technology (UIST 2007), pp. 3–12. ACM Press, New York (2007)
22. Nichols, D.M.: Implicit rating and filtering. In: Proceedings of the 5th DELOS Workshop on Filtering and Collaborative Filtering, Budapest, pp. 31–36 (1997)
23. Pickens, J., Golovchinsky, G., Shah, C., Qvarfordt, P., Back, M.: Algorithmic mediation for collaborative exploratory search. In: Proceedings of the 31st Annual International ACM SIGIR Conference: Research & Development in Information Retrieval, pp. 315–322 (2008)
24. Reddy, M.C., Jansen, B.J.: A model for understanding collaborative information behavior in context: a study of two healthcare teams. Inf. Process. Manag. **44**(1), 256–273 (2008)
25. Shah, C.: Collaborative information seeking: a literature review. Adv. Librariansh. **32**, 3–33 (2010)
26. Shah, C.: Collaborative Information Seeking: The Art and Science of Making the Whole Greater than the Sum of All. Information Retrieval Series. Springer, Berlin (2012)
27. Shah, C., Gonzalez-Ibanez, R.: Exploring information seeking processes in collaborative search tasks. In: Annual Meeting of the American Society for Information Science, Pittsburgh, PA (2010)
28. Shah, C., Leeder, C.: Exploring collaborative work among graduate students through the C5 model of collaboration: a diary study. J. Inf. Sci. **42**(5), 609–629 (2015)
29. Shah, C., Gonzalez-Ibanez, R.: Spatial context in collaborative information seeking. J. Inf. Sci. **38**(4), 333–349 (2012)
30. Shah, C., Radford, M.L., Connaway, L.S.: Collaboration and synergy in hybrid Q&A: participatory design method and results. Libr. Inf. Sci. Res. **37**(2), 92–99 (2015)
31. Smeaton, A.F., Lee, H., Foley, C., Givney, S.M., Gurrin, C.: Físchlár-DiamondTouch: collaborative video searching on a table. In: SPIE Electronic Imaging - Multimedia Content Analysis, Management, and Retrieval, San Jose, CA, vol. 6073 (2006)
32. Sweller, J.: Cognitive load during problem solving: effects on learning. Cogn. Sci. **12**(2), 257–285 (1988)
33. Turnitin: The Sources in Student Writing - Secondary Education. Technical Report (2013)
34. Twidale, M.B., Nichols, D.M.: Collaborative browsing and visualization of the search process. Aslib Proc. **48**, 177–182 (1996)
35. Watson, D., Friend, R.: Measurement of social-evaluative anxiety. J. Consult. Clin. Psychol. **33**(4), 448–457 (1969)
36. Wilson, T.D.: Models in information behaviour research. J. Doc. **55**(3), 249–270 (1999)

Appendix A
Computer-Mediated Communication (CMC)

Communication has been recognized as a core component of coordination, cooperation, and collaboration [5, 8, 22]. We also saw that while communication is an essential element of social and collaborative activities, it is not sufficient, and that one could simply study communication without guaranteeing any higher-level processes such as coordination or collaboration. Here we will review several theories related to computer-mediated communication (CMC), several of which can inform computer-mediated collaboration, whereas others stand on their own for explaining communication itself.

The widespread use of communication technologies has brought about new forms of socio-collaborative work. Social and collaborative activities can be performed through various communication media (e.g., email, IM, audio, video) and vary on several dimensions including concurrency (synchronous vs. asynchronous) and location (colocated vs. distributed) [7, 17]. Literature suggests that such work demands extensive information sharing, coordination, awareness [23], and division of labor and persistence [14]. Theories and studies within the context of CMC can explain how different communication media (e.g., email, audio, video) across varying dimensions (e.g., synchronous vs. asynchronous, colocated vs. distributed) can facilitate or hinder interaction and collaboration, and thereby performance of teams. This section outlines some of CMC theories to help understand such potential and shortcomings of various communication contexts within the framework of SIS.

A.1 Social Presence Theory

Social presence theory is one of the earliest theories in CMC, which can explain the kind of interactions during a socio-collaborative work. Presence is considered an integral part of mediated environments. Social presence is defined as the degree to

C. Shah, *Social Information Seeking*, The Information Retrieval Series 38,
DOI 10.1007/978-3-319-56756-3

which a person is aware of another person in a mediated communication context [24]. This theory suggests that different communication media enable different levels of social presence experience. While face-to-face (F2F) communication has the highest level of social presence, CMC has a considerably lower level of social presence due to lack of nonverbal cues and reduced feedback. Since SIS requires extensive communication for information sharing and awareness, contexts with low social presence such as those in distributed and asynchronous dimensions may require extra efforts to compensate the limited affordances of these dimensions or may call for additional system features to facilitate communication and awareness. Early research also suggests that social presence is related to increased satisfaction [9, 21], but there is also evidence that a misfit between the medium and a task's social need can negatively influence the experience of social presence [3] and communication performance [13]. Along these lines, there must be a fit between an SIS task and the degree of social presence to increase the outcomes of collaboration, and systems should support the necessary level of social presence. For example, simple tasks with unambiguous answers benefit from media which have only low social presence, while judgment tasks call for media which allow high social presence [3].

A.2 Media Richness Theory

Another theory in CMC is media richness theory [4] which considers media according to their capability to provide feedback in terms of the number of channels they support (e.g., audio, visual). "Rich" media such as F2F communication allow excessive information, whereas "lean" media like text allows little. The main argument in this theory is that there is a match between the equivocality of communication tasks and the communication media. More specifically, the more equivocal the communication task, the richer the media it calls for.

Early research has sorted out certain task categories in terms of their need for information richness [12, 20] and has showed mixed findings on the need for information richness with regard to a task in collaborative work. A recent literature review suggests that collaborative work demands extensive information sharing, coordination, and awareness [23], and significant amounts of coordination require richer media [26]. Past studies have found that F2F and audio-only interactions do not differ in terms of task outcome for problem-solving tasks [2], but participants' performance on design tasks was significantly better in F2F, copresent than audio-only, remote conditions [16]. Other studies could not find any advantages for using video-mediated communication (VMC) in collaborative environments [1, 16, 30]. In contrast, social tasks, involving negotiation or conflict resolution, show some benefits of F2F or VMC [6] not for task outcome but for increased participant satisfaction [16]. More recent studies testing the effectiveness of CMC compared to F2F in collaborative working found CMC to be more effective (e.g., [10]), which can be explained by the task-oriented nature of CMC.

The task-oriented nature of CMC was also shown in the early studies of CMC. Walther [28] investigated the effects of CMC on social relationships and found that the impersonal style of communication in CMC was reduced when participants had enough time to complete their task. Several studies in the CMC literature showed that certain personal communication was lower in CMC than F2F highlighting the task-oriented nature of CMC. For example, one study showed that task performance of CMC participants was initially poorer when compared to the performance of verbal interactions, but improved as they gained experience of the CMC context [15]. Participants in this study adopted a specific way of giving directions, where they were more precise compared to F2F interactions. Along with these lines, individuals working collaboratively on an information seeking task may find different ways for communicating awareness or search findings when encountered with communication constraints in contexts such as text chat.

A.3 Social Information Processing (SIP) Theory

The SIP theory of CMC interaction [29] assumes that communicators in CMC can reduce interpersonal uncertainty, form impressions, and develop affinity in online settings as they can do in F2F context and rejects the view that the absence of nonverbal cues restricts the communicators' capability to exchange information. SIP theory posits that communicators exchange social information through the content, style, and timing of online messages. The rate of information exchange is slower online due to instrumental and relational constraints as well as inefficiency in communicating online. When time is limited, interaction can be expected to be impersonal and task oriented; and when not restricted communicators can reach levels of impression and relational development just like they would in F2F settings.

Some early studies considered the relative availability of higher-order information seeking strategies in CMC and F2F. Studies of initial interactions in F2F settings have identified several distinct types and subtypes of information seeking strategies. For instance, Tidwell and Walther [27] argued that, unlike F2F settings, online systems offer individuals only limited opportunities to observe others unobtrusively or to gain information about them indirectly. They further argued that if CMC users adapt available cues to perform interpersonal functions, then they would rely on interactive strategies to a greater extent in CMC than in F2F settings. They examined the information seeking strategies of CMC and F2F dyads engaged in acquaintance and decision-making tasks. Their results support the adaptation view that CMC users employed a greater proportion of self-disclosures and questions than did F2F partners. Additionally, the correspondence between the frequency of the interactive strategies and partners' ratings of one another's communication effectiveness was significantly more positive in CMC than in F2F communication. Along with SIP theory, F2F partners seem to draw on visual, auditory, and verbal cues at their disposal, and CMC partners adjust their strategies for effective interpersonal information acquisition. Later, the theory took also into consideration the variations in the motivation to reduce uncertainty across different types of media and anticipated future interaction in predicting interactions in CMC.

A.4 Social Identification/De-Individuation (SIDE) Theory

SIDE theory assumes that CMC's lack of nonverbal cues filters out interpersonal and individual identity information [11]. CMC may promote de-individuation by reducing the number of channels that are used for personal interaction. De-individuation is defined as the process whereby submergence in a group produces loss of identity for individuals [18]. Communicating without nonverbal information, and in physical isolation, promotes greater group identification and self-categorization in line with social identity. CMC groups interpret the content of others' messages as signals for creating or reinforcing group norms [11]. When CMC context makes group identity salient, individuals overly attribute similarity and common norms, resulting in social attraction to the group and group members. A recent study revealed that the text-only users developed greater group-based self-categorizations, which affect group attraction which was indirectly affected through increased stereotyping of out-group members [19].

A.5 Hyperpersonal Communication Model

Walther [28] argued that four sets of effects, namely, sender, receiver, channel, and feedback, may create *hyperpersonal communication* that goes beyond the interpersonal interaction in F2F context. Receiver and source effects come from the roles individuals play in the communication process. The channel facilitates goal-enhancing messages by allowing greater control over message construction than is available in F2F context. A CMC user may take his/her time in reviewing and editing message and may take advantage of an asynchronous channel to effectively consider responses. Asynchronous channels also allow individuals to exchange social comments more easily in task-oriented settings. Finally, hyperpersonal feedback may allow receivers to send selective messages.

Numerous empirical studies in CMC literature demonstrated that the use of email and computer conferencing reduced interpersonal affect and group solidarity. Experiments with groups with no history working on a task in a limited time showed that CMC was more task oriented than were F2F meetings. CMC was significantly higher than F2F on certain social categories of conversation, leading to conclusions about the task-oriented nature of CMC. Walther [28] suggested that within the context of group decision-making, reduced socio-emotional communication and increased task orientation can enhance group work. In addition, impersonal communication can lead group members to use a greater proportion of their work time for instrumental tasks. As socio-emotional concerns such as conflict take time and effort away from task resolution, any mechanism that reduces the need to expend effort should enhance the efficiency of a group's efforts. A study on a problem-solving discussion confirmed this notion with a finding of an inverse relationship between the frequency of personal remarks and decision-making success in CMC

[25]. In other words, groups do not accomplish as much work on a task when they generate great amounts of conversation over the communication medium [25].

A.6 Summary

CMC theories present different perspectives toward the benefits of collaborative information seeking in CMC. Team members can benefit from varying affordances of media at different times of an SIS task. On one hand, team members may especially desire a rich media with high social presence, at the beginning of a task when they perform brainstorming and decision-making on strategy and division of labor. In that sense, initial synchronous and collocated or audio-supported media context may foster such interactions. After the strategy is determined and responsibilities are shared, on the other hand, individuals may gain the advantages of lean media with low social presence as impersonal communication generated by CMC allows group members to focus most of their time and efforts on instrumental task increasing efficiency. Therefore, distributed and asynchronous contexts may generate affordances that would be advantageous for team members working separately on their assigned parts of the task. However, since awareness is an integral part of an SIS task, the communication context should still enable members to exchange information so as to know each other's steps. Altogether, theories of CMC can inform us on the guidelines to design better systems that would improve the outcomes of teams working on an SIS task.

References

1. Anderson, A., Newlands, A., Mullin, J., Mariefleming, A., Dohertysneddon, G., Vandervelden, J.: Impact of video-mediated communication on simulated service encounters. Interact. Comput. **8**(2), 193–206 (1996)
2. Chapanis, A., Ochsman, R.B., Parrish, R.N., Weeks, G.D.: Studies in interactive communication. I – The effects of four communication modes on the behavior of teams during cooperative problem-solving. Hum. Factors **14**(6), 487–509 (1972)
3. Chou, S., Min, H.: The impact of media on collaborative learning in virtual settings: the perspective of social construction. Comput. Educ. **52**(2), 417–431 (2009)
4. Daft, R.L., Lengel, R.H.: Information Richness. A New Approach to Managerial Behavior and Organization Design. Research in Organizational Behavior, pp. 191–223. JAI Press, Greenwich (1984)
5. Denning, P.J., Yaholkovsky, P.: Getting to "We". Commun. ACM **51**(4), 19–24 (2008)
6. Fish, R.S., Kraut, R.E., Root, R.W., Rice, R.E.: Evaluating video as a technology for informal communication. In: Proceedings of the SIGCHI Conference on Human Factors in Computing Systems CHI 92, pp. 37–48 (1992)
7. Golovchinsky, G., Pickens, J., Back, M.: A taxonomy of collaboration in online information seeking. In: Proceedings of JCDL 2008 Workshop on Collaborative Exploratory Search, Pittsburgh, PA, June (2008)

8. Gray, B.: Collaborating: Finding Common Ground for Multiparty Problems. Jossey-Bass, London (1989)
9. Hostetter, C., Busch, M.: Measuring up online: the relationship between social presence and student learning satisfaction. J. Scholarsh. Teach. Learn. **6**(2), 1–12 (2006)
10. Lantz, A.: Meetings in a distributed group of experts: comparing face-to-face, chat and collaborative virtual environments. Behav. Inform. Technol. **20**(2), 111–117 (2001)
11. Lea, M., Spears, R.: Computer-mediated communication, de-individuation and group decision-making. Int. J. Man Mach. Stud. **34**(2), 283–301 (1991)
12. McGrath, J.E., Arrow, H., Gruenfeld, D.H., Hollingshead, A.B., O'Connor, K.M.: Groups, tasks, and technology the effects of experience and change. Small Group Res. **24**(3), 406–420 (1993)
13. Mennecke, B.E., Valacich, J.S., Wheeler, B.C.: The effects of media and task on user performance: a test of the task-media fit hypothesis. Group Decis. Negot. **9**(6), 507–529 (2000)
14. Morris, M.R., Horvitz, E.: SearchTogether: an interface for collaborative web search. In: ACM Symposium on User Interface Software and Technology (UIST), Newport, RI, pp. 3–12, October (2007)
15. Newlands, A., Anderson, A.H., Mullin, J.: Adapting communicative strategies to computer-mediated communication: an analysis of task performance and dialogue structure. Appl. Cogn. Psychol. **17**(3), 325–348 (2003)
16. Olson, J.S., Olson, G.M., Meader, D.K.: What Mix of Video and Audio is Useful for Small Groups Doing Remote Real-Time Design Work?, pp. 362–368. ACM Press, Denver (1995)
17. Pickens, J., Golovchinsky, G.: Collaborative exploratory search. In: Proceedings of Workshop on Human-Computer Interaction and Information Retrieval, pp. 21–22. MIT CSAIL, Cambridge, MA, October (2007)
18. Postmes, T., Spears, R., Lea, M.: Breaching or building social boundaries?: SIDE-effects of computer-mediated communication. Commun. Res. **25**(6), 689–715 (1998)
19. Postmes, T., Spears, R., Lea, M.: Intergroup differentiation in computer-mediated communication: effects of depersonalization. Group Dyn. Theory Res. Pract. **6**(1), 3–16 (2002)
20. Rana, A.R., Turoff, M., Hiltz, S.R.: Task and Technology Interaction (TTI): a theory of technological support for group tasks. In: Proceedings of the Thirtieth Hawaii International Conference on System Sciences, vol. 00(c), pp. 66–75 (1997)
21. Richardson, J.C., Swan, K.: Examining social presence in online courses in relation to students? perceived learning and satisfaction. JALN **7**(1), 68–88 (2003)
22. Shah, C.: Toward Collaborative Information Seeking (CIS). In: Proceedings of Collaborative Exploratory Search Workshop at JCDL 2008, abs/0908.0 (2009)
23. Shah, C.: Collaborative information seeking: a literature review. Adv. Librariansh. **32**, 3–33 (2010)
24. Short, J., Williams, E., Christie, B.: The Social Psychology of Telecommunications, vol. 7. Wiley, London (1976)
25. Smolensky, M.W., Carmody, M.A., Halcomb, C.G.: The influence of task type, group structure and extraversion on uninhibited speech in computer-mediated communication. Comput. Hum. Behav. **6**(3), 261–272 (1990)
26. Straus, S.G., McGrath, J.E.: Does the medium matter? The interaction of task type and technology on group performance and member reactions. J. Appl. Psychol. **79**(1), 87–97 (1994)
27. Tidwell, L.C., Walther, J.B.: Computer-mediated communication effects on disclosure, impressions, and interpersonal evaluations: getting to know one another a bit at a time. Hum. Commun. Res. **28**(3), 317–348 (2002)
28. Walther, J.B.: Computer-mediated communication: impersonal, interpersonal, and hyperpersonal interaction. Commun. Res. **23**(1), 3–43 (1996)
29. Walther, J.B., Burgoon, J.K.: Relational communication in computer-mediated interaction. Hum. Commun. Res. **19**(1), 50–88 (1992)
30. Whittaker, S., O'Conaill, B.: The Role of Vision in Face-to-Face and Mediated Communication, pp. 23–49. Lawrence Erlbaum Associates, Mahwah (1997)

Glossary

Annotations In this work, annotations primarily refer to notes and other information added to a Web resource.

Answerers Refers to humans that answer askers' questions through an online Q&A or a social media/networking service. They may be known social connections, strangers, or experts.

Askers Refers to the humans that ask questions to satisfy their needs through an online Q&A or a social media/networking service.

Co-browsing Also known as social or collaborative navigation. A process of allowing a set of users to navigate (or browse) and share information with a possible immediate interface.

Collaboration This is a process involving various agents that may see different aspects of a problem. They engage in activities through which they can go beyond their own individual expertise and vision by constructively exploring their differences and searching for common solutions. In contrast to cooperation, collaboration involves creating a solution that is more than merely the sum of each party's contribution. The authority in such a process is vested in the collaborative rather than in an individual entity (see Chap. 6 for a detailed discussion).

Collaborative Q&A Q&A services that facilitate the ability to edit and improve phrasing of a question and/or the answer to a given question over time via user collaboration. WikiAnswers, for example.

Community Q&A (CQA) User-driven environments where people searching for personalized answers post various types of questions to an online Q&A community that are then answered by members of that community. Also known as knowledge exchange communities. Yahoo! Answers, for example.

C. Shah, *Social Information Seeking*, The Information Retrieval Series 38,
DOI 10.1007/978-3-319-56756-3

Computer-supported cooperative work (CSCW) A field of research that addresses how the coordination of collaborative activities can be supported by computer systems.

Environment A set of objects and attributes that may include users, systems, and their context.

Expert-based Q&A Q&A services in which answers are provided by a group of experts rather than an open community. Many include pricing systems that allow askers to compensate answerers. AllExperts, for example.

Face-to-face Refers to information seeking or other encounters that occur in person.

Human-computer interaction (HCI) Research concerning the design and use of computer technology interfaces between machines and people.

Human relevance judgments An important means of evaluation in which actual humans gauge an answer's relevance within social information seeking platforms.

Information behavior/human information behavior The study of the interactions between people, information, and the situations (contexts) in which they connect.

Information need This involves fact-finding, exploration of a topic, content consumption (e.g., read a document, view a video, buy a product), negotiations (e.g., auctions), etc.

Information retrieval (IR) The area of study concerned with searching for documents, information within documents, and metadata about documents, as well as searching structured storage, relational databases, and the World Wide Web.

Information search process (ISP) A foundational information seeking model initially proposed by Kuhlthau that focuses on stages of users' behavior during information seeking processes.

Information seeking (IS) The process or activity of attempting to obtain information in both human and technological contexts. IS, in this book, is seen as incorporating IR (see Chap. 1).

Knowledge sharing An activity through which information is exchanged between people. Here, knowledge sharing occurs via social information seeking processes.

Library and information science (LIS) An interdisciplinary field that applies the perspectives and tools of information science and other domains to libraries, focuses on the organization and dissemination of information, and studies the political economy of information.

Multi-session information seeking A newer IR framework that accounts for multistep information seeking processes, collaborative information seeking, and/or the systems that foster these interactions.

Online Q&A Community-based online question-answer services. Examples include Yahoo! Answers and Stack Overflow.

Participants Refers to the humans that are parts of a study, an experiment, and/or a collaboration. In some cases, they may not even use a system. With respect to a user study, this refers to the subjects who participate.

Peers Refers to humans who belong to the same age, professional, knowledge, or social group.

Peer-to-peer (P2P) system A computer or network distributed application architecture that equally splits tasks between peers without using a central server, so that each computer in a network communicates with all other computers. These systems display information sharing potential.

Personalization System configuration for a given user based on their profile, preferences, and/or behavioral patterns.

Potential answerers Online Q&A users who could efficiently and effectively answer an asker's question. They should be identified to reduce askers' wait time and facilitate a site's development (see Chap. 4).

Qualitative Refers to data or research that can be observed but not measured using numerical metrics.

Quantitative Refers to data or research that can be measured and typically deal with numbers.

Query A question, especially one that expresses doubts or checks validity and accuracy. Here, we generally refer to queries posed in online information seeking environments.

Recommendation System configuration for a given user based on their matched profile, preferences, and/or behavioral patterns with other users in the network.

Rising stars Online Q&A users who consistently provide quality posts and earn a respected reputation from other community members (see Chap. 4).

Search engine A software system that is designed to search for information in a corpus, a database, or the World Wide Web to answer users' inquiries. Examples include Google and Bing.

Sense-making The process by which people give meaning to experience.

Social and collaborative information seeking (SCIS) A larger model of information seeking behavior that accounts for both social information seeking and collaborative information seeking. It incorporates individual-based information seeking activities as well as special cases of collaborative and social processes (see Chap. 7).

Social annotations Annotations associated with a Web resource that can be modified or removed without modifying the resource itself. These could affect search results (see Chap. 5).

Social bookmarking A process by which users can store and share links to Web pages using online bookmark management services (see Chap. 5).

Social capital In this text, the total number of resources embedded in online social networks or the potential to access resources in social networks for some purposeful action (see Chap. 3).

Social information seeking Human behavior in which people look for information through social channels such as social media services, social networking sites, and community-driven content providers. Also known as social search or social information retrieval.

Social live streaming services (SLSSs) Social networking sites that allow users to broadcast content in real time. Examples include Periscope and Facebook Live.

Social media Forms of electronic communication, such as Websites and microblogging platforms, through which users create online communities to share information, ideas, personal messages, and other content.

Social networking site (SNS) Any of the numerous online platforms used by people to build social networks or social relations with other people who share interests and/or real-life connections.

Social Q&A Question-answering (Q&A) services that allow users to ask questions to friends or acquaintances within social networking sites or social search engines.

Social search Searching beyond social Q&A platforms. Social search describes the process in which individuals seek to satisfy an information need through their social connections in Web 2.0 environments.

Struggling users Refers to active online Q&A users who experience difficulty with providing quality content (see Chap. 4).

System Refers to machines or automated mechanisms.

Usability Refers to a system's multifaceted user-friendliness. It typically involves testing for system's effectiveness and efficiency, as well as user satisfaction.

Users Refers to the humans who are using a given system.

Virtual reference (VR) Refers to online library reference transactions via computer-mediated communication, such as Instant Messaging or email.

Web 2.0 A modern state of the Web in which pages have evolved from static to dynamic with user-generated content and social media (see Chap. 3).

Index

C. Shah, *Social Information Seeking*, The Information Retrieval Series 38,
DOI 10.1007/978-3-319-56756-3

Printed in the United States
By Bookmasters